American Romanian Academy of Arts and Sciences

CLASH OVER ROMANIA

Vol. II

British and American Policies toward Romania: 1938 - 1947

Dr. Paul D. Quinlan

Author: Dr. Paul D. Quinlan

CLASH OVER ROMANIA, Vol. II. British and American Policies toward Romania: 1938 – 1947, the 2nd Edition.

The 1st Edition was published in 1977 (ISBN-13: 978-0686232636). Copyright © 1977 by the American Romanian Academy of Arts and Sciences.

Editor: Dr. Oana Leonte

Contributing Editor: Ioana L. Ene

Cover: George Roca

American Romanian Academy of Arts and Sciences, ARA Publisher www.AmericanRomanianAcademy.org

Printed in the United States

To Maureen,

Natasha, and Annemarie

Content

Acknowledgements

I want to thank Dr. Arthur G. Kogan of the Historical Office of the Department of State and the staffs of the National Archives and the Public Record Office for their patience and helpful assistance. Although much of the American material was still classified when I did my research, I was given a special security clearance by the State Department and the Department of the Army and allowed to use their unopened records.

I also wish to express my appreciation to General Cortlandt Van R. Schuyler, American military representative on the Allied Control Commission for Romania, for letting me use his unpublished diary, as well as answering many of my questions. Many people read the manuscript and made helpful suggestions. This list includes Mircea Ionnitiu, private secretary of King Michael, and his brother Nicolae Ionnitiu, who generously granted me numerous interviews; former Romanian diplomat Radu Florescu, Sr; assistant United States political representative Roy M. Melbourne; and especially Dr. Radu Florescu, Jr., of Boston College for his patience and constructive guidance. Thanks are also due to the staffs of the Library of Congress, the Franklin D. Roosevelt and the Harry S. Truman Libraries, and manuscript collections at Harvard and Yale Universities.

Dr. Paul D. Quinlan

Introduction

During the turbulent era of the late 1930's and 1940's the states of Eastern Europe and the Balkans were constantly involved in a struggle to maintain their territory and independence. Situated between Germany and Russia, these countries became the battleground of their larger neighbors. One of the most important of the Balkan nations was Romania. Strategically located along the Black Sea and the south-western border of the Soviet Union, as well as controlling the mouth of the Danube River, Romania had helped to block the Russians from extending their control to the Straits and the Mediterranean since the end of the eighteenth century. Moreover, Romania was rich in raw materials, being the number one oil producing nation in Europe outside of the Soviet Union.

This is a study of British and American policies towards Romania from 1938 through 1947. Overall, first Britain and later both Britain and the United States tried to maintain an independent and friendly Romanian state. At the same time, the Western Powers saw Romania's independence as affecting their own security.

British and American relations with this small oil-rich Balkan state provide an interesting and informative story in itself. More important, events in Romania had an impact on Western policies in general, and help to explain the origins of World War II and the Cold War. To date there has been no study of British and American relations with Romania for this period. The only study of a similar nature involves

Germany's relations with Romania from 1938 through 1944 by Andreas Hillgruber, *Hitler, König Carol und Marshall Antonescu*. It has only been since the mid 1960's that the Western governments have begun to open their archives for the war period providing sufficient primary sources for such a study. Because of the lack of primary documents historians have been unaware of the importance and role of Romania.

This study is based mainly on recently published and unpublished documents of the British and American governments. Some of the documents just help to confirm what has already been known, but many contain information never before brought to light. For example, the part played by the United States in the attempt to overthrow the Groza government in August 1945 has remained almost totally unknown to historians. Western representatives in Romania have not published their memoirs, and high government officials like James Byrnes never mentioned the abortive coup in their works. Unfortunately the British Foreign Office has somehow "misplaced" most of its documents on this embarrassing crisis, but thanks to the American State Department the story can be told.

Other primary material dealing with the topic was consulted, including my good fortune to have had access to General Cortlandt Van R. Schuyler's extensive unpublished diary, as well as interviews and correspondence with several of the chief participants in these events. Numerous secondary sources were also utilized, including studies by contemporary Romanian historians.

Those areas of Romanian history which are involved with British and American policies were given some necessary explanation. This was essential where little had been written about prior to this study. Aspects of Romanian history which are not concerned with British and American policies towards Romania were only alluded to or omitted entirely.

CHAPTER I

Historical Background

Romania, since ancient times a crossroad between Europe and Asia, seldom has been an area of serious concern of Britain's foreign policy. Historically, England's interests in that turbulent, oil-rich, Balkan country have been confined primarily to trade and finance. Yet during the first and second World Wars Romania was viewed by the British as being important to their own security, and during the latter period had a considerable influence in shaping English foreign policy.

During World War I Britain and Romania fought together as allies. In order to get Romania to go to war with the Central Powers, Britain, along with France, Russia, and Italy, had reluctantly agreed to Romania's political and extensive territorial demands.[1] Later, at the Paris Peace Conference of 1919, heated debates erupted over the extent and validity of these commitments.

At the Peace Conference much of the difficulty between the Allies and Romania involved the latter's territorial claims. The heads of the major Allied powers, especially Lloyd George and Woodrow Wilson, felt these demands

---

[1] According to the political convention of 17 August 1916 the Allies promised to safeguard Romania's present frontiers (which included Southern Dobrogea), and recognized her right to annex Transylvania, Bucovina, and the Banat. In return, on 27 August Romania declared war on the Central Powers

were too extensive. The British delegation was sympathetic to the principle of national self-determination and supported many of Romania's aspirations.[2] At the same time, they wanted a settlement that would lead to permanent peace and stability, and feared that an agreement which gave too much land to Romania at the expense of her neighbors would jeopardize this.[3]

The British wanted to prevent Romania from annexing the entire Banat. They favored dividing Bucovina between a Ruthenian state and Romania, as well as giving part of Southern Dobrogea back to Bulgaria.[4]

Lloyd George distrusted Romania's claim that the great majority in Bessarabia approved annexation.[5] During most of 1919 Allied leaders remained at loggerheads, but in the end Britain had to yield to most of Romania's objectives. The Big Four were divided, and the Romanian army, which already occupied most of the disputed areas, was the only major force in Central Europe to hold back the frightening menace of Bolshevism. Moreover, Bucharest had already recognized these areas as forming part of the new Romanian state.[6] The Allies were faced with a fait accompli.

---

[2] Sherman David Spector, *Rumania at the Paris Peace Conference* (New York, 1962), 99-100.

[3] David Lloyd George, *The Truth about the Peace Treaties* (London, 1938), II 920

[4] Spector, *op. cit.*, 100. With the exception of the word Bucharest, Romanian spellings will be used for Romanian names.

[5] *Ibid.*, 93-94

[6] On 1 December, 1918, representatives of the Transylvanian Romanians meeting at Alba Iulia proclaimed the union of Transylvania with Romania. Much has been written on the

At Paris, Romania achieved almost all of her goals.[7] The Allies recognized her new frontiers. Romania signed peace treaties with Austria, Bulgaria, and Hungary, a collective treaty on frontiers, and a special treaty on 28 October, 1920, which gave de jure recognition to the union of Bessarabia with Romania.[8] This last treaty was not signed by the United States, and, of course, the Soviet Union.

Despite the tension between Britain and Romania during the Peace Conference, relations were friendly between the two countries during the inter-war period. Britain's interests were confined primarily to commerce and finance, especially during the twenties, as well as dynastic connections. Queen Marie, the beautiful and talented wife of the Hohenzollern King of Romania, Ferdinand - he ruled from 1914 to 1927 - was the former Princess Marie of

---

formation of Greater Romania by the Romanians themselves. For example, see *Unification of the Romanian National State: The Union of Transylvania with Old Romania* (eds. Miron Constantinescu; Ștefan Pascu, Bucharest, 1971); *La desagregation de la monarchie Austro-Hongroise 1900-1918* (eds. C. Daicoviciu; Miron Constantinescu, Bucarest, 1965).

[7] Romania was forced to give up part of the Banat to the new Yugoslavian state and some of her territorial claims in Transylvania to Hungary. Romania claimed approximately thirty-six thousand square miles of Transylvania. In the end she retained thirty-two thousand square miles.

[8] Romania signed the Treaty of St. Germain with Austria and the Treaty of Neuilly with Bulgaria on 10 December, 1919. She signed the Treaty of Trianon with Hungary on 4 June, 1920. The collective treaty on frontiers, which recognized the new borders of those states that had acquired territory from the now defunct Hapsburg Monarchy, was signed on 28 October, 1920.

Edinburgh, a granddaughter of Queen Victoria. Romania borrowed heavily from Britain during the war and early post-war period; her total debt amounted to over twenty million pounds after funding.[9] The British Government favored cancelling all inter-ally debts, but because of American demands for repayment, London was forced to notify her debtors that they would have to pay.[10] After the war Britain signed several commercial agreements with Romania.[11] In the nineteen twenties almost ten percent of Romania's imports and six percent of her exports were with Great Britain.[12]

Since the latter part of the nineteenth century, the bulk of Britain's investments in Romania have been in oil. On the eve of World War I, twenty-one percent of the foreign investments in the Romanian oil industry came from Britain; the only country to invest more was Germany.[13] Britain was Romania's largest oil importer before the war. By 1930 there were seventeen English oil companies operating in Romania

---

[9] Arnolld J. Toynbee, *Survey of International Affairs 1926* (London, 1928), 103-104.

[10] *Papers Relating to the Foreign Relations of the United States* (Washington, 1943-1972). Foreign Relations, I ,406-409.

[11] The British granted credits totaling one hundred thousand pounds in 1919 and 1920, signed a Corn Agreement on 22 January, 1920, an Oil Agreement on 9 August, 1920, and a Commercial Treaty in May, 1923.

[12] Joseph S. Roucek. *Contemporary Roumania and Her Problems* (Stanford, California. 1932), 336-337, England imported oil, wheat, corn, and timber from Romania, and exported textiles, metal, and metal goods.

[13] Maurice Pearton, *Oil and the Romanian State* (Oxford. 1971), 68.

with a total capital of forty-one million dollars.[14] Britain remained her main importer until the early nineteen thirties. After 1932, however, because of lower prices in the United States, English purchases declined. [15] The British Government's main activity in Romania was promoting suitable economic and financial conditions for the development of the oil trade and protecting British investments.

During most of the inter-war period, British involvement in Romania's foreign affairs was limited, especially during the nineteen twenties. While both countries participated in various European and international conferences and worked to maintain the peace treaties, little of this had a direct bearing on British-Romanian relations. England returned to her traditional foreign policy of "nonintervention" in Eastern Europe. This did not mean that she was indifferent to political developments in that part of the Continent.

The British Government closely watched events throughout Europe. Basically "nonintervention" meant that since this area was not considered vital to Britain's security, Her Majesty's Government tried to avoid pledges and alliances that might involve her in conflicts which were not in her own best interest. This did not prevent her from trying to influence developments which she felt could endanger the peace and stability of Europe. At the same time, Britain avoided involvement in the French alliance system in Eastern Europe and steadily refused to be drawn into guaranteeing these states. For Romania, though, the

---

[14] Roucek, *Contemporary Roumania and Her Problems*, 266-267.
[15] Pearton. *op. cit.*, 199.

13

situation was just the opposite. The Romanian Government viewed its alliances as a vital part of its security system. Having achieved her territorial objectives, Romania's goal was to protect her new frontiers and maintain the status quo. For Romania, maintaining the status quo involved preventing revision of the peace treaties, especially the Treaty of Trianon. Despite England's critical attitude towards Romania at the Peace Conference, the British Government never officially supported Hungarian revisionism during the war years. [16] The Romanians, however, especially during the nineteen thirties, were often fearful that Britain would revise her policy. Various English governments manifested a willingness to discuss revision of the Treaty of Versailles, and a revision of that treaty could open the doors to changes in the Trianon Treaty.[17] It was well-known that many in Britain sympathized with Hungary.[18] In 1933, 168 members of the House of Commons tried to get a motion passed which would have had the British Government bring the question of revision of Trianon before the Assembly of the League of Nations at the earliest opportunity.[19] Support for Hungary was found not only among revisionists, but also in Conservative circles,

---

[16] A. Macartney, *A History of Hungary* 1929-1945 (New York, 1956), I, 82.

[17] The National Coalition governments of Ramsey MacDonald, Stanley Baldwin, and Neville Chamberlain.

[18] Arnold J. Toynbee, *Survey of International Affairs 1927* (London, 1929), 205- 207; Roucek, *Contemporary Roumania*, 151-152; Macartney, History of Hungary, 1, 82.

[19] R. W. Seton-Watson, *Treaty Revision and the Hungarian Frontiers* (London, 1934), 67.

and among the British aristocracy where there was some sympathy for Hungary's ruling class. On the academic level, the well-known Oxford historian R. W. Seton-Watson defended Romania, while C.A. Macartney championed the cause of Hungary. The most famous English critic of the Trianon Treaty was the powerful newspaper publisher Lord Rothermere, who caused a considerable amount of alarm in the Little Entente countries with his campaign for "Justice for Hungary." Yet his influence on British policy was negligible.[20]

Romania based her security on her alliances, the peace treaties, the League of Nations, and her friendship with France.[21] With the growth of Fascism in the thirties these became increasingly threatened. At the same time, British-Romanian relations became more involved. The prospects that Britain might try to appease Germany and Italy disturbed Romania, especially since this could result in the weakening of her security system. During the discussions

---

[20] Macartney, *A History of Hungary*, I, 82.

[21] R. Deutsch, "The Foreign Policy of Romania and the Dynamics of Peace (1932-1936),"*Revue Roumaine d'Histoire*, 5 (1966), I, 125-1 27. Romania signed the following alliances. Polish-Romanian Alliance of 3 March, 1921; Treaties helping to form the "Little Entente" were signed by Romania with Czechoslovakia and Yugoslavia in April and June of 1921, respectively; Treaty of Friendship between Romania and France of June, 1926; the Balkan Pact, 9 February, 1934, signed with Yogoslavia, Greece, and Turkey. See Eliza Campus. "Le caractere europeen des traites bilateraux conclus par la Roumanie dans la decade 1920-1930," *Revue Roumaine d'Histoire*, 12 (1973), VI, 1068-1081.

for a Four Power Pact in 1933 the British Government indicated its willingness to consider treaty revision. [22] Romania strongly opposed this. On several occasions Nicolae Titulescu, Romania's skillful Foreign Minister, urged the British Government to reverse its position.[23] He warned the English Prime Minister Ramsay MacDonald that the Pact "would ruin the League of Nations and inevitably bring on a war."[24] The efforts of the Little Entente statesmen were influential in weakening the Pact.[25] Romania was a strong

---

[22] The Four Power Pact called for Britain, France, Germany, and Italy to work together for the maintenance of peace. One of the methods by which peace was to be guaranteed was through treaty revision. By the summer of 1933, however, when the Pact was finally completed it had been so watered down with modifications, especially those of France, that the whole document was largely a collection of generalities. In the end it was only ratified by Italy and Great Britain, and it utterly failed to have any effect in stopping Hitler from withdrawing from the League of Nations and the Disarmament Conference in October, 1933. For a thorough examination of the Pact see, Konrad H. Jarausch, *The Four Power Pact 1933* (Madison Wisconsin, 1965).

[23] During much of the period from 1927 to 1936, Romania's foreign policy was directed by Nicolae Titulescu. His policy was based on intimacy with the West, preservation of the peace treaties, and the reconciliation of Romania and the Soviet Union.

[24] Pavel Pavel, *Why Rumania Failed* (London, 1944), 128; Dinu C. Giurescu, "La diplomatie roumaine et le Pacte des Quatre (1933)." *Revue Roumaine d'Histoire*, 8 (1969), 82-83, 85-87.

[25] I.M. Oprea, *Nicolae Titulescu's Diplomatic Activity* (Bucharest, 1968), 116-120; Gerhard L. Weinberg, *The Foreign Policy of*

supporter of the League of Nations. During the Ethiopian crisis, Romania was one of the staunchest advocates of upholding the authority of the League. In order to make the League's policy effective she was willing to have oil included in the sanctions even though this would have hurt severely her own hard-pressed economy. Romania supplied forty-six percent of Italy's oil. But the British Government would not consent to an oil embargo, despite the strong criticism by the Labour and the Liberal Parties.[26]

Britain continually refused to entangle herself in Eastern Europe. When France tried to reorganize her system of alliances in Eastern Europe in 1934 and include the Soviet Union, the most Britain would do was to give her "benevolent approval" to the project.[27] The failure of the Western Powers to act during the remilitarization of the Rhineland was especially alarming to Romania. In a

---

Hitler's Germany (Chicago, 1970), 52; Jarausch, *Four Power Pact*, 95-97.

[26] Brice Harris, Jr., *The United States and the Italo-Ethiopian Crisis* (Stanford, California, 1964), 99; A.J. Barker, *The Civilizing Mission: A History of the Italo-Ethiopian War of 1935-1936* (New York, 1968), 135, 198. See also Ion Babici, "Actions de solidarite du peuple roumain avec la lutte heroique du peuple d'Ethiopie contre l'agression fasciste (1935-1936)," *Revue Roumaine d'Histoire*, 6 (1967), II 257-273; Franklin D. Laurens, *France and the Italo-Ethiopian Crisis* 1935-1936 (The Hague, 1967); Henderson B. Braddick. "The Hoare-Laval Plan: A Study in international Politics," *Review of Politics*, 24 (1962), 351-364.

[27] Robert Machray, *The Stuggle for the Danube and the Little Entente* 1929-1938 (London, 1938), 143; William Evans Scott, *Alliance Against Hitler* (Durham, North Carolina, 1962), 258.

conversation with the American Minister to Bucharest, Titulescu declared:

> "What the allies needed was a Hitler or a Mussolini. The French... should have immediately and promptly announced their intention of sending their forces into the demilitarized zone. We would then have seen the British get busy in Berlin to have the German troops withdrawn."[28]

Under these conditions it is understandable that Romania felt compelled to establish closer relations with Germany in order to protect her own security. In spite of England's attitude towards Eastern Europe there were signs of growing concern and sympathy for Romania. The ever-increasing influence of Nazi Germany in South Eastern Europe, as well as the development of Fascism in Romania were disturbing to Great Britain. This anxiety was manifested in part by the improvement of King Carol's reputation in England. Carol, the eldest son of Queen Marie and King Ferdinand -rumored to be the only one of her six children fathered by Ferdinand - acquired world fame as an international playboy in the twenties.[29] His exploits received

---

[28] *Foreign Relations 1936*, I, 227; Oprea, *Titulescu's Diplomatic Activity*, 137-139: Nicolae Titulescu. *Discursuri* led. Robert Deutsch. Bucuresti. 1967), 482-485. American Minister was Leland Harrison.

[29] Carol was born on 16 October, 1893. He became Crown Prince in 1914 after the death of his grandfather King Carol I. In 1917 he contracted a morganatic marriage with a general's daughter. The marriage did not last long, and several years later he married Princess Helen of Greece. Their only son, Prince Michael, was born in 1921. Four years later Carol

a great deal of coverage by the British press who dubbed him the "royal rapscallion" and "Carol the Cad."[30] Carol lived in England for a short time with his celebrated red-headed Jewish mistress, Madame Magda Lupescu, after he renounced his rights to the throne rather than give up Magda in 1925. In 1928 the British Government expelled him from the country for allegedly conspiring to launch a surprise coup d'etat and seize the Romanian throne from his infant son. His reputation sank even lower after he recovered the throne in 1930. British Labour circles sharply criticized him for his anti-democratic policies. As Fascism grew in Romania, however, the attitude of the British press changed. "The bad boy of the Balkans" began to be depicted

---

deserted his wife and renounced his rights to the Romanian throne. In 1930 he returned to Romania and reclaimed the throne.

[30] A.L. Easterman, *King Carol, Hitler and Lupescu* (London, 1942), 94. Carol created a sensation at the funeral of George V in London in 1936. According to the British press the Romanian Legation had to quickly hire a masseur on the morning of the funeral to work on the King who was not feeling very well after a nightlong drinking bout. In the last minute confusion of the funeral procession, the masseur, who allegedly even worked on Carol in his car on the way to the funeral, became bewildered by the marching troops, lost his head, and marched a considerable distance in the procession with the official dignitaries. The press displayed pictures of a strange looking man in the parade wearing white trousers and a felt hat. The Romanians claimed the whole story was false, and that the "Marching Masseur" was in reality a member of the Romanian delegation wearing his native costume.

as a fighter of Fascism and a friend of Great Britain.[31] The old royal lover stories were forgotten. Another sign of the growing concern for Romania was the invitation by the British Government to Carol in the fall of 1937 to make his first official state visit.

At the same time, Carol wanted to establish closer relations with England. In July, 1937 he unexpectedly arrived in London on a "shopping" trip. During his seven day stay he talked to the King and Queen and several members of the British Cabinet, including the Prime Minister Neville Chamberlain. In conversation with the noted British journalist Wickham Steed, Carol declared he wanted to change England's impression that Romania was a French colony and "wished for specially cordial relations" between the two countries.[32]

United States involvement in Romania was even more limited than Britain's. Before World War One the State Department showed little concern for the Balkans. [33]

---

[31] Easterman, *Carol, Hitler and Lupescu*, 100, 116. Writing about Carol's "shopping" trip to London in July, 1937, the American journalist Vernon McKenzie stated that he "received the best press" he ever had in England up to that time. For an interesting account of the changing attitude of the British see Vernon McKenzie, *Through Turbulent Years* (New York, 1938), 131-136. For more information see Chapter II.

[32] Pavel Pavel, *Why Rumania Failed*, 143; New York Times, July 23-25, 1937; The Times, London, July 20-27, 1937.

[33] A. Thomas Devasia, "The United States and the Formation of Greater Romania, 1914-1918: A Study in Diplomacy and Propaganda," *Doctoral Thesis Boston College*, 1970, 40. Until the

Romania did not open a legation in the United States until 1918. To Americans, Romania was a far-off land of gypsies, royal scandals, and dancing peasants in colorful costumes. As late as 1929, State Department officials expected the new Romanian Minister to show up in Washington wearing rouge and corsets. In 1930 there were only 146,000 Americans of Romanian extraction living in the United States, and most of them came from areas that belonged to the Austrian Empire before the First World War, especially Transylvania.[34]

The first time that Eastern Europe became a factor in American foreign policy was during World War One. [35] During most of the War, the United States Government was reluctant to get involved in the problem of Romanian unification, and was not a signer of the Treaty of Bucharest of August, 1916. It was not until November, 1918, that the Wilson Administration finally endorsed the principle of Romanian unity.[36]

---

war America's interest in Romania centered around trade and occasional efforts to secure better treatment for Jews.

[34] Robert H. Ferrell, "The United States and East Central Europe before 1941," *The Fate of East Central Europe: Hope and Failure of American Foreign Policy* (ed. Stephen D. Kertesz, Notre Dame, Indiana 1956), 24; Devasia, *op. cit.*, 202.

[35] Ferrell, op. cit., 25.

[36] Victor S. Mamatey, *The United States and East Central Europe 1914-1918* (Princeton, New Jersey, 1957), 377-378. For Romanian activities in the United States during the war see also I. Gheorghiu; C. Nuțu, "The Activity for the Union Carried Out Abroad," *Unification of the Romanian National State: The Union of Transylvania with Old Romania* (eds. Miron

At the Paris Peace Conference the American delegation was the most critical of Romania's territorial demands of the Big Four.[37] Wilson called for an impartial examination of territorial claims based on the principle of national self-determination. But his principles ran counter to many of Romania's objectives. On the question of Transylvania, the United States delegation urged a more easterly boundary "so that the best ethnic frontiers could be erected;" the Americans wanted to join Northern Bucovina to an independent Ruthenian state, as well as force Romania into returning the entire Southern Dobrogea to Bulgaria.[38] They refused to approve the union of Bessarabia with Romania. Robert Lansing, the American Secretary of State, continually blocked the Conference from recognizing the new status of Bessarabia, and urged that no changes be made in Russian territory. The United States believed that the Bolsheviks did "not rule by the will or the consent of any considerable proportion of the Russian people" and that their regime would be overthrown shortly.[39] This being the case, they wanted to wait until a more representative government was established in Russia before making a final decision on territorial questions. But in the end, Wilson was forced to compromise his principles and reluctantly endorsed most of

---

Constantinescu; Ștefan Pascu, Bucharest, 1971), 127- 143 passim: Vasile Stoica, *In America pentru Cauza Românească* (Bucharest, 1926).

[37] Spector, *Peace Conference*, 95-113 passim.

[38] Ibid., 103; Ferrell, *United States and East Central Europe*, 43.

[39] *Foreign Relations 1920*, III, 461-468; *Foreign Relations 1932*, II, 506-507.

the changes approved by Britain, France, and Italy. Romania's new boundaries finally were officially recognized in August, 1921, when the United States signed separate peace treaties with Austria and Hungary. The only exception was Bessarabia, whose new status Washington flatly refused to sanction.

During the inter-war period United States involvement in Romania was confined mainly to economic matters. Relations were friendly between the two countries, especially after the mid-twenties. A number of problems, chiefly economic, created some tension in American-Romanian relations in the early post-war period. Romania borrowed heavily from the United States during the war. Of the twenty countries to borrow from America, the Romanian debt was the ninth largest approximately forty-four million dollars before funding.[40] It was not until the end of 1925 that a payment agreement was finally arranged. The United States Government blamed Romania for this delay, claiming that she did not want to pay her debts.[41] Another sore spot was Romania's failure to pay her bills to a number of large American companies. [42] At the same time, the State Department protested that the Romanian Government was giving priority to other foreign payments, which was

---

[40] Harold G. Moulton; Leo Pasvolsky, *War Debts and World Prosperity* (New York, 1932), 91, 430-431.

[41] *Foreign Relations 1924*, II, 614, 619, 635, 641

[42] *Ibid*. The largest debts were with the International Harvester Company for more than four hundred thousand dollars, the Baldwin Locomotive Works, the Transoceanic Corporation whose notes were held by the Chase National Bank and the Equitable Trust Company, and the Bencoe Export Company.

viewed as conflicting with prior pledges made to the United States. [43] Not all of the protests, however, came from Washington. The Romanian Government objected to the Immigration Act of 1924, which greatly impeded immigrants going to America from Southern and Southeastern Europe.[44]

One of the most serious disputes involved American oil interests in Romania. The largest share of American capital invested in that country was in oil.[45] Unlike Britain, there was only one American oil company in Romania, the Romano-Americana, which was owned and operated by the Standard Oil Company of New Jersey. A pioneer in the Romanian oil industry, since the beginning of the century Romano-Americana had been one of the country's largest oil firms. In the late thirties Standard's investments in Romania were approximately twenty-six million dollars.[46]

In the fall of 1923 it became known that the Romanian Government intended to pass a new mining law designed to reduce foreign control over the oil industry. Under this bill, in order for a foreign company to acquire new oil lands, Romanian citizens would have to hold fifty-five percent of that company's stock and comprises two-thirds of its board

---

[43] *Foreign Relations 1924*, op. cit.

[44] *Ibid*. 213-214, 222

[45] Roucek, *Contemporary Roumania*, 267. By the late nineteen-thirties direct American investments totaled about forty-six million dollars. American Legation to Secretary of State, August 10, 1939, State Department Dispatch, No.1026, 871.00/698, 38, National Archives.

[46] American Legation to Secretary of State, August 10, 1939, State Department Dispatch, 38.

of directors. This bill ignited a storm of protests from foreign-owned oil companies and their respective governments. The American Government was especially upset. Washington warned Romania that this bill would be disastrous to foreign oil investment.[47] This proposed law along with the other problems the United States was having with Romania caused the State Department to consider bringing the American Minister home for consultation.[48] "This action," the American Secretary of State Charles Evans Hughes wrote, "is contemplated with a view to adopting a policy calculated to improve this situation as well as to call the attention of the Rumanian officials clearly to the concern with which our Government views recent developments."[49] The United States Minister in Bucharest, Peter Jay, however, was reluctant to go this far. He notified the Department that this action "would be a severe shock to the Liberal Government and would come at a particularly embarrassing time."[50] He suggested that before further action was taken he be allowed to inform the Romanian Foreign Minister what the State Department was contemplating in order to see if the Romanians would change their policy.[51] This recommendation was approved. It produced the desired results. Shortly afterwards, the Romanian Government began to comply with most American demands. From this time on relations between the two countries improved.

---

[47] *Foreign Relations 1924*, II, 609.

[48] *Ibid.*, 614.

[49] *Foreign Relations 1924*, II, 61 4.

[50] *Ibid.*, 615.

[51] *Ibid.*

Beginning in 1926 several commercial treaties were concluded between Romania and the United States.

Romania adhered to the Kellogg- Briand Pact.[52] During the inter-war period there were protests from various groups in the United States over the treatment of ethnic and religious minority groups in Romania. Jewish-American organizations were especially vocal. At times they tried to persuade the State Department to complain about anti-Semitism in Romania, but the most the American Government would do was to informally bring these protests to the attention of Romanian officials. Washington tried to avoid these issues which it viewed as concerning "the domestic administration and politics of Rumania".[53]

On the lighter side, in the fall of 1926, Queen Marie made a trans-continental goodwill tour of the United States - "to put Rumania on the map," she told one American audience. Throughout the country, large, generally friendly crowds flocked to see a real queen and her royal companions. In New York she received a ticker tape parade up Broadway, and in Washington she was the guest of President Cooledge, being the first reigning queen to receive this honor. As she was leaving New York for home (her visit being cut short by the news of her husband's sudden illness), she was presented with a gift that many a Balkan ruler of that era must have cherished - a bullet-proof car.

---

[52] Gheorghe Matei, *La Roumanie et les problemes du desarmement (1919- 1934)* (Bucarest, 1970), 28-29; Oprea, *Titulescu's Diplomatic Activity*, 51-52.
[53] *Foreign Relations 1927*, III, 640.

By the beginning of the Roosevelt presidency only two major political questions remained between the two countries the status of Bessarabia and the problem of war-debts. On 10 August, 1920, the American Secretary of State, Bainbridge Colby, announced that the United States would not recognize any dismemberment of the Russian Empire unless it was first approved by a representative Russian government. [54] For the next twelve years the State Department based its refusal to recognize the union of Bessarabia with Romania on Colby's statement. The Romanian Government protested repeatedly, arguing, among other things, that the position of the United States constituted "public discrimination" against Romania. It was not until 1932 that the State Department began to reconsider its position. In a memorandum to the Under Secretary of State, the Chief of the Division of Near Eastern Affairs urged that the question be brought to a close if this could be done without causing any injury to American interests, I do not see that we gain anything particularly by upholding the Colby principle so rigidly in the case of Bessarabia when it has been treated somewhat lightly in other instances of the alienation of Russian territory.[55]

In the following year, Bucharest stepped up its protests because of the prospect that the United States would recognize the Soviet Union. The Romanians feared that if this happened before the Bessarabian question was solved it "would drag on indefinitely."[56] They repeatedly argued that

[54] *Foreign Relations 1920*, III, 427, 430,
[55] *Foreign Relations 1932*, II, 508.
[56] *Foreign Relations 1933*, II, 660.

there were no valid reasons why the United States should not recognize the union, and that to do so would remove a major stumbling block to world peace. Finally, not seeing any further justification for maintaining the Colby principle, and desiring to remain on good terms with Romania, the State Department advised the president to give de facto recognition to the union.[57] To accomplish this as simply as possible, Cordell Hull, Roosevelt's Secretary of State, favored the inclusion of Bessarabia within Romania's immigration quota. He told the President that this would "have the effect of according American recognition to Rumanian sovereignty over Bessarabia."[58] "It is sensible," noted Roosevelt, as he approved Hull's policy.

For the rest of the decade relations between the two countries were confined primarily to economic affairs. At the same time, the United States Government closely watched Romania's political developments. With the growth of Fascism, the State Department became worried about the future of Romania. American ministers in Bucharest sympathized with the non-Fascists, but carefully refrained from getting involved in domestic affairs. The American people became more aware and sympathetic towards the small states of Central and South Eastern Europe as they were increasingly threatened by Fascism. This attitude towards Romania, however, was not manifested in official policy until the end of the decade.

---

[57] *Foreign Relations 1933*, II, 681.

[58] *Ibid.* De jure recognition was never given by the United States.

CHAPTER II

The British Commitment to Romania

The winter of 1937-1938 marked the beginning of a new, more turbulent phase in Romania's history during the inter-war period. On the international level, the rise of Germany and Russia and the renewal of their interest in South Eastern Europe threatened the balance of power in that area. At the same time, French influence, which had been dominant since the early postwar years, was rapidly declining. Romania was becoming increasingly trapped between Germany's Drang nach Osten and Russia's desire to reestablish the frontiers of the Tsarist empire.[1]

Romania's domestic situation was equally depressing. The great depression hit Romania very hard, especially the poor, hard-working peasants. The economy did not begin to improve until the mid-thirties, and when war broke out in 1939, agriculture had barely recovered from its earlier losses.[2]

---

[1] A brief article on the historiography of the war period by contemporary Romanian historians can be found in Traian Udrea; Ioan Chiper, "La seconde guerre mondiale dans l'historiographie Roumaine," *Revue Roumaine d'Histoire*, 13 (1974), IV, 647-664.

[2] Henry L. Roberts, *Rumania: Political Problems of an Agrarian State* (New Haven, Connecticut, 1951), 170.

Romania's living standards were among the lowest in the Balkans.[3] Romania's political situation was unstable, marked by frequent changes of government, widespread corruption, and growing radical movements. While parliamentary democracy was able to stagger through the depression, its end was near. The country's most democratic-minded political party, the National Peasant Party, was never able to regain the popularity it had in the late twenties, when it received approximately eighty percent of the vote in 1928. In the election of December, 1937, its total had fallen to twenty percent. The leadership of the party was divided; many of its most capable men had deserted; and an increasing number of its supporters were attracted to the Fascist Iron Guard.[4]

The outlook for Romania's other large traditional party, the Liberal Party, was not much brighter. Although the Liberals were able to make somewhat of a comeback after 1933, their leadership was also split, and their Premier, the able but unscrupulous Gheorghe Tătărescu, was a friend and follower of the king - or whoever happened to be in power, for that matter. Moreover, their party program and especially their economic policies were moving in the direction of an authoritarian corporatist society.[5] As the

---

[3] Lucreţiu Pătrăşcanu, *Sous trois dictatures* (Paris, 1946), 53-56.
[4] Roberts, *Rumania*, 176. The Peasant Party which held power from 1928 to 1930 and again in 1932-1933 was powerless to halt the depression. Basically it was the depression and the inability of the Peasants to stop it that undermined the popularity of the party. See Roberts, Chapters VII and VIII.
[5] *Ibid.*, 187-202 passim.

traditional parties declined in popularity, the strength of right-wing, semi-fascist, and Fascist groups grew. These developments further lowered the already poor impression English and American statesmen had of Romanian politics. Franklin Mott Gunther, the American Minister in Bucharest from 1937 to 1941, described the political system as "always characterized by internal party strife, political greed, corruption and frequent changes of Government." [6] Unfortunately, corruption in government was so prevalent that some saw it as a national characteristic. "Rumania," Tsar Nicholas II supposedly exclaimed, "is neither a state nor a nation, but a profession."

Since his dazzling airplane coup in June, 1930, King Carol was the key figure in Romania's domestic and foreign politics. [7] Tall, slender, with wavy blond hair and immaculately dressed in his Bond Street clothes, he was then, as now, and enigmatic figure. His father is reputed to have compared him to a piece of Swiss cheese: "He has so many holes." Greedy and un-scrupulous, he was endowed with above average intelligence, possessed remarkable energy and a natural charm. As King, Carol endeavored to erect a

---

[6] Gunther to Secretary of State, June 13, 1938, State Department Dispatch, No. 378, 871.00/640, 1-2. Gunther was a career diplomat, having entered the State Department in 1907. He held various secretarial posts in Europe. Asia, South and Central America. He served as United States Minister to Egypt in the late twenties, and, for a short time, was Minister to Equador. He was assigned to Romania in July 1937.

[7] Andreas Hillgruber, *Hitler, König Carol und Marschall Antonescu* (Wiesbaden, 1954), 9.

government in which the monarch was the dominant figure. He disliked the Romanian party system, and had little if any, belief in representative government.[8] In order to increase his own power and popularity, and steal some of the thunder away from the Fascists, he adopted some of their techniques. Although moderately popular in Romania, his political activites and earlier playboy image gave him a poor reputation in England and the United States.

During the nineteen thirties Fascism became a strong force in Romanian politics. The most popular and fast-growing radical movement was the "Legion of the Archangel Michael," or the Iron Guard, as it was best known in the West. In the election of 1931 the Iron Guard won less than thirty-one thousand votes, and failed to elect a single representative to Parliament. In the election of December, 1937, however, the Guard received fifteen and one-half percent of the votes, returned sixty-six deputies to the chamber, and became the third largest party in the land. At first, Carol tolerated the Guard and had ideas about winning it over to his side.[9] But as the strength and violence of the Guard grew, and as it came to represent a serious threat to his own position, Carol became worried.

---

[8] Nicholas M. Nagy-Talavera, *The Green Shirts and the Others* (Stanford, California, 1970), 276; Roberts, Rumania, 189.
[9] Florea Nedelcu, "Carol al II-lea și garda de fier - de la relații amicale la criză - (1930-1937)," *Studii, Revista de istorie*, 24 (1971), V, 1009-1013; Nagy-Talavera, op. cit., 288. For a recent history of the Iron Guard see Mihai Fătu; Ion Spălățelu, Garda de fier, organizație teroristă de tip fascist (Bucuresti, 1971).

There were close ties between the extreme right in Romania and the Foreign Division of the Nazi Party under Alfred Rosenberg. This agency occasionally dabbled in Romanian politics, giving money and propaganda to several radical groups, as well as attempting to bring about some unity and cooperation among the warring parties of the Romanian right.[10] Before 1938, the Foreign Division's main support went to the National Chirstian Party under the leadership of the Transylvanian poet, Octavian Goga, and Professor Alexandru Cuza, a patriarch of European anti-Semitism, and not to the Iron Guard.[11] Ironically, for a movement that emphasized youth, Goga was in his mid-fifties, and Cuza was around eighty! The right wing parties, including the Iron Guard, frequently proclaimed their sympathy and desire to bring about closer relations with Nazi Germany.[12] In the fall of 1937, Corneliu Z. Codreanu, the zealous leader of the Iron Guard, issued a statement clearly outlining his foreign views.

> I am against the great democracies the West. I am against the Little Entente. I am against the Balkan Entente, and have not the slightest sympathy for the League of Nations, in which I do not believe. I am in favor of a foreign policy attached to the Rome-Berlin

---

[10] Hillgruber, *Hitter, König Carol und Marschall Antonescu*, 11-13; Weinberg, *Foreign Policy of Hitler's Germany*, 324; Hans-Adolf Jacobsen, *Nationalsozialistische Aussenpolitik* 1933-1938, Frankfurt am Main, 1968), 80-84. See also *The Trail of the Major War Criminals Before the International Military Tribunal*, V, 25, PS-007.

[11] Hillgruber, op. cit., 11-12.

[12] *Ibid.*, 12.

axis and of an alliance with the revolutionary Nationalist Powers directed against Bolshevism. Forty-eight hours after the victory of our organization we shall have an alliance with Rome and Berlin.[13]

On 20 December, 1937, Romania held parliamentary elections. The results were surprising. For the first time under the electoral law of 1926, the government in power failed to win enough votes to control Parliament.[14] The Liberals, who controlled the government at the time, received only thirty-six percent of the vote; the National Peasants obtained twenty percent, the Iron Guard fifteen and one-half, and the National Christian Party of Goga and Cuza nine percent. What was even more surprising was Carols appointment of the anti-Semitic poet and Fascist, Octavian Goga, as Premier.

Carol actually had few alternatives. He could not recall the defeated Liberals, and his extremely bad relations with Iuliu Maniu, the head of the National Peasants, precluded

---

[13] Bullitt to Secretary of State, November 1937, State Department Dispatch, No.599, 871.00/547. For Codreanu's own story see Corneliu Z. Codreanu, *Eiserne Garde* (Berlin, 1939).

[14] Under this law the party which won forty percent of the votes received as a bonus half of the seats in Parliament plus a number of the remaining seats corresponding to its percentage of the total votes cast. The Liberals, who were in power at that time, passed the bill in order to bolster their shaky position. In practice, the law immeasurably aided the party in power in controlling elections. For a detailed study of the election see I. Scurtu, Lupta partidelor politice alegerile parlamentare din decembrie 1937," *Studii, Revista de istorie*, 20 (1967), I, 145-162.

his appointment. It was very unlikely that he would appoint the Iron Guard, which he was beginning to view as his chief enemy. [15] On the other hand, Goga would be heavily dependent upon the King because of his party's poor showing in the election, and the poet was also a good friend of Madame Lupescu.[16] Moreover, Carol saw to it that many cabinet positions remained in the hands of his loyal supporters. [17] A number of diplomats, including Franklin Mott Gunther and the American Minister to Hungary, John Montgomery, also believed that Carol nominated Goga in order to appease the right, especially with the hopes of weakening the Iron Guard.[18]

Goga's appointment was disturbing to the Western democracies. The French Government feared this would disrupt Romania's traditional foreign policy and significantly increase the influence of Germany, as well as unleash a brutal campaign against the Jews. The English and American governments, although apprehensive about growing German influence, were more worried over the Jewish question. The American Embassy in Paris notified the State Department that the British were looking "for trouble

---

[15] Nedelcu, "Carol al II-lea și garda de fier," 1013-1027.

[16] Hillgruber, *Hiller, König Carol and Marschall Antonescu*, 14; Nagy-Talavera, Green Shirts, 294.

[17] Florea Nedelcu, "Cu privire la politica externă a României în perioada guvernării Goga-Cuza," *Studii privind politica externă a României 1914-1939,* (1969), 185; Hillgruber, *op. Cit.*

[18] Montgomery to Roosevelt, January 28, 1938, President's Secretary File, Franklin D. Roosevelt Library; *Foreign Relations* 1938, II, 672-674.

from the situation in Rumania."[19] Roosevelt authorized the Romanian Minister in Washington "to send a personal message to King Carol expressing the hope that he would keep Rumania within the sphere of democracy." [20] The French were especially alarmed. Not only was Romania their main ally in the Balkans, but also she was a member of both the Balkan and Little Ententes. Camille Chautemps, the French Premier, told the American Ambassador Bullitt that "Carol's action in choosing Goga was a severe blow to France." Chautemps expected Goga to follow the foreign policy of his predecessors for the moment, "but after the elections ... Rumania would move further into the German-Italian orbit."[21]

Bucharest tried to allay these fears by claiming that Romania's foreign policy would remain basically the same. In a press interview on January 4 the new Foreign Minister, Istrate Micescu, asserted that "the Rumanian Government remains faithful to the treaties which bind it to France, Poland, and the Little and Balkan entente."[22] "We have never thought," Goga added, "that the traditional ties with France

---

[19] Bullitt to Secretary of State, December 31, 1937, State Department Telegram, No.1795, 871.00/554.
[20] Moffat's Conversation with the Romanian Minister Charles A. Davila, December 31, 1937, State Department Memorandum, 871.00/557; Nedelcu, *Politica externă a României în perioada guvernării Goga-Cuza*, 190.
[21] *Foreign Relations 1938*, I, 1-2; Nedelcu, *op. cit.*, 189-190.
[22] Gunther to Secretary of State, January 20, 1938, State Department Dispatch, 871.00/591, 13. See also *Documents Diplomatiques Francais* 1932-1939, (Paris, 1972), 2e Serie, VII, 796, 813-816; Oprea, *Titulescu's Diplomatic Activity*, 162.

could be harmed in any way whatsover." Goga also announced on several occasions that he desired "to maintain the closest relations with England."[23] But at the same time, the new government emphasized extending Romania's friendship to "other nations."[24] In spite of its reassurances, the Goga Government failed to calm Western statesmen.

No sooner had the Goga Government taken office than it began a cruel campaign against the Jewsz[25] London and Paris protested, with the French, whose interests in Romania were greater, taking the lead. At first the British were reluctant to support the strong countermeasures France advocated. Sir Ronald Lindsay, British Ambassador in Washington, told the American Under Secretary of State that if France stopped shipping arms to Romania it would drive the latter "more quickly into the arms of Germany and Italy."[26] But when mild protests failed, the British intensified their threats. At the end of January, Yvon Delbos and Anthony Eden, the French and British Foreign Ministers, respectively, threatened to regard the treaties which recognized Romania's ownership of Transylvania and

---

[23] Gunther to Secretary of State, January 20, 1938, State Department Dispatch, 13-14.

[24] *Ibid.*, 12.

[25] The actions against the Jews largely centered around restrictive measures which deprived thousands of them of their Romanian citizenship, closed down Jewish businesses, and dismissed hundreds from the professions. There were also frequent reports of Jews being beaten according to the American Legation in Bucharest.

[26] Sumner Welles's Conversation with Lindsay, January 5, 1938, State Department Memorandum, 871.00/565.

Bessarabia as being annulled if the Goga Government continued its attacks on the Jewsz.[27] While this was going on, the American Government made several informal protests concerning the Jewish situation, but refused to participate directly with England and France.[28] This cautious approach was in accordance with the State Department's policy of staying out of Romania's domestic affairs when it did not directly involve American citizens and interests.[29]

The French protested the loudest. On 9 February the French Minister in Bucharest confided to Gunther that he received

> telegraphic instructions from his Government to protest vehemently the apparent trend of this government ... away from traditional alliances. The treatment of Jews and the application ... of the minorities treaty. Thierry added that his government was "very angry" with the Government of Goga and that he would present alternatives of it either mending its ways or facing withdrawal of French support constituting munitions, French 75s, military secrets, et cetera.[30]

---

[27] *Foreign Relations 1938*, I, 5. Also Nedelcu, *Politica externă a României în perioada guvernării Goga-Cuza*, 206.

[28] *Foreign Relations 1938*, I, 6; *Foreign Relations 1938*, 11, 674; *Time*, January 24, 1938,16.

[29] *Foreign Relations 1938*, II, 674-675.

[30] Gunther to Secretary of State, February 9, 1938, State Department Telegram, No. 21, 751.71/33.

The English Minister received similar instructions from London, but with the emphasis on the Jewish question.[31] Shortly afterwards, Thierry, in a "spirited conversation" with Carol which lasted for several hours, presented his demands.[32] At the same time, the British Minister, in a

> much milder form … asked Goga whether Rumania was prepared to suspend any coercive measures against the Jewish population until this matter had been given further consideration at Geneva. Goga said yes to this question.[33]

The next day Goga was forced to resign.

The hectic career of the Goga Government had lasted only six weeks. In its stormy period in office, among other things, it helped to cause a decline in trade, a paralyzing of the stock market, and an overall business depression; public confidence in the government decreased, and disturb- ances developed everywhere; the Russian Government recalled its Minister, and the approaching electoral campaign appeared to be turning into a full-fledged war.[34] The protests of the French and British governments helped to get Goga removed, but the crucial reason had to do with Romania's domestic affairs.[35]

---

[31] *Ibid.*

[32] *Documents on German Foreign* Policy 1918-1945, (Washington, 1949), Series D, V, 250.

[33] *Ibid.*

[34] Gunther to Secretary of State, February 21, 1938, State Department Dispatch, No 179, 871.00/610; *The Times*, London, February 12, 1938.

[35] Hillgruber. Hitler, *König Carol und Marschall Antonescu*, 15-16; German Foreign Policy, V, 250-251; Gunther to Secretary of

New elections had been scheduled for March. Goga, whose party was only the fourth largest, was desperately trying to increase his popular support. In order to reduce the fighting among the extreme right - already several people had been murdered, dozens gravely wounded, and approximately four hundred and fifty arrested - and achieve some unity for the election, he entered into negotiations with Codreanu. With the help of the Germans, on February, Goga and Codreanu reached a limited agreement.[36]

In an effort to end the violence between their two parties Codreanu agreed to reduce his electoral activities. The prospects of unity among the rightwing radicals, however, was alarming to Carol. This, coupled with the likelihood that the Iron Guard would significantly increase its strength in the coming election, caused the King to take drastic counter-measures.[37] He cancelled the elections and prepared a royal coup d'etat. On 10 February, Carol offered Goga the premiership of a new authoritarian government based on royal authority. But Goga turned it down. He insisted on holding the elections. As a result Carol simply dismissed him.[38] Bitter to the end, that night on the radio the poet

---

State, February 11, 1938, State Department Telegram. No. 23, 871.00/596.

[36] Hillgruber, op. cit., 15.

[37] Ibid. Eugen Weber, "Romania," The European Right, A Historical Profile (eds. Hans Rogger; Eugen Weber, Berkeley, California, 1965), 551.

[38] German Foreign Policy, V, 250-251; Carol realized Goga was hardly fit to be Premier. Why he wanted him to remain in office is questionable. Probably he hoped to keep the right divided and retain some of its support.

ended " his farewell address with the cry: "Israel you have won!" In the mean time, Carol carried out a coup d'etat from above. The time for opera bouffe was over.

Carol now created a government based upon ideas he had harbored since he first came to power: a royal dictatorship with Fascist trappings and a strong emphasis on youth. He abolished the Constitution of 1923 and promulgated a new corporatist constitution, which was ratified by a plebiscite with supposedly ninety-nine percent of the voters approving. Martial law was extended to all parts of the country; the power of the legislative bodies was greatly weakened; ministers were to be selected by the king, and were solely responsible to him; and universal suffrage was suppressed. Under the new constitution only men and women who worked in certain occupations and were over thirty could vote. According to the American Legation in Bucharest this was "aimed directly at the youthful Iron Guardist."[39] Political parties were outlawed, their club rooms closed, and their newspapers rigorously censored. "The brunt of the entire movement," wrote Gunther, "was taken by the lron Guard, against which it was largely aimed."[40] Within the next several months thousands of Guardists were arrested, including Codreanu, who was sentenced to ten years in prison for treason.[41]

Gheorghe Tătărescu, a reputed francophile, was appointed Foreign Secretary. Carol, however, now directed

---

[39] Gunther to Secretary of State, June 13,1938, State Department dispatch, 3.
[40] *Ibid.*, 4.
[41] Klaus Charle, *Die Eiserne Garde* (Berlin-Wien, 1939), 32.

the country's foreign affairs. "Rumanian foreign policy," declared the American Minister, "is the King's policy."[42] In order to allay fears in the West, the new Romanian Government announced on 16 February that it was continuing its traditional foreign policy.[43] Special emphasis was given to Romania's friendship with France. In the same statement the government noted:

> The constant efforts of Great Britain to safeguard peace and to defend the rights laid down by the Treaties obviously place us on the lines followed by British policy. A wide development of Anglo-Rumanian relations in all spheres will therefore be one of our principal tasks.[44]

After Goga's dismissal, relations between Romania and the Western democracies returned to a more normal basis. The French Ambassador to Turkey called the change of Government "a piece of good news ... a decided set-back for the Iron Guard and for Hitlerism in Romania."[45] While the campaign against the Jews did not end, it died down considerably.[46] One of the surprising outcomes of the Goga interlude and subsequent dictatorship of the King was the enhancing of Carol's reputation in England. He came to be viewed as a strong ruler and the savior of Romania from

---

[42] Gunther to Secretary of State, op. cit., 7.

[43] *Documents on International Affairs* 1938 (ed. Monica Curtis, London), 290-291.

[44] *Documents on International Affairs* 1938, I, 290.

[45] Bullitt to Secretary of State, February 11, 1938, State Department Telegram, No. 229, 871.00/599.

[46] Gunther to Secretary of State, June 13,1938, State Department Dispatch, 5.

Fascism.[47] The invitation to make a state visit to England, which had been cancelled after Carol nominated Goga, was renewed. The American Minister to Romania also was impressed with the King's achievements. A lengthy report from Gunther to the State Department on Carol's dictatorship concluded with the remarks:

> The country, professional politicians excepted, has not taken unkindly to the dictatorial regime. Quiet and calm prevail, and there is marked satisfaction at the absence of the bitter political strife which formerly constituted so prominent a part of public life.[48]

> A later report by the American Legation pointed out that law and order are established, political strife is eliminated, the peasant is peaceful, and the country is probably accomplishing more work than at any other time in its history.[49]

While Carol was establishing his dictatorship and driving the Iron Guard underground, Romania's international situation was also significantly changing. The deteriorating position of France in South Eastern Europe was further weakened by the union of Austria and Germany

---

[47] See *The Times*, London, February 12, April 1, 19, November 15-18, 1938. *The Manchester Guardian*, November 15-18, 1938; *The Evening Standard*, November 15-18, 1938, *Fortnightly* (January-June, 1938), 580-587, *Fortnightly* (January-June, 1939), 315-319; *New Statesman and Nation* (January-June, 1939), 450-451.
[48] Gunther to Secretary of State, June 13,1938, State Department Dispatch, 11.
[49] American Legation to Secretary of State, August 10, 1939, State Department Dispatch, 42.

in March, 1938. With the Anschluss, French hegemony over South Eastern Europe ended The old balance of power was replaced by an unstable equilibrium between three power groups: France-Great Britain, Germany- Italy, and Soviet Russia. As a result of this, Romania's position became more insecure. With the decline of her traditional ally France, Romania began moving closer to Germany and towards a position of neutrality in inter national affairs. The Anschluss accelerated this. The new power balance forced Romania to follow a cautious policy of maintaining good relations with both the Fascist and the democratic powers. "Carol," Gunther wrote, is "standing back and waiting to see what will happen."[50]

Britain's criticisms of the Goga government failed to dampen Carol's desire to improve relations between the two countries. Throughout the winter of 1938, the reports of the American Minister in Bucharest frequently mentioned the Romanian Government's growing interest in Britain. The English, and not the Romanians, cancelled Carol's state visit.[51] Even the Goga Government supported the visit. The renewed invitation to Carol scheduled the visit for the end of March. But unfortunately for Carol, the sudden German action against Austria forced him to cancel it. Gunther

---

[50] Gunther to Secretary of State, June 13, 1938, State Department Dispatch, 6.

[51] Jerome et Jean Tharaud, *L'envoye de I'Archange* (Paris, 1939), 210.

reported that the King did this "with great reluctance."[52] The American Minister believed that Carol's decision was

> inspired by a feeling of caution that it would not do to appear too closely aligned at the present moment with the western powers in case they prove ineffectual in arresting the march of events in Central Europe.[53]

British involvement in Romania developed slowly. Since May, 1937, the British Prime Minister as Neville Chamberlain, a man whose name has become almost synonymous with appeasement. His beliefs, however, were close to those of most British statesmen and the bulk of public opinion of his time.[54] In his late sixties, confident and energetic, although at times naive, he abhorred war and believed that it had to be avoided at almost all costs. Having little respect for the military power of France and the Soviet Union, he felt that England and Gemany would be the two dominant powers in the future.[55] In order to avoid a war with Germany, Chamberlain hoped to reach an understanding with Hitler based on the recognition of the common interests of both nations. It was inconceivable to him that a foreign ruler could willfully seek the mastery of Europe which must ultimately lead to a conflict with

---

[52] Gunther to Secretary of State, June 13, 1938,'State Department Dispatch, 6; New York Times, March 16, 1938.

[53] Gunther to Secretary Of State, March 16, 1938, State Department Telegram, No. 43, 871.001 CAROL 11/133.

[54] F. S. Northedge, *The Troubled Giant: Britain Among the Great Powers 1916-1939* (New York, 1966), 481.

[55] *Ibid.*, 481-482.

Britain.[56] Chamberlain's views on British policy towards South Eastern Europe were in keeping with the traditional outlook of British statesmen, a philosophy which caused many in Romania to doubt that in a conflict England would help them. Moreover, there was a widespread belief that in order to appease Hitler the English were willing to give Germany a free hand in Eastern Europe.[57]

One English statesman who wanted to see London assume a more important role in Romania was Sir Reginald Hoare, the British Minister in Bucharest. The American Minister to Romania, who had served with Hoare before had a high opinion of him, notified Washington "that he had been urging his Government to assume a vital interest here."[58] Gunther considered this

> an interesting thought... and not illogical when one considers the geographic situation of Rumania: if Great Britain is ever seriously to attempt to stem the German Drang nach Osten, a strong Rumania in which Great Britain has a vital interest would be a serious stumbling block in the path of Mr. Hitler.[59]

---

[56] *Ibid.*, 482.

[57] Pierrepont Moffat, January 3, 1938, State Department Memorandum, 871.00/560; Pavel Pavel, *Why Rumania Failed*, 157-158; Mircea Malița, *Romanian Diplomacy: A Historical Survey* (Bucharest, 1970), 108.

[58] Gunther to Secretary of State, March 17, 1938, State Department Dispatch, No. 215, 740.00/345, 1-2.

[59] Gunther to Secretary of State, March 17, 1938, State Department Dispatch, No. 2. Sir Reginald Hoare was a career diplomat. He entered the diplomatic service in 1905. He served in Constantinople, Rome, Peiping, Leningrad, Warsaw, and

In the spring of 1938, despite Britain's policy of appeasement and traditional outlook towards South Eastern Europe, there were further signs of growing English interest in Romania. There was talk of British loans, and numerous visits by noted Englishmen to Romania to investigate the possibility of capital investments.[60] The Romanian press was especially favorable to Britain, and an English chair was established at Bucharest University.[61]

Foreign Minister Nicolae Petrescu-Comnen - the third in as many months - described the interest which the English manifested in the development of the economy as "unprecedented."

During the summer, indications of British involvement in Romania continued. The American Legation reported that "for the first time England is resorting to propaganda here both cultural and economic."

> In the cultural field there have been a series of lectures, the organization of a British Institute for the teaching of English and emphasis on newspaper propaganda through Reuter's which it is understood is now controlled by the British Government.[62]

In June, the versatile Tătărescu showed up in London on an unofficial visit to strengthen economic relations between

Cairo. From 1931 to 1935, he was Minister to Persia. In 1935 he was appointed to Romania.

[60] American Legation to Secretary of State, August 10, 1939, State Department Dispatch, 32.

[61] American Legation to Secretary of State, August 10, 1939, State Department Dispatch, 32.

[62] Gunther to Secretary of State, October 20, 1938, State Department Dispatch, No. 571, 871.00/652, 7.

the two countries. Later, Lord Lloyd, the head of the British Council, visited King Carol. This flurry of British activity climaxed with the English purchase of two hundred thousand tons of Romanian wheat in order to help the latter solve her huge wheat surplus problem.[63] These activities worried the tall, pot-bellied German Ambassador in Bucharest, Wilhelm Fabricius. In July, he advised the Foreign Ministry

> that prompt and satisfactory deliveries in the armaments field are the best means for combating the fanciful designs of the British for erecting an economic bulwark against German expansion.[64]

By the end of August, the Germans had altered their tactics. Fabricius told Comnen that Germany was interested in buying "wheat in considerable quantities to help Rumania out of her difficulty." But Fabricius pointed out, "it is out of the question for us to make an offer so long as M. Milita Constantinescu continued his British policy."[65] At the same time, he advised Berlin to be cautious in making purchase offers for fear of helping British transactions. On a number of occasions in conversations with Romanian officials,

---

[63] Letter from Leith-Ross to Sargent. January 16, 1939, F.O. 371/23831 R395/21/67, F. Public Record Office; L. Zvkova, "British Economic Policy in the Balkans on the Eve of World War 11," *Studia Balcanica*, 4, (1971), 176-177.

[64] *German Foreign Policy*, V, 290.

[65] *Ibid.*, V, 319. Constantinescu was the Governor of the Romanian National Bank and Minister of National Economy. Berlin viewed him as one of the chief instigators behind the attempt to bring Romania and England closer together economically.

Fabricius dangled the possibility of large German purchases of various items, but only if the Romanians orientated their policy away from England.

The prime concern of the British Foreign Office during the summer of 1938 was the crisis over Czechoslovakia. Above all else, Britain wanted to avoid getting into a war with Germany, and sought to negotiate a peaceful settlement of the crisis with Hitler. The Romanian Government was also deeply involved in the crisis, and like the British, dreaded the prospects of war. Unlike Britain, Romania had a treaty with Czechoslovakia. As a member of the Little Entente, Romania was committed to help the Czechs if they were attacked by Hungary. Both Britain and Romania feared, however, that if a conflict broke out between Germany and Czechoslovakia they would be forced into it. In some ways Britain and Romania worked closely during the crisis. The suspicious Germans notified Berlin that "Rumania had been kept informed by Great Britain about every phase of the present crisis. [66] More important, on several occasions, the two governments joined together in urging the Czech leaders to make concessions.[67]

The Romanian Government was especially concerned with the question of permitting the transit of Russian forces across its territory. Since the end of World War I, relations between Romania and Russia had been poor. The two countries did not reestablish diplomatic relations until June, 1934, and the Soviets never recognized the loss of Bessarabia.

---

[66]*German Foreign Policy*, II, 337.

[67] *Ibid*; Josef Lipski, Diplomat in Berlin 1933-1939: *Papers and Memoirs* (New York 1968), 376.

Romania feared Russia more than she did Germany.[68] The French and German governments were also enmeshed in the transit question, but Britain refused to get involved. On a number of occasions during the spring and summer of 1938, France asked the Romanians to grant the Soviets permission to cross their territory, but England never supported these efforts.[69] Where as the british wanted the Czechs to make

---

[68] As Romania's Foreign Minister from 1932 to 1936, Titulescu sought to improve relations with the Soviet Union, especially with an eye on getting Soviet recognition of the status of Bessarabia. It was through Titulescu's efforts that relations between Romania and Russia, broken since the First World War, were reestablished. Shortly before he was dismissed from the government by King Carol in August, 1936, he was on the verge of a concluding Mutual Assistance Pact with the Soviets which included the latter's de facto recognition of the loss of Bessarabia. It was in part the strong opposition both from within and outside Romania to Titulescu's attempts to establish closer relations with the Russians that led to his downfall. The Mutual Assistance Pact was never signed. For a recent study of Titulescu's diplomatic activities see I. M. Oprea, *Nicolae Titulescu's Diplomatic Activity* (Bucharest, 1968).

[69] France tried to persuade Romania to allow Soviet troops and planes to cross her territory to aid Czechoslovakia if the latter was attacked by Germany. The Russians informed the French in the spring of 1938 that they would not be able to aid the Czechs without getting such approval from either Romania or Poland. The Romanians especially feared Russian troops on their territory and refused to make any concessions on this point. The Romanians, however, hinted that they might close their eyes to Russian planes, and, on several occasions, did nothing to stop Czech crews from flying Soviet aircraft over their land. But this was not sufficient for Moscow. In the end

concessions, it is understandable that they would not support these efforts which, if successful, could only encourage the Czechs to resist German demands. England viewed neu trality as the safest course. The Munich Agreement further shifted the balance of power in South Eastern Europe in favor of Germany, as well as increased her influence over Romania. Romania's strategic location and her numerous resources made her a potentially valuable ally for Hitler. Since 1934 Berlin had concentrated primarily on developing commercial relations with Romania, being especially interested in the latter's oil. At the same time, she saw the establishment of close economic ties with Romania as a means of bringing her within the political orbit of the Reich.[70] By the end of 1938, one-third of Romania's trade was with Germany. One of the cardinal principles of Carol's foreign policy was to maintain friendly relations between the two countries. While Carol feared the growing power and influence of Germany, he agreed to her commercial

---

nothing materialized. *German Foreign Policy*, II, 283, 250, 337, 426-427, 434, 499, 500-501, 573-576, 746, 936; *Foreign Relations 1938*, I, 42, 502, 507-508, 583, 653. Boris Celovsky, *Das Münchener Abkommen* 1938 (Stuttgart, 1958), 320.

[70]This was the basic policy of the German Government towards Romania, despite the occasional meddling in Romania's internal affairs by the Foreign Division of the Nazi Party under Rosenberg. The latter's activities helped to hinder relations between the two countries. Hillgruber, *Hitler, König Carol und Marschall Antonescu*, 12, 80-86; Weinberg, *Foreign Policy of Hitler's Germany*, 230, 324-325; Jocobsen. Nationalsozialistische Aussenpolitik, 82.

treaties, partly because of Romania's economic situation and also for reasons of power politics.[71]

The Munich settlement further stimulated Carol's desire to bring about closer relations with Great Britain. In order to offset the growing supremacy of Germany in South Eastern Europe, the resourceful King hoped that England would assume a more important role. [72] Moreover, he was convinced that in a future war, barring a Communist triumph, England would ultimately be victorious. [73] "Therefore in his view," stated the astute German Minister to Romania, "it is advisable to be on the side of Great Britain."[74] Carol also hoped to establish closer economic relations with Britain, especially with an eye to borrowing money in order to purchase much needed military equipment.

In the future, with the disruption of Czechoslovakia, one of Romania's chief suppliers of military hardware, England

---

[71] Essentially, Germany provided Romania with the highest prices for her goods, as well as other economic advantages Romania could not obtain elsewhere. A student of the Romanian economy, Henry Roberts, wrote: "In the absence of remunerative world prices and the failure of the other great powers to provide any assistance, Germany's policy ... was a benefit faute de mieux." Roberts, *Rumania*, 216. Also Deutsch, *Foreign Policy of Romania*," 130-131; Antonin Basch, *The Danube Basin and the German Economic Sphere* (New York, 1943), 179, 184, 191-192.

[72] Viorica Moisuc, "Orientations dans la politique exterieure de la Roumanie apres le Pact de Munich," *Revue Roumaine d'Histoire*, V, 1966), II, 327-330; Hillgruber, *Hitler, König Carol und Marschall Antonescu*, 23.

[73] *German Foreign Policy*, II, 574.

[74] *Ibid.*

would become more significant in Carol's plans for strengthening his armed forces.

Important changes also took place in Britain's foreign policy as a result of the Munich Pact. Prime Minister Chamberlain viewed the agreement as not only saving Europe from war, but also as an important steppingstone to better English-German relations. But unfortunately for King Carol, in order not to antagonize Germany, London's policy toward South Eastern Europe became cautious and hesitant once more.

In November, the King of Romania finally made his long-awaited official state visit to England. [75] He was accompanied by his son, Crown Prince Michael, Foreign Minister Petrescu-Comnen, and a number of other high government officials. The reception he received manifested the change of his image in England. Carol spent three days in London, where he received a very warm welcome. The press praised his courage in resisting Fascism in Romania.[76] He met the King, the Prime Minister, and other government officials, as well as a number of important businessmen. He was the guest at several lavish banquets, a parade was given in his honor, and he was made a Knight of the Garter.[77] The trip was very successful for propaganda and prestige

---

[75] The date for the visit was finally set on 17 October. See N. P. Comnene, *Preludi del grande dramma* (Roma, 1947), 277. The visit took place from 15 to 18 November.

[76] See *The Times* (London), *The Manchester Guardian*, and *The Evening Standard* for 15-18 November.

[77] *The Times*, London, November 15-18, 1938; *New York Times*. November 16, 1938.

purposes. For this great-grandson of Queen Victoria, who ten years earlier had been forced to leave the country, it was a great personal triumph. But, in practical terms, the visit was disappointing.

On the night of 16 November, Chamberlain and his Foreign Minister, Lord Halifax, had discussion with Carol. Carol wanted to find out how a far Britain was willing to get involved in Romania and how much assistance she was willing to give.[78] He was particularly interested in acquiring loans and credit to buy armaments, and a large increase in British purchases of wheat and oil. Chamberlain was evasive and noncommittal. He told Carol that Britain had not assigned Central and South Eastern Europe to Hitler as a sphere of interest, but "that natural forces seemed ... to make it inevitable that Germany should enjoy a preponderant position in the economic field."[79] Much of the conversation was on general European problems. On the economic proposals in which Carol was especially interested Chamberlain replied that he would like to re-examine them.[80] Carol's discussions with London political leaders and businessmen also produced few definite results. With the exception of a promise to send a trade mission to

---

[78] *Documents on British Foreign Policy* 1919-1939 (London. 1949-1954), Third Series, III, 231-232.

[79] *Ibid.,* 232.

[80] *Ibid.,* 233; Hillgruber, *Hitler, König Carol und Marschall Antonescu,* 25-26. Carol was especially interested in the following loans and credit, trade mission. Danube development, naval base, mercantile marines, timber, and silos.

Bucharest, three days after he arrived Carol left empty handed.

On the way back to Romania Carol visited Paris, where there were more lavish ceremonies and journalistic fanfare. But the practical results were also dismal.[81] The French, however, agreed to raise their minister in Bucharest to the rank of ambasador.[82]

While outwardly during the following winter there appeared to be a relaxation of international tensions, the British Foreign Office became increasingly worried about Hitler's future plans. What was beginning to trouble the Foreign Office the most was not whether Hitler would act, but in what direction. Reports from the British Embassies on the Continent reflected the growing fear that after Hitler finished with Czechoslovakia he would turn towards Poland, the Ukraine, or Romania. Joseph Kennedy, the wealthy American Ambassador to England, believed that in February Halifax

> came to the opinion ... that England must fight if Hitler enters Rumania. He is not inclined to think an entrance into Hungary should provoke a war because he says Hungary is at the present minute honeycombed with Nazism. But on a step into

[81] Charles A. Micaud, *The French Right and Nazi Germany 1933-1939* (New York, 1964), 190.

[82] Britain refused to take similar action. Her policy was to assign ambassadors only to the larger states. As the country with the third largest population in Eastern Europe, the Romanian Government believed that it was important enough for foreign governments to give their ministers in Bucharest the rank of ambassador.

Rumania he believes that England cannot wait any longer.[83]

The British also began to show interest in the condition of Romania's army. In November, when Carol saw Hitler at the Berghof in Bavaria following his London visit, discussions began about an extensive economic treaty between Germany and Romania. [84] The sudden, cold-blooded murder of Codreanu by the secret police, however, caused the Germans to abruptly cancel the discussions, and they were not resumed until the end of the following January. [85] In February the German Government sent Dr. Helmut Wohlthat, the Ministerial Director for special duties in the Reich Ministry of Economics, to Bucharest to continue

---

[83] Kennedy to Secretary of State, March 18, 1939, State Department Telegram, No. 360, 740.00/630.

[84] Carol had reservations about going to Germany, and it was only at the end of October that he decided to include it in his trip. His discussions with Hitler and Goring involved a host of political problems including Germany, Romania, and Eastern Europe, as well as talks about greater economic cooperation between the two countries. These economic discussions must have been furthered by Carol's failure to accomplish anything substantial in London and Paris. Hillgruber, *Hitler, König Carol und Marschall Antonescu*, 25-29; *German Foreign Policy*, V, 338-342, 344-347.

[85] On 30 November, shortly after Carol returned from his discussions with Hitler, he had Codreanu and thirteen of his followers killed. Hitler was furious, especially because he felt it might be concluded that this happened with his approval. For the next several months relations were strained between the two countries. Hillgruber, *Hitler, König Carol und Marschall Antonescu*, 29; Nagy-Talavera, Green Shirts, 301.

the negotiations. Many Romanians felt that Germany's economic objectives were too far reaching and that they would cause serious economic and political problems for their country.[86] Indeed, this was no normal economic treaty. Fabricius told the Foreign Ministry that if Wohlthat's proposals were agreed to Germany would achieve predominance in Romania.[87] During the middle of March the negotiations reached a climax. The Romanian Government was in a precarious position. There were aspects of the treaty which Carol was very reluctant to go along with.[88] On the other hand, he feared antagonizing Hitler, and diplomatic relations had just begun to return to normal since the Codreanu murder.

Fearing the growing German influence in Romania as well as the developing crisis in Czechoslovakia, Viorel V. Tilea, the recently appointed Romanian Minister to England, tried to persuade the British Government to make several gestures to show its concern for his country.[89] The English had recently stepped-up their economic activity in Romania again, and in February, Lord Sempill, who represented a private British business group, talked with Carol and a

---

[86] Hillgruber, *Hitler, König Carol und Marschall Antonescu*, 46. See also Moisuc, "Politique exterieure de la Roumanie." 331, 333-334.

[87] *German Foreign Policy*, V, 393.

[88] Gunther to Secretary of State, April 5, 1939, State Department Dispatch, No. 834, 762.71/89, 2-3.

[89] *British Foreign Policy*, IV, 283-284; Gunther to Secretary of State, April 5, 1939, State Department Dispatch, 2-3; Christopher Thorne, *The Approach of War 1938-1939* (New York, 1967), 114.

number of other high government officials.[90] The Germans were worried. Upon arriving in Bucharest on 8 March, after a brief return to Germany, Wohlthat explained to the Foreign Ministry that it was fortunate he arrived when he did because of increasing British and French pressure against the treaty.[91] On 14 March, Tilea called on the British Foreign Office for an interview. To the Deputy Under Secretary of State Sir Orme Sargent, he pointed out his anxiety about the threatening situation in Eastern Europe, and urged him to announce the upcoming commercial mission to Romania at once, and to raise the British Legation in Bucharest to an embassy. But to Tilea's disappointment, Sargent merely replied that his suggestions would be considered.[92]

Nevertheless, Tilea was not a man who could be put off easily. Young, ambitious, and a passionate Anglophile, since his arrival in London at the beginning of February he had been busily trying to bring about closer Anglo-Romanian relations.[93] So far he had nothing to show for it. But this

---

[90] Lord Sempill's report of his visit to Romania, March 24, 1939, F.O. 371 /23832 R2005/113/37; *German Foreign Policy*, V, 395-396.
[91] *Ibid.*, 410.
[92] *British Foreign Policy*, IV, 283-284. See also Foreign Office Minute discussion of proposed trade mission to Romania. March 2, 1939, F.O. 371 /23832 R1470/113/37; Foreign Office to Hoare, March 4, 1939, F.O.371/23832 R1495/113/37.
[93] Foreign Office to Bucharest, February 3, 1939. F.O. 371/23831 R826/113/37; Conversation between Leith-Ross and Tilea, February 2, 1939, F.O.371/23831 R827/113/37; Conversation between Hudson and Tilea, February 22, 1939, F.O.371/23832

situation was about to change rapidly. In the early morning hours of March 15, German troops swiftly occupied the rest of Czechoslovakia. Berlin announced that the Wehrmacht had been sent in to end the "reign of terror" against Germans and to maintain law and order. On the same day, German troops entered the newly proclaimed "independent" Slovakia, which now became a German protectorate. Englishmen were startled and outraged.[94] Hitler had broken his Munich promise. The view that he could be stopped by paper treaties was shattered. Moreover, many feared further German aggression in a matter of days[95]

On the afternoon of the 16th, Tilea hurried to the Foreign Office. The excited Romanian Minister told Sargent that

> his government, from secret and other sources had good reason to believe that within the next few months the German Government would … proceed to disintegrate Rumania in the same way as they had disintegrated Czech-Slovakia, with the ultimate object of establishing a German protectorate over the whole country.[96]

Tilea then asked "how far they could count upon Great Britain in the event of their having in the near future to face and resist as they certainly would a German threat of this

---

R1342/113/37. For recent account of Tilea see Sidney Aster, *1939* (New York, 1973), chapter three.

[94] Martin Gilbett; Richard Gott, *The Appeasers* (Boston, 1963), 233; William Rock, *Appeasement on Trial* (New York, 1966), 203-211.

[95] Gilbert, *op. cit.*, 234.

[96] *British Foreign Policy*, IV, 284.

kind."[97] He also requested that Britain loan Romania ten million pounds for the purchase of war materials.[98] This time Sargent was worried. Without promising anything though, Sargent explained that his proposals raised "questions of high policy," and that he would contact Lord Halifax. At 6 a.m. on the following morning, Tilea received "a mysterious telephone call from Paris." The caller, whose voice Tilea immediately recognized, informed him of the far-reaching economic demands the Germans were making on Romania.[99] Later that morning, he received a telegram from Bucharest telling him to warn the British Government of the potentially grave consequences to all European natins of the growing belief that Hitler was the sole arbiter of their fate.[100]

That afternoon Tilea rushed back to the Foreign Office. This time he spoke to Lord Halifax. He told the Foreign Minister that

> during the last few days the Roumanian Government had received a request from the German Government to grant them a monopoly of Roumanian exports, and to adopt certain measures of restriction of Roumanian industrial production in German interests. If these conditions were accepted, Germany

---

[97] *Ibid.*

[98] *Ibid.*

[99] *The Times,* London, November 20,1968. Who this was is still unknown.

[100] Viorica Moisuc, *Diplomația României și problema apărării suveranității și independenței naționale în perioada martie 1938 - mai 1940* (București, 1971), 137-138.

would guarantee the Roumanian frontiers. This seemed to the Roumanian Government something very much like an ultimatum... In the view of his Government it was of the utmost importance that His Majesty's government should consider with all urgency whether they could give a precise indication of the action they would take in the event of Roumania being a victim of German aggression. If it was possible to construct a solid block of Poland, Roumania, Greece, Turkey, Yugoslavia with the support of Great Britain and France it was to be expected that the situation might be saved.[101]

In stressing the urgency of the situation, Tilea warned that "it was by no means to be excluded that the German Government would make an almost immediate thrust upon Roumania." [102] Tilea, who had little previous diplomatic experience, exaggerated. [103] Nevertheless, Halifax was alarmed. The Roumanian Minister's warning, coming just after Hitler's seizure of Bohemia and Moravia, produced a startling shift in British foreign policy. The occupation of the rest of Czechoslovakia destroyed the longheld British belief that Hitler was interested only in taking over lands with a large German population. Englishmen now feared that

----

[101] *British Foreign Policy*, IV, 366-367.

[102] *Ibid*.

[103] Letter Radu Florescu Sr., to the author, June 25, 1976; Gunther to Secretary of State Department Dispatch, State, April 5, 1939, 3; British Foreign Policy, *op. cit.*, 398-399; Gunther to Secretary of State, April 4, 1939, State Department Dispatch, No. 830, 762.71/87, 1-2. See explanatory footnote on page 42.

Hitler's real goal was to conquer Europe and Romania appeared to be the next victim.[104] The Cabinet felt something had to be done at once. Halifax, who was becoming increasingly disillusioned with appeasement over the last several months, took the lead. Hesitant at first, Chamberlain was swept along by the force of public opinion.[105]

The day after his talks with Tilea, Halifax notified his ambassadors in France, Russia, Poland, Turkey, Greece, and Yugoslavia of the new German threats and to inquire what these states would do to help Romania.[106] Shortly before, the Chiefs of Staff had told government officials that if Berlin controlled Romania's oil the effects of a British wartime blockade would be largely nullified. Furthermore, German domination of Romania would allow them to directly threaten Greece, Turkey, and the Eastern Mediterranean.[107] Any hopes Halifax had for a quick solution, however, were now dealt a dash of cold water. The replies from the Continent were evasive. They all wanted to know what Great Britain intended to do!

---

[104] Lord Halifax, *Fullness of Days* (New York, 1957), 208-209; Northedge, *Troubled Giant*, 568; B. H. Liddell Hart, *The Liddell Hart Memoirs* (New York, 1965), 219-220.

[105] Kennedy believed that if Chamberlain opposed taking action to defend Romania there would have been a break between the Prime Minister and Halifax. Kennedy to Secretary State , March 18,1939, State Department Telegram.

[106] *British Foreign Policy*, IV, 360-361; *The Diplomatic Diaries of Oliver Harvey* 1937-1940 (ed. John Harvey, London, 1970), 262.

[107] The Diaries of Sir Alexander Cadogan 1938-1945 (ed. David Dilks, New York, 1971), 160.

In the meantime, the Foreign Office had been trying to work out a plan by which military assistance could be given to Romania in case of a German attack. The British never had the illusion that they could defend Romania's frontiers with English soldiers.[108] They decided to try to form a bloc of states in Eastern Europe which would be able to provide direct military aid to Romania, as well as to each other, in case of attack. As a first step they proposed that the governments of Poland, France, and Russia join with them in making a four-power declaration of solidarity to resist aggression.[109] The Foreign Office notified these governments of its four-power plan on the 20th.

While the Foreign Office was trying to devise a plan to protect Romania, a curious fact came to light which might have caused the British to postpone their plans to help Romania. [110] On the day after Tilea's conversation with Halifax, Hoare reported that the Romanian Foreign Minister told him that the Germans had never threatened them with an Two days later Hoare saw the King who also stated that there had been no ultimatum. He added, however, that "Roumania would resist German pressure but could not do so indefinitely without support."[111] While these statements

---

[108] B*ritish Foreign Policy*, IV, 460.

[109] *Ibid*., 400; William R. Rock, *Neville Chamberlain* (New York, 1969), 175-176.

[110] *British Foreign Policy*, IV, 370.

[111] *Ibid*., 398. If this is the truth of the matter, as the evidence indicates (an ultimatum has never shown up in any archive to date), where did the idea of an ultimatum come from? Did Tilea invent it, or was he acting on instructions from Bucharest? In a recent letter to this author, M. Radu Florescu,

perhaps reduced the urgency of assisting Romania, Britain's policy remained the same. In the same telegram notifying the British ambassadors of the four-power declaration the Foreign Office pointed out

> that in spite of doubts as to accuracy of reports of German ultimatum to Roumania, recent German absorption of Czecho-Slovakia shows clearly that German Government are resolved to go beyond their hitherto avowed aim of consolidation of German race ... In the circumstances thus created it seems to His

---

who at the time was Counsellor of the Romanian Legation in London and acted as charge d'affaires when Tilea was away, wrote: "There was no ultimatum." Tilea "called it an ultimatum" because of "his inexperience in handling diplomatic business." Other evidence supports this. Before he left Bucharest for his London post, Tilea had received a broad mandate from King Carol to do all he could to bring the two nations closer together. On 20 March Hoare informed the Foreign Office that he was "inclined to conclude that before leaving for London" Tilea had received from Carol "some sort of general instructions to ue every effort to convince ... H. M. Government of the necessities of the situation in South-Eastern Europe and that he set about his task with impulsive naivete." This also agrees with the reports of Gunther, who around the beginning of April. 1939, had several conversations with Tilea. Following these talks he notified the State Department that Tilea "admitted to me that he only followed his instructions without using the word ultimatum." Gafencu described it as an "excess of zeal." Letter. Radu Florescu Sr., to the author, June 25, 1976; *British Foreign Policy*, IV, 399; Gunther to Secretary of State, April 5, 1939, State Department Dispatch, 3; Aster, 1939, 66-67.

Majesty's Government in the United Kingdom to be desirable to proceed without delay to the organization of mutual support on the part of all those who realize the necessity of protecting international society from further violation of fundamental laws on which it rests.[112]

A Foreign Office memorandum written about a week later described Germany's activities in the East as a prelude to an attack in the West.[113] Numerous reports were also coming into the Foreign Office that Hungary was preparing an invasion of Romania. Pock-marked faced Ernest Urdăreanu, Carol's right-hand man, informed Hoare on 21 March that "Hungarian mobilization is acquiring threatening proportions and Roumanians have almost certain knowledge that twenty-five German divisions are on the Hungarian frontier."[114] On the following day in a high level discussion between British and French officials, Chamberlain stated "Germany might well apply the modern technique and deliver her attack in the guise of an attack by Hungary."[115]

At the same time, the French Government, which had been receiving similar information about the situation in

[112] British Foreign Policy, *op. cit.*, 400; Harvey, Diplomatic Diaries, 263.

[113] British Foreign Policy, *op. cit.*, 615.

[114] *Ibid.*, 433; Moisuc, "Politique exterieure de la Roumanie," 336: Malita, *Roumanian Diplomacy*, 108; G. Bonnet, *Fin d'une Europe* (Genf, 1948), 157.

[115] British Foreign Policy, op. cit., 460.

Romania, strongly supported Britain's activities.[116] Daladier warned the French Cabinet that when Germany controls Romania's oil supplies, she will be able to wage war against all Europe. [117] The Quai d'Orsay informed the British Embassy that France would support Romania regardless of the reply from Poland, Russia, and Yugoslavia. [118] The United States also encouraged Britain not to abandon Romania. Kennedy said to Halifax that America would be "more readily moved" to support Britain if she aided Romania, than if she did nothing. If, having abandoned Romania, England became involved in a conflict with Germany in defending Greece or Turkey, America might not come to her aid.[119]

The replies to Britain's four-power declaration were disappointing; only France supported it without attaching reservations. Strange as it would seem later, Poland, not Russia, was the crucial factor. Both Britain and France had grave doubts about the effectiveness of the Red Army, especially after the recent officer purges, and believed that Poland had the strongest fighting force in the East. [120] Colonel Beck, the Polish Foreign Minister, replied that Poland could not associate with Russia for fear of provoking

---

[116] *British Foreign Policy*, IV, 396-397; Gunther to Secretary of State, April 5, 1939, State Department Dispatch, 3.
[117] Bonnet, *Fin d'une Europe*, 155.
[118] British Foreign Policy, *op. cit.*, 397; Sir John Slessor, *The Central Blue: The Auto biography of Sir John Slessor, Marshal of the RAF* (New York, 1957), 230.
[119] British Foreign Policy, *op. cit.*, 380.
[120] L. S. Amery, My Political Life (London, 1955), 111, 309, 318; Keith Feiling, *The Life of Neville Chamberlain* (London, 1946), 403.

Germany. Beck added,however, that "Poland might be able to… if Soviet Russia were omitted."[121] The Romanians also were reluctant to associate with Russia. Grigore Gafencu informed the British Minister that instead of a four-power declaration the

> Western Powers should state in precise terms that they will not allow any further changes of the frontiers and will support any state that defends its independence with all the military force at their disposal.[122]

On 22 March, Halifax and Bonnet agreed that because of the hostile feelings towards Russia they would have to postpone attempts to obtain her support for Romania.[123] For the next several days both men worked closely in trying to devise a plan that would secure Poland's support.

On the day following the Anglo-French discussions, Romania signed the controversial economic treaty with Germany. The English were disappointed, but continued with their plans to protect Romania. Both the British and American Governments felt that the effectiveness of the treaty as a factor in Germany's expansion program would depend upon its application. [124] Since 15 March, the Romanian Government had been as fearful of an invasion by

---

[121] *British Foreign Policy*, IV, 453.

[122] *Ibid.*, 421. Gafencu became Romania's Foreign Minister in December 1938.

[123] *Ibid.*, 459.

[124] Gunther to Secretary of State, April 5, 1939, State Department Dispatch, 3; *British Foreign Policy*, IV, 619, 311.

Hungary as it was of Germany.[125] When Hitler occuped Bohemia and Moravia, Hungarian troops attacked Ruthenia. Carol feared that the Hungarians might next make a grab for Transylvania, and rushed troops to the border. The Romanians, as well as the British and French, believed that Hungary worked closely with the Reich and that her foreign policy was largely dominated by Berlin. In the Anglo-French discussions on 22 March, Chamberlain asserted that "an attack by Hungary would be treated in the same way as an attack by Germany."[126] By signing the economic treaty with Germany, the Romanians hoped not only to placate Berlin, but also to make sure that Hitler kept a leash around Budapest.

On 27 March, Halifax notified Hoare of London's latest plan. Under this arrangement Britain and France would come to the aid of Romania and Poland if they were threatened, as long as the latter would also agree to help Romania if she were the victim. Romania was to be encouraged to make a similar promise to Poland, but because of her smaller army it would not be mandatory that

---

[125] Gunther to Secretary of State, April 5, 1939, State Department Dispatch, 3; *British Foreign Policy*, IV, 619, 311.

[126] British Foreign Policy, op. cit., 460. In a conversation with Sir Orme Sargent, M. Radu Florescu, the Romanian Charge d'affaires, asked if "the proposed guarantee would operate against an attack by Hungary as well as by Germany. I assured him that if Roumanian independence were threatened by Hungary, who obviously in that case would be collaborating with Germany, the guarantee contemplated under our scheme would apply." British Foreign Policy, *op. cit.*, 576.

she agree to this.[127] Romania favored this plan, but was hesitant about making a commitment to Poland especially since the threat of encirclement might provoke Germany. Poland was even more hesitant about making a promise to Romania. What Romania preferred was a direct Anglo-French guarantee with no mention of any other countries.[128]

Since the German annexation of Memel on 22 March, the fear had been growing in Britain that Poland might be Hitler's next victim. At the end of the month the English became alarmed. Amidst conflicting reports of an imminent German attack, Chamberlain announced on 31 March in the House of Commons a British guarantee to Poland.[129] The French Government gave Poland a similar guarantee. Because of the urgency of the situation, they eliminated the stipulation about Poland aiding Romania. Several days later Colonel Beck visited London to work out a formal treaty. The crafty Foreign Minister was reluctant, when pressed by the British and French, to agree to support Romania; the most Beck would promise was to discuss the matter with the Romanian Government. [130] Meanwhile, the Romanians stepped up their efforts to get London and Paris to give them a direct guarantee. With the Italian annexation of Albania on April, the focus of attention shifted once more. As the threat to Romania subsided, the British Government

---

[127] *British Foreign Policy*, IV, 51 5-51 7.

[128] *British Foreign Policy*, V, 80-81.

[129] *Parliamentary Debates House of Commons*, 5th Series, V, 345, 1939.

[130] Anna Cienciala, *Poland and the Western Powers 1938-1939* (Toronto, 1968), 232-233

decided to wait until the Poles and the Romanians met before going ahead with their guarantee plans. London still hoped to create a bloc in Eastern Europe in which the different states would be pledged to aid each other, and not one based solely on English and French promises of support. The Romanians, however, were becoming worried. They felt they were being forgotten. To help Tilea out, on April Alexandre Cretianu, the Secretary General of the Romanian Ministry of Foreign Affairs, was sent on a secret mission to England and France. Although he failed to persuade Halifax of the need for an immediate declaration by the British, in Paris he was pleased to hear that his feelings were shared by Daladier. The French Government now began to press London to act right away, warning that Romania was still Hitler's main objective.[131] Finally on 13 April, under strong pressure from Paris Daladier threatened to give a guarantee to Romania even if he had to do it alone and without awaiting the outcome of the Polish talks, the British Government announced its pledge to support Romania's independence.[132] A French guarantee was given on the same day. In less than a month Britain had largely reversed its

---

[131] *British Foreign Policy*, V, 114; *Rock Appeasement*, 242-243.

[132] The announcement stated "in the event of any action being taken which clearly threatened the independence of Greece or Roumania, and which the Greek or Roumanian Government respectively considered it vital to resist with their national forces, His Majesty's Government would feel themselves bound at once to lend the Greek or Roumanian Government, as the case might be, all the support in their power." H. C. Debs., 5 s., V. 346, 1939; Viscount Templewood, *Nine Troubled Years* (London, 1954), 246-248.

traditional foreign policy towards Eastern Europe. King Carol was delighted with the outcome.[133] While he would have preferred a treaty specifically guaranteeing Romania's frontiers, he had a British and French promise to support Romania against an attach by Germany or Hungary, and he had his way in preventing the pledge from being connected with Poland. [134] The American Legation in Bucharest reported that the guarantee "brought considerable satisfaction to this country even though she exercised much restraint in accepting it for fear of wounding German susceptibilities."[135]

Throughout the March crisis Romania had also requested economic assistance from England, especially a loan of ten million pounds for the purchase of war materials. On 20 March the Foreign Office announced it would send a trade mission to Romania. At the end of April the trade mission was sent under the leadership of Sir Frederick Leith-Ross, Chief Economic Adviser to the Foreign Office. The outcome of the visit was the granting of five million pounds in credit and the promise to purchase two hundred

---

[133] British Foreign Policy, op. cit., 298. Gunther wrote "a feeling of profound satisfaction prevails in high official circles over Chamberlain's statement." Gunther to Secretary of State, April 15,1939, State Department Telegram, No 74.

[134] The guarantee did not cover a Soviet attack on Romania. *British Foreign Policy*, V, 66.

[135] American Legation to Secretary of State, August 10, 1939, State Department Dispatch, 32.

thousand tons of Romanian wheat from the next harvest.[136] Although Romania had hoped for more, the British were too hard-pressed in trying to strengthen their own military forces. Gunther explained to Roosevelt that Britain was doing what she could and was hardly in a position to do more.[137] Unfortunately for Romania, she was not able to obtain credit in the United States because of the Johnson Act which prevented loans to World War One debt defaulters. In the summer of 1939 the Romanian Government ordered war materials and motor vehicles from a number of American firms; but the lack of available cash forced her to do most of her trading in Europe.[138]

During the rest of the spring and summer of 1939, Carol tried to follow a policy of neutrality, while maintaining friendly relations with all sides, especially Britain and Germany. While Hitler was upset with the British- French guarantee, the Romanians were surprised that he took it as calmly as he did.[139] Both Poland and Romania feared that the Germans would interpret the guarantee as an attempt to encircle them. When Gafencu visited London in April, he

---

[136] Sir Frederick Leith-Ross, *Money Talks* (London, 1968), 265; Gunther to Secretary of State, May 13, 1939, State Department Telegram No. 107, 871.24/170.

[137] Gunther to Roosevelt, June 19, 1939, President's Secretary's File, Roosevelt Library.

[138] In 1934 Romania stopped paying her World War I debt to the United States Government. See Davila's conversation with Hull, June 13, 1934, Hull Papers, Box 61, Library of Congress.

[139] *British Foreign Policy,*.V, 301; Max Domarus. *Hitler: Reden und Proklamationen 1932-1945* (München, 1963-), II, (Erster Halbband), 1141.

told Halifax that a stipulation directly binding Poland and Romania was not necessary, because if Germany invaded one of them the end result would be a general war and the other would be forced into it.[140] Halifax could do little but accept Gafencu's argument. During the months following the March crisis one of the chief concerns of the British was trying to persuade the Russians to promise their support to Poland and Romania against a German attack. But whereas each side greatly distrusted the other, it was almost impossible to reach a satisfactory agreement. Both Poland and Romania feared a Russian guarantee of their independence would open the way for Soviet interference.[141] Furthermore, Hitler warned Gafencu that if Romania accepted a Russian guarantee Germany might be forced to take drastic measures.[142] Gafencu told Halifax that the only way his Government would conset to an agreement with the Soviets would be if Romania was not mentioned by name.[143]

As the negotiations between Russia, Britain, and France progressed, the Soviets demanded the right to send troops into Romania and Poland if war appeared imminent. Both

---

[140] *British Foreign Policy*, V, 299; Malita, *Roumanian Diplomacy*, 109.

[141] V. A. Varga, "Atitudinea guvernului român burghezo-moșieresc față de tratativele anglo-franco-sovietce din anul 1939," *Studii, Revista de istorie*, 13 (1 960), IV, 57-71 passim.

[142] Grigore Gafencu, *Last Days of Europe* (New Haven, Connecticut, 1948), 70; *British Foreign Policy*, V, 309-310.

[143] Bullitt to Secretary of State, April 28, 1939, State Department Telegram, No. 848, 740.00/1218 SEC. 2; Cristian Popișteanu, *România șiAntanta Balcanică* (Editura politică, Bucuresti, 1968), 253-254.

Poland and Romania strongly opposed this. The Romanians feared that if they allowed Russian troops to enter their country they would take back Bessarabia which still appeared on Soviet military maps with the inscription "Under Romanian military occupation" if not try to establish a Communist government. Actually, Britain made little effort to persuade the Romanian Government to give way. London's main concern at this time was the growing threat of a German attack on Poland. In any case, the German-Soviet Nonagression Pact of 23 August brought to a sudden halt Britain's efforts to tie Russia into her system of guarantees. The Nonaggression Pact not only wrecked Britain's attempts to extend her alliance system, but also made World War II almost inevitable. At the same time, it had grave consequences on Romania.

Because of the growing German threat to South Eastern Europe, since 1937 Britain's interest in Romania had been gradually increasing. During the same period, King Carol looked to England to help offset the developing hegemony of Germany. But it was Tilea's warning to the Foreign Office, coming just after Hitler took over the rest of Czechoslovakia, that triggered a chain reaction causing England to reverse her traditional foreign policy towards Eastern Europe. Romania, Poland, and Greece all received guarantees. Regardless of the consequences, Britain was fatefully committed to defend these countries from Germany.

CHAPTER III

Early War Years

The German-Soviet Nonagression Pact was a great blow to Romania - the two great powers in Eastern Europe were now partners. In order to gain a free hand against Poland, Hitler made important concessions to the Soviets, including the recognition of Bessarabia as a Russian sphere of interest. Paragraph three of the secret additional protocol to the Nonaggression Pact stated:

> With regard to South Eastern Europe, attention is called by the Soviet side to its interest in Bessarabia. The German side declares its complete disinterestedness in these areas.[1]

The Non aggression Pact forced the Romanian Government to follow an even more cautious foreign policy than before. Armand Calinescu, the Romanian Prime Minister, wrote: "Spectacular German-Soviet pact. I consider the situation to be very serious."[2] On 25 August Bucharest let Warsaw know that in a Polish-German conflict Romania would remain neutral.[3] The following day Gafencu told

---

[1] *Nazi-Soviet Relations* 1939-1941 (eds. Raymond Sontag; James Biddle, Washington, 1948) 78.

[2] Grigore Gafencu, Prelude to the *Russian Campaign* (London, 1945), 253.

[3] On 3 March 1921 Poland and Romania had signed a formal alliance providing for military assistance if either were attacked by Russia. It did not cover a German attack.

Fabricius that "Rumania was determined to remain neutral in any conflict between Germany and Poland if even France and Britain were to come in."[4] On 6 September, King Carol, after consulting with his Crown Council, formally declared Romania's neutrality.

Although the Romanian Government had no definite proof that the Nonaggression Pact contained a secret protocol, they feared that a secret agreement had been concluded over territory in Eastern Europe which included Bessarabia.[5] This fear was greatly increased when Russian troops invaded Poland on 17 September. In view of Poland's hopeless military situation, Romania declined to fulfill its obligation to aid the Poles under the 1921 alliance against Russia. On 21 September the Romanian Government delivered a declaration of neutrality to the Soviets. The Nonaggression Pact and the Russian entry into Poland, however, had a great impact on Romania's attitude towards the Soviet Union. An attack by Russia now became Romania's main concern. On 19 September, two days after Russia invaded Poland, Călinescu wrote:

"The Russian advance changes the situation. The German danger is farther off. Now the Russian danger is primary."[6] Preparing for the worst, Romania began to move troops to the Dniester River. The British were as startled by the German-Soviet Pact as the Romanians. Besides ending

---

[4] *German Foreign Policy*, VII, 363.

[5] Gafencu, *Prelude to the Russian Campaign*, 253-254; Jay Pierrepont Moffat Correspondence, August-September 1939, V. 43, Harvard University.

[6] Gafencu, *Prelude to the Russian Campaign*, 254.

Britain's hope of Russian troops helping to defend the Poles, the entry of the Soviets into Hitler's camp closed the most important supply route into Poland. When war broke out on 1 September, the Poles were practically isolated. The rapid turn of events caused Britain and France to look to Romania as the only available supply route into Poland.[7] Moreover, during the first days of September, the Western Powers and King Carol both feared a possible German attack on Romania after Poland was defeated. In a Foreign Office memorandum of 5 September to the Deputy Chiefs of Staff and the Allied Demands Committee, Orme Sargent stated it was in Britain's "vital interest" to strengthen Romania

> by whatever means we can … [Her] territory offers the only channel through which we can supply, and indeed communicate, with Poland. Moreover, it will be necessary, if the Polish Army is to be saved for further use, that it should be able to retreat into Roumanian territory without being interned, and be enabled there to refit.[8]

Winston Churchhill, at the time First Lord of the Admiralty, wanted to send British destroyers into the Black Sea under the Romanian flag.[9] Bucharest, on the other hand, was trying to get the French to supply them with enough

---

[7] The Baltic was ruled out as a supply route for a number of reasons. One of the most important was Germany's air power in this area.

[8] Foreign Office Memorandum, September 5,1939, F. O. 371/23737 R7286/21/67.

[9] Halifax to Churchill, September 22,1939, F. O.371/23754 R7981/2613/67.

equipment for fifteen divisions.[10] Neither of the Western Allies, however, considered sending an expeditionary force into Poland or Romania, nor did they try to pressure Romania into sending troops to Poland. A note of 9 September by Halifax, which was shortly afterwards sent to the French Government, explained why London desired to keep Romania neutral. Two of the paramount reasons were the inability of Britain to provide much assistance and the number and strength of Romania's potential invaders. In addition to Germany, Halifax wrote,

> Russia, Hungary, and Bulgaria all ... covet slices of Roumanian territory. If Roumania declares war it seems probable that Germany will urge one or all of these countries to attack Roumania, and indeed very little urging might be required. In the view of His Majesty's Government...we avoid the humiliation of a cheap victory for Germany at the expense of a country we have guaranteed and to whose assistance we are bound to come.[11]

Thanks to the Wehrmacht, the question of a supply route into Poland was quickly settled. By the middle of September, Poland's much touted army was in shambles, and, consequently, Allied plans to send aid through Romania were abandoned. Now the immediate concern of the West was to use Romania as an evacuation route for the Polish Government and what was left of her nineteenth century

---

[10] Roumanian Minister's Conversation, September 13, 1939, F. O. 371/23852 R7512/1716/37.

[11] E. Phipps to Quai dlOrsay, September 12, 1939, F. O. 371/23840 R7572/22/37.

army. On 13 September Tilea told Halifax that his government would allow transit through Romania for the Poles.[12] At the same time, the Romanian Government came under pressure from Berlin. The Germans warned Romania not to grant asylum to the Poles, and to close her Polish borders.[13] Yet, in spite of the German threats the Romanians largely kept the promise they made to the English. In a lengthy memorandum to the Foreign Office describing events in Romania during this period John LeRougetel, British Counsellor in Bucharest, pointed out that Romania

> paid a good deal more than lip service to their allies... The British Military Mission to Poland came and went in the thinnest of civilian disguises. Remnants of the Polish armies were disarmed, interned and left to face the rigours of a Balkan winter with the clothes in which they stood up, but no very serious attempt was made to prevent their escaping. The entire Polish treasure passed through the country in a few hours and had been shipped from Constanta in a British tanker under the very noses of an infuriated Gestapo.[14]

---

[12] Roumanian Minister's Conversation, September 13,1939, F. O. 371/23852. Also Gheorghe Zaharia. "La Roumanie et la resistance antifasciste du centre et du sud-est europeen en 1935-1941,"*Revue Roumaine d'Historie*, 12 (1 973), II, 290-291.
[13] *German Foreign Policy*, VIII, 47-48, 52-53, 61-62.
[14] LeRougetel's Memorandum, December 30, 1942, F. O. 371/33278 R9059/9059/37; Alexandre Cretzianu, *The Lost Opportunity* (London, 1957), 29-30; Henri Prost, *Destin de la Roumanie* 1918-1954 (Paris, 1954), 137.

During the middle of September approximately eighty thousand Polish civilians and soldiers poured over the borders into Romania.[15] The Romanian Government did what it could, especially for the civilians, but the number of refugees was too large. Military camps and civilian centers were set up to provide some of the much needed food, clothes, and medical supplies. The government even provided a stipend of one hundred lei a day to some.[16] Many Poles received shelter in private homes. The Romanian Red Cross and the YMCA also did their share.[17] Many eventually made their way to France where they helped to form the backbone of the future Polish Army in exile.[18]

The only serious difficulty between the Allies and Romania involved the flight of the leaders of the Polish Government. On 17 September the Romanian Government offered the Polish leaders asylum or transit through their country as long as they would divert themselves of their government positions and enter as private citizens.[19] But when the Polish leaders entered Romania on the following day they issued a stirring proclamation "calling upon all

---

[15] *The Times*, London, October 16, 1939; Moisuc, Diplomatia Romaniei, 255.

[16] *The Times*, op. cit., November 16, 1939. The *New York Times* reported that the staffs of the British Consulates in Lvov and Cernăuți helped hundreds of British subjects and Polish Jews escaping from Poland. New York Times, September 19, 1939.

[17] *The Times*, London, November 16, 1939.

[18] Hans Roos, *Polen und Europa: Studien zür Polnischen Aussenpolitik* 1931-1939 (Tubingen, 1957), 168; Stanislaw Mikolajczyk, The *Pattern of Soviet Domination* (London, 1948), 8.

[19] *Foreign Relations* 1939, II, 691.

Poles to stand by their Government which would establish itself in an Allied country."[20] The Poles also refused to declare themselves private citizens. Shortley afterwards Berlin began to send strong protests to the Romanian Government warning that they would view the departure of the Polish leaders as "an unfriendly act and a violation of neutrality."[21] As a result, Romania was forced to change its position and interned the Poles.

Bucharest now came under strong pressure from Britain and France to release the Polish leaders. Hoare was instructed that if he could not persuade the Romanian Government to free President Moscicki he should try to smuggle him out of the country![22] Leger, the Secretary-General of the French Ministry of Foreign Affairs, declared to the American Ambassador Bullitt that Romania's action was "a monstrous example of cowardice and indecency."[23] Leger also urged the United States Government to help the Poles. Oddly enough, however, it was not long before the Allies and the Polish representatives in France began to view the internment of the government as a godsend. By this time the members of the Polish Government had become discredited, and it became apparent that it would be much easier to form a new government in exile without interference from the old. Indeed, the French Government

---

[20] Ibid; Hillgruber Hitler, Konig Carol und Marschall Antonescu, 58.
[21] *German Foreign Policy*, VIII, 102-103.
[22] Hoare to Cadogan, September 20,1939, F.O. 371/23840 R8066/122/37.
[23] *Foreign Relations* 1939, II, 690.

seemed secretly to hope that the Romanians would keep the Polish leaders. Added to this Hoare had been warning London repeatedly that Romania would not free the Poles at this time because she feared that Germany or Russia or both might use it as an excuse to declare war. He believed that putting pressure on Romania would only stir them up against the Allies. "Let the Roumanians play for time,"urged Hoare, "and let us keep their good-will ... The day may come when we shall find it necessary to demand that Roumania shall take a firm line with Germany."[24] At the same time, the Romanian Government said that when German pressure subsided they would allow the Poles to leave.[25]

The American Government did not begin to become openly involved until the end of September. Cordell Hull, Gunther, and the State Department wanted to keep Washington out of it.[26] On the other hand, Bullitt and Biddle, the American Ambassadors to France and Poland respectively, and close friends of Roosevelt, bombarded the President with requests that he personally intervene.[27] Bullitt described the problem as "an issue of international decency." [28] Much to the dislike of Gunther, he was instructed to see what he could do to free the Poles, especially President Moscicki. On 26 October Gunther conveyed a verbal request from Roosevelt to King Carol to

---

[24] Hoare to Cadogan. September 20,1939, F.O. 371/23840.
[25] *Foreign Relations* 1939, II, 694-697.
[26] Moffat Correspondence, August-September 1939, V. 43.
[27] Ibid.
[28] *Foreign Relations*, op. cit., 697.

release Moscicki. Roosevelt told Hull: "I want for my own conscience to have made some further move in behalf of the poor old ex-President of Poland."[29] While still fearful of Berlin, Carol was very sympathetic to Roosevelt's request desiring "nothing better" than to see Moscicki go, he explained to the American Minister, and promised to do what he could. For the next several months Gunther continued to urge the Romanians to act, until finally on 25 December, to the dismay of the Germans, the ex-Polish President was allowed to leave.[30] The rest of the Polish leaders were split up and kept under surveillance by the Romanians. Further protests by the United States accomplished nothing. On 21 December, 1940, Marshal Rydz-Smigly managed to escape.[31] Beck, though, suffered a nervous breakdown shortly after entering Romania and was placed in a sanatorium near Sinaia. In 1940, the German News Agency announced that he had been arrested while trying to escape with a British passport. Several years later he contracted tuberculosis and died at Stanesti near

---

[29] *Foreign Relations* 1939, II, 701; Gunther to Hull, September 29, 1939, President's Secretary's File, Roosevelt Library. Moscicki had resigned as president, and Wladyslaw Raczkiewlca was nominated as his successor at the end of September.

[30] *Foreign Relations*, op. cit., 705-706; *German Foreign Policy*, VIII, 575-576. Gafencu told Fabricius that Moscicki was allowed to go to Switzerland for reasons of health. Fabricius called this "an affront." "It had evidently been intended to present us with a fait accompli... I nevertheless strongly remonstrated with Gafencu."

[31] *The Times*, London, December 21, 1940.

Bucharest on 5 June, 1944.[32] By the end of September, 1939, Romania's international position was less secure than ever before. Not only did she still fear an attack by Germany and Hungary, but also, from 17 September, an attack by Russia. From this time, fear of Russia increasingly determined Romania's foreign policy. On 20 September, Molotov, in a talk with the Romanian Minister in Moscow, questioned her neutrality because of reports that Polish troops and planes were being concentrated along the Soviet-Romanian border.[33]

In the following month, Molotov asked the Turkish Foreign Minister Sarajoglu whether Turkey would remain neutral if Russia seized Bessarabia. [34] Moreover, with German, English, and French armies concentrated in the West, Russia had a free hand in the East.

On 27 September, Tilea, "speaking personally and without instructions from his Government," asked Under Secretary of State Alexander Cadogan if the British guarantee to Romania also applied to an attack by the Soviets. [35] This was a ticklish question. The guarantee as announced covered aggression from any quarter, even Russia. After briefly explaining some of the difficulties

---

[32] *The Times*, London, June 19, 1944: *Archiv für Aussenpolitik und Landerkunde* (hrsg. von A. I. Berndt; G.Leibbrandt, Berlin, 1944), 248.

[33] Alexander Cretzianu, "The Soviet Ultimatum to Roumania (26 June, 1940)," *Journal of Central European Affairs*, 9 (1950), 397; See also *New York Times*, September 24, 1939.

[34] *Foreign Relations* 1939, I, 485.

[35] Roumanian Minister's Conversation, September 27, 1939, F. O. 371/23852 R8126/1716/37.

involved, Cadogan told Tilea he would have to submit the question for consideration.[36] On the following day Gafencu asked Hoare the same question.[37] Actually, this issue had been raised previusly on 7 April, 1939, by Tilea in a conversation with Cadogan several days before Britain and France gave their guarantee to Romania. At that time, Cadogan informed Tilea that

> the whole basis of the arrangement... was that of resistance to the threat of German domination in Europe and that all we were trying to do was devised with that object. We had never considered the question of guaranteeing either Poland or Roumania against the Soviet.... Monsieur Tilea said that in reporting this conversation to Bucharest he would say that this point had not been considered and... he would not "for Roumanian reasons" repeat what I had said about the whole arrangement having been based on the idea of resistance to German domination, and he expressed the hope that if we reported the conversation to Sir R. Hoare the latter would be given the same information as he was giving his Government. I said that I had no objection to omitting from any message to Sir R. Hoare reference to the fact that the arrangement was aimed against Germany, though of course Sir R. Hoare

---

[36] *Ibid*.
[37] Hoare to Foreign Office, September 28, 1939, F. O. 371/23846 R8130/328/37.

knew perfectly well, from the instructions which had been sent to him, that this was in fact the case.[38]

On 29 September the British War Cabinet decided against extending the guarantee. It was Halifax's view that there "would be many disadvantages in... adopting such a course."[39] In explaining their decision to the French, the British argued that they could not give Romania any "effective assistance" if she were attacked by Russia. "If we were to declare war on Russia because she invaded Roumania," the English believed, "the extension of the war, far from benefiting Roumania, would have the immediate effect of forcing Great Britain to disperse her efforts in order to guard against Russian attacks in other fields, and to that extent render the fundamental object of winning the war more arduous and protracted."[40] Moreover, Britain was trying to avoid any situation which might bring Russia and Germany closer together.[41] While Romania followed a policy of cautious neutrality, her sympathies were with the Western Powers.[42] Both the English and French governments

---

[38] *British Foreign Policy*, V, 66; Foreign Office Minute, January 27, 1940, F. O. 371/24968 R1425/9/37. Gafencu's memoirs indicate that Tilea had not disclosed the information he received in April about the guarantee not applying to Russia.

[39] Cabinet Conclusions, September 29,1939, F. O. 371/23846 R8278/328/37.

[40] Foreign Office to Phipps, October 6, 1939, F.O. 371/23846 R8278/328/37.

[41] Halifax to Churchill, September 22, 1939. F. O. 371/23754.

[42] Eliza Campus, "Pozitia internationala a Romaniei in anii 1938-1940," *Studii, Revista de istorie*, 26 (1973), VI, 1156-1157; Nagy-Talavera, *Green Shirts*, 305.

agreed with Romania's policy, believing that her Western sympathies could be a valuable asset against Germany. They especially feared Romania becoming a satellite of the Reich, largely because of her strategic geographical position and valuable oil resources. Nevertheless, neither Western Power favored extending their guarantee to cover a Russian attack. The British felt it would be best to tell Bucharest that the guarantee only applied to Germany and Hungary, but France, fearing that this might force Romania closer to Germany, wanted to avoid giving a definite answer for the present. [43] The Quai d'Orsay suggested informing the Romanians that Allied response would depend upon a number of circumstances, especially on the attitude of Turkey.[44] For the next several weeks, neither government could agree on a reply to give to the Romanians.In the meantime, the Romanians continued to raise the issue. Around the end of October a compromise was agreed to by London and Paris. On 3 November, Hoare told Gafencu privately that the instructions he received from London "made it plain that neither His Majesty's Government nor the French Government believed it to be possible for them to intervene actively in the defence of Roumania against Russia."[45] Tilea was given a similar reply by Cadogan.[46] At

[43] Foreign Office to Phipps, October 6,1939, F.O. 371/23846.
[44] Sargent's Minute, November 11, 1939, F.O. 371/23846 R9915/328/37; Campbell to Foreign Office, May 2, 1940, F.O. 371/24902 R5729/4156/67.
[45] Hoare to Foreign Office, November 4, 1939, F.O. 371/23846 R9747/328/37.

the same time, the Romanians were asked not to raise the question "officially" because they would be given an "unsatisfactory answer."[47] The British hoped this would settle the issue. In an interoffice memorandum, Orme Sargent, who was responsible for European affairs at the Foreign Office, commented: "As far as the Roumanians are concerned we need not do anything more."[48] After a conversation with King Carol on 17 November, Lord Lloyd reported to London that "it is satisfactory to know that the King in general accepted our attitude as regards the limitation of our guarantee to Roumania."[49] But unfortunately for the English, the issue would not stay buried. In a conversation on 4 December, Tilea asked Halifax to reconsider the whole question.[50] Three days later Tilea told the British Foreign Minister that it was "necessary" for England and France to come to a "definite decision."[51] What caused the Romanians to urgently renew this issue were the recent indications by the Soviets that they were preparing to take back Bessarabia. In a conversation with the French Ambassador in Moscow, Deputy Foreign Commissionar

---

[46]Roumanian Minister's Conversation. October 30, 1939, F.O. 371/23846 R9447/328/37.

[47] Sargent's Minute, November 11, 1939, F.O. 371/23846.

[48] *Ibid*.

[49] Lloyd to Foreign Office, November 20, 1939, F.O. 371/23759 R11145/8672/67.

[50] Roumanian Minister's Conversation, December 4, 1939, F.O. 371/23852 R11078/1716/37.

[51] Roumanian Minister's Conversation, December 7, 1939, F.O. 371 /23846 R11217/328/37; *The Diaries of Sir Alexander Cadogan 1938-1945* (ed. David Dilks, New York, 1971), 236.

Potemkin stated that Odessa has been a dead port since the loss of Bessarabia.[52] On 6 December the Moscow published "Communist International" contained an article accusing the Romanian Government of exploitation and oppression in Bessarabia.[53] During the fall of 1939, there were growing indications that Roumania would move closer to Germany unless Britain and France extended their guarantee.[54] The French Government had been warning the British of such a development. In order to encourage the Romanians that the possibility of an extension existed, France wanted to notify them that the attitude of the Allies was largely dependent upon Turkey's willingness to support Romania and open the straits to Western warships. The French urged the British to support discussions between Romania and Turkey, but until the middle of November London rejected this.[55]

Not sure of Turkey's attitude towards a Soviet attack on Romania, the British feared that if the Turks did promise their support this would put them in an embarrassing position. "In this event we might be at a loss... to know what to reply," wrote Sargent, "since we have. never considered the possibility of sending naval, still less military, forces into

---

[52] Cretzianu, "Soviet Ultimatum," 397.

[53] Steinhardt to Secretary of State, December 6, 1939, State Department Telegram, No. 1032,761.71/161.

[54] Hoare to Foreign Office, October 10, 1939, F. O. 371/23840 R8680/122/37; Foreign Office Minute, December 1, 1939, F. O. 371/23840 R11193/122/137; Gafencu, Prelude to Russian Campaign, 257.

[55] Foreign Office Minutes, November 9, 10, 11, 1939, F.O. 371/23846 R9915/328/37.

the Black Sea to help Roumania."[56] During the latter part of November, however, the British Government became convinced that the Turks would only promise to support Romania if it appeared that a Russian attack was just a prelude to an invasion of Turkey.[57] On 9 December the French Ambassador to England, Corbin, urged Halifax to give "something more than a merely negative answer... to the Roumanian Government's enquiry."[58] This time Halifax replied that he "thought it would not be impossible to reconcile the points of view taken by our two government."[59] This was simply a shift in tactics not policy. On the previous afternoon Numan Menemencioglu, Turkish Secretary General, told Halifax, Cadogan, and Sargent that he felt it was doubtful that the Russians were preparing to do anything more in the Balkans than take Bessarabia back, and that Turkey's frontier began with Bulgaria and not Romania. That night Cadogan noted in his memoirs that the Turks would throw Romania "to the wolves." On the 11th Hoare was instructed to inform Gafencu and Tilea that Britain would consider extending her guarantee "if Italy's neutrality were to be assured and if Turkey were to declare her intention of going to war with Russia in the case of Russian aggression against Roumania." If Britain was certain of this

---

[56] Sargent's Minute, November 11, 1939, F.O. 371/23846.

[57] War Cabinet Conclusions, November 21, 1939, F.O. 371/23846 R10442/328/37; Foreign Office Minute, November 17, 1939, F.O. 371/23846 R10183/328/37; Knatchbull- Hugessen to Foreign Office, December 22, 1939, F.O. 371/23847 R11928/328/37.

[58] Halifax to Campbell, December 9, 1939, F.O.371/23847 R11371/328/37.

[59] *Ibid*

an entirely new situation would be created which His Majesty's Government would at once study in consultation with the French government, with a view to seeing what contribution they could make to the defence of Roumanian territory.[60]

In the same telegram Hoare was informed that the Foreign Office was convinced that these conditions could not be fulfilled.[61] The Romanians sent inquiries to Rome and Ankara. The response of the Italians was the more favorable. On 16 December Count Ciano told former Romanian Foreign Minister Victor Antonescu that in the event of Soviet aggression Italy would assist Romania with arms, munitions, and aircraft.[62] But as the English expected, Turkey prove to be the major stumbling block. Gafencu later wrote: "How was a formal promise to be obtained from Turkey... seeing that the Ankara Government had constantly refused to enter into engagements directed against the U.S.S.R.?"[63] On 3 January Tilea notified Hoare that, "Though the Turkish Government had given encouragement to the Roumanian Government, they had never explained precisely what they intended to do to help them."[64] The Romanian Government never bothered to raise the issue with London again.

---

[60] Foreign Office to Hoare, December 11, 1939, F.O. 371/23846 R11217/328/37; Gafencu, *Prelude to Russian Campaign*, 274.

[61] Foreign Office to Hoare, op. cit.

[62] Gafencu, *Prelude to Russian Campaign*, 277.

[63] *Ibid.*, 274.

[64] Hoare to Foreign Office, January 3, 1940, F.O. 371/24884 R202/5/67.

After Hitler conquered Poland, the Allies feared he might next invade the Balkan Peninsula.[65] During the fall and winter of 1939, the English and French Governments discussed several projects designed to strengthen and protect the Balkans and Romania from a German attack. These plans centered around the formation of a Balkan bloc and the construction of a joint Allied and Balkan army. The French took the lead in developing these plans.[66] Although the British supported these efforts in principle, their cautious policy helped to hold back the French from carrying them our.[67] In September, during two meetings of the Allied Supreme War Council, the French suggested that the Allies ought to have an army at either Salonika or Istanbul to stop a German advance towards the Mediterranean or the Straits.[68] In December, Daladier called for joint Allied

> diplomatic action in Turkey, Romania, Greece and Yugoslavia; material help to these countries; a study of the forms in which assistance could be given to

---

[65] J. R. M. Butler, Grand Strategy (vol. II of History of the Second World War: United Kingdom Military Series, ed. J. R. M. Butler, London, 1957), 64; Amery, *My Political Life*, III, 344-345; Harvey, *Diplomatic Diaries*, 320.

[66] Maxime Weygand, *Memoires* (Paris, 1950), III, 21-25; Maurice G. Gamelin, *Servir* (Paris, 1947), III, 205-209.

[67] Sir Llewellyn Woodward, British Foreign Policy in the Second World War (London, 1970-1971), I, 22-23.

[68] *Ibid.*, 23.

them, and an effort to persuade them to unite in order to resist attack.[69]

In spite of Britain's desire to help the Balkans and keep them from coming under the control of Germany, the limited resources of the Allies caused London to oppose much of this.[70] More important, Britain feared this might provoke Italy into abandoning her neutrality.[71] The Allies were never able to reach a final agreement on these projects. While Britain encouraged the Balkan states to settle their differences and join together for defensive purposes, she constantly rejected the more ambitious French schemes. As fighting broke out in the West in the spring of 1940, these plans were largely abandoned. Although England was unwilling to send troops to the Balkans or extend her guarantee to cover a Russian attack, during the winter and spring of 1940 maintaining the friendship of Romania was important to Britain's plans for defeating Germany. The

---

[69] *Ibid.*, 28. The French also desired to draw the main center of warfare away from the western front, and increase the size of their own forces with the addition of Balkan armies. Woodward, *op. cit.*, 22.

[70] Gamelin, *op. cit.*, I, 206.

[71] Woodward, *British Foreign Policy*, 23-30; Gamelin, *Servir*, 208. See also Z. Avramovski, "Attempts to Form a Neutral Bloc in the Balkans (September December 1939)," *Studia Balcanica*, 4, (1971), 133. On several occasions the British and French tried to determine what Italy's reaction would be. The Italians, however, were unwilling to enter into discussions. In the meantime, the French General Staff went ahead and discussed these plans with Romania and Yugoslavia. Woodward, *op. cit.*, 29-30.

British were well aware how heavily dependent Hitler was on Romanian oil. Several English studies during the winter of 1940 showed that oil supplies were "probably the weakest link in the chain of Germany's war potential; her position in this respect may become desperate unless she can obtain further outside sources of supply." [72] Germany's chief supplier of oil was Romania.[73] The British Government tried to limit Germany's oil import in various ways. The two most successful methods were through the Allied blockade of German seaports and by using persuasion and pressure on the Romanian Government. By blockading Germany's seaports, Hitler was forced to use the few existing railroad lines as well as river barges on the Danube in order to transport oil from Romania. Making the situation more difficult for the Germans was the shortage of vehicles to transport oil, especially railroad tank-cars. While the Romanians under pressure agreed to let the Germans purchase a maximum of one hundred thirty thousand tons of oil each month, they refused to let them ship the oil in Roumanian tank-cars.[74]

The shortage of tank-cars, combined with the lengthy freezing of the Danube from December until the end of March, sharply reduced the amount of oil that reached Germany. At the same time, the Roumanian Government allowed the Allies to greatly increase their purchases of oil,

---

[72] Slessor, *Central Blue*, 265-266.
[73] W. N. Medlicott, *The Economic Blackade* (London, 1952), I, 51.
[74] Halifax to Mr. Hankey, April 6, 1940, F.O. 371/24974 R4302/26/37. This agreement was concluded on 29 September, 1939.

and refused to compel British and French owned oil companies to sell to the Germans. [75] By the spring, Germany's oil supply had fallen considerably below what she needed.[76]

Some of the activities of the English would provide good material for a cloak and dagger story. One scheme was to place sand and other abrasives, or a special material which would catch fire, in the axle-boxes of tank-cars going to Germany. This created, as one agent put it, "a constant succession of minor pinpricks" for the Germans.[77] In order to keep Danubian river barges out of the hands of the Germans, London chartered as many of them as they could, even setting up a special company, the Goeland Company, to carry this out. By the end of 1939, however, the Goeland Company had been able to charter only 148 of the 2,725 vessels on the river.[78] Danubian river pilots were also bribed into not working for the Germans. Fearing a large increase in oil deliveries to Germany in the spring when the Danube

---

[75] Halifax to Mr. Hankey, April 6, 1940, F.O. 371/24974 R4302/26/37; *German Foreign Policy*, IX, 41-42, 168. From a high of 134,191 tons and 126,497 tons in April and July 1939, respectively, Germany's oil import from Romania had fallen sharply since the war began. In January and February of 1940 her oil import was only 15,000 and 18,000 tons. Gafencu's Note to Halifax, February 19, 1940. F. 0. 371/24972 R2312/26137; *German Foreign Policy*, IX, 41-42.

[76] Hillgruber, *Hitler, Konig Carol und Marschall Antonescu*, 84-85.

[77] Bickham Sweet-Escott, Baker Street Irregular (London, 1964), 22; Hermann Neubacher, *Sonderauftrag Sudost* (Gottingen, 1956), 44.

[78] Medlicott, *Economic Blockade*, I ,254-256.

would be ice-free, the British hoped either to destroy Romania's oil fields which they had done during the First World War or block traffic on the river. In order to avoid a probable rupture of relations with Romania, and because of the technical difficulties involved, the Western Powers tried to get the consent of the Romanian Government for the destruction of the Ploesti oil fields. [79] The Allies never seriously considered doing this without Romania's cooperation. [80] For months the British tried to reach an agreement with Bucharest, promising to pay for expected damages as well as temporarily erecting an embargo on exports to Romania.[81] But in the end, the Romanians refused to give in, and the project was abandoned. On 5 April British saboteurs attempted to block traffic on the Danube at the Iron Gates Canal by sinking barges and by blowing up the large boulders on the Yugoslavian side of the river.[82] The plan was not well executed, and the Gestapo kept a close watch on the operation.

The Germans informed Gafencu, but at first he refused to do anything. Finally, under strong German pressure, the Romanians agreed to search the barges. In their hulls over

---

[79] Cabinet Paper, February 27, 1940, F. O. 371/24972 R2687/26/37; Foreign Office Memorandum, February 5, 1940, F.O. 371/24971 R17451/426/37; Hoare to Foreign Office and Minutes. May 27-June 6, 1940. F.O. 371/24983 R6415/195/37.
[80] Hoare to Foreign Office and Minutes, op. cit.
[81] Foreign Office Memorandum. February 20. 1940. F.O. 371/24972 R2382/26/37. The embargo extended from January 25 to February 20, 1940. See also Moisuc, *Diplomația României*, 274.
[82] *Die Geheimakten des französischen Generalstabes* (Berlin, 1939-1940), *Deutsches Weissbuch des Auswärtigen Amtes*. VI, 82-83.

one hundred English soldiers were discovered, along with explosives and a cannon.[83] Afterwards, London constantly denied this embarrassing failure.[84] Throughout this period Romania's sympathies were with the Western Powers. Most Romanians believed the Allies would eventually win the war; but as Hoare wrote to the Foreign Office: "What worries Roumanians is... what is going to happen to themselves in the meantime." [85] At the same time, the Romanian government tried to maintain friendly relations with Germany. Over half of Romania's trade was with Germany, and the Reich was her main supplier of war materials. The possibility that Romania would turn to Hitler for protection against the Soviets was a constant fear in London and Paris. Despite frequent German hints that only they could give protection against the Russians, the Romanians were not sure where Hitler stood. In December, however, Fabricius told Gafencu that "if war should become intense in the West, it will not be possible to prevent the U.S.S.R. from realizing certain plans."[86] Fortunately for the Romanians, the Russo-Finish War gave them a temporary respite. In the spring Soviet interest in Romania was renewed. On 29 March in a speech before the Supreme

---

[83] Deutsches Weissbuch, VI, 83; Neubacher, *Sonderauftrag*, 43. See also Robert St. John, *Foreign Correspondent* (Garden City, New York, 1957), 118-122.

[84] Romania retaliated by tightening controls on the river..

[85] Hoare to Foreign Office. February 16, 1940, F.O. 371/24983 R2505/195/37; *German Foreign Policy*, IX, 61.

[86] Gafencu, *Prelude to Russian Campaign*, 257. For the most recent account from the German side see the article by J. W. Brugel in *Vierteljahrshefte für Zeitgeschichte*, October, 1963.

Soviet, Molotov referred to Bessarabia as an unsolved question between the two countries and intimated that an improvement in relations would require a settlement of that question. [87] In April, Moscow began to reproach the Romanians for allegedly provoking border incidents.[88] More important, the Russians began a major troop buildup behind Romania's frontier.[89] On 19 April, Carol and several of his ministers vowed to meet any attack on Romania with armed resistance. Bucharest could at least match the Soviets when it came to saber rattling. Throughout the winter the government had been telling the people that the army would never give up Bessarabia. Supposedly impregnable defenses were being constructed, including the digging of a moat which would be flooded with oil so as to protect the country with a ring of fire. But the Romanian people seemed to be the only ones who took all this seriously. "Because of

---

[87] *Foreign Relations* 1940, III,191-193; Gafencu, *Prelude to Russian Campaign*, 288.

[88] The Anglo-French guarantee probably helped to delay Soviet action against Romania because the Russians were not sure how far it extended. Adam Ulam wrote that "until the spring of 1940, the Soviets could not be sure that a move against Romania would not involve them in a war with the Allies, the contingency feared by them most, next to an attack by Germany." Adam Ulam, *Expansion and Coexistance* (New York, 1968), 288.

[89] Major J. P. Ratay to War Department, May 25, 1940, Milltary Attache Report No. 2543. National Archives. Ratay's report stated 26-30 infantry divisions, 9 cavalry, and 14 armored brigades. See also Ratay to War Department, July 15, 1940, Military Attache Report No. 2546.

its foppish officers, in sharply cut uniforms, corsets and cosmetics," wrote C. L. Sulzberger, then New York Times Balkan Bureau manager, "the Rumanian army had a dismally low reputation."[90] "Stories continually come to my attention regarding the pitiful inadequacy of military equipment and supplies, as well as the lack of morale, in Rumania's army," reported Gunther to the State Department. "The present revelation of graft and slipshod methods of equipping the army was brought about by the delivery of 50,000 pairs of shoes badly needed for the troops on maneuvres, without laces."[91] No wonder Western military experts put so little stock in Romania's military! As usual though, it was not so much what Romania did that determined her fate, as what happened amongst the major powers. As German armies overran the West and Romania's belief in an Allied victory rapidly diminished, Carol felt he had little choice but to look to Berlin as his only hope for protection.

By the end of May it was evident to Carol that France was doomed. Britain's position was desperate. On 27 May the Romanians even tried to get the United States to intervene in their behalf.[92] At the beginning of April,

---

[90] C. L. Sulzberger, *Long Row of Candles* (New York, 1969), 79.
[91] Gunther to Secretary of State, October 20, 1938, State Department Dispatch, No. 572,871.00/653,2.
[92] Romanian purchases of United States goods had increased in the previous fall and winter. In September the Romanian Government ordered five hundred Ford trucks valued at roughly one million dollars, and equipment for the construction of border fortifications which came to almost half a million dollars. In December an additional order was placed

Constantine Oumansky, the Soviet Ambassador to Washington, had mentioned to Hull that "his government had no intention to interfere with Bessarabia." Gafencu now told Gunther that he was ready to open discussions with the Soviets, and asked if Washington would try to obtain "a clarification of Russian intentions."[93] A week and a half later, the State Department replied that "it would be inopportune and would serve no useful purpose for the American Embassy at Moscow to take steps along the lines suggested."[94] In the same telegram Gunther was notified for his own "confidential information" that during "a conversation with Molotov... Thurston made some inquiries regarding the Rumanian situation. Molotov showed himself to be disinclined, however, to discuss the matter." Isolated and fearful of a Soviet attack, on 29 May Carol decided to align Romania with Germany.

In an attempt to conciliate Hitler, Tătărescu informed Fabricius that Romania desired "closer cooperation... not

---

with Ford for one thousand more trucks. The terms were for between thirty and forty percent down and the rest payable upon delivery. The cost of these purchases was more than half the total cost of Romanian imports from the United States for 1938 ($6,500,000). Hibbard to Secretary of State, September 28, 1939,State Department Dispatch, No. 1077, 871.24/180; Hibbard to Secretary of State, December 11, 1939, State Department Dispatch, No. 1105,871.24/193.

[93] *Foreign Relations* 1940, I, 468. In his message to Washington Gunther also wrote: "Naturally he is seeking a way out of succumbing to German offer of protection with all the consequences which that would entail."

[94] *Foreign Relations*, I,468.

only in all economic fields but in all fields." Beyond "that they wanted to have proposals as to how the German Government visualized the future preservation of the south-eastern area."[95] The provisional German-Romanian oil pact of March was completed, and Romania promised to improve transportation facilities. [96] Ion Gigurtu, a pro-German businessman, became Minister of Foreign Affairs[97] In June, in order to further win favor with Hitler, British and French ships on the Danube were seized and turned over to the Germans.[98]

But Carol's last minute efforts were not able to prevent the Soviets from taking Bessarabia, as well as Northern Bucovina an area which had never belonged to Russia and was not even mentioned in the German-Soviet Pact. On 26 June, Romania was given a twenty-four hour ultimatum by the Russians to concede these areas. In a last ditch effort Carol sought help from Germany and Italy. The next day Fabricius was instructed by Berlin to tell Carol that "in order to avoid war between Rumania and the Soviet Union, we

---

[95] *German Foreign Policy*, IX, 466-467. See also A. Simion, "Les conditions politiques du diktat de Vienna (30 aout 1940)," *Revue Roumaine d'Histoire*, II, (1972), III,448.

[96] German Foreign Policy, *op. cit.*, 467. N. N. Constantinescu, "L'exploitation et le pillage de 1'economie roumaine par l'Allemagne hitlerienne dans la periode 1939-1944," *La Roumanie pendant la deuxieme guerre mondiale* (eds. Ion Popescu-Puţuri "and Others." Bucarest, 1964), 108.

[97] As a result of Carol's new foreign policy, on 31 May Gafencu resigned as Foreign Minister.

[98] Hoare's Memorandum, February 21,1941, F. O. 371/29975 R4962/2/37.

can only advise the Rumanian Government to yield to the Soviet Government's demands."[99] The governments of Italy, Turkey, and the Balkan countries also recommended a peaceful settlement. [100] As a result of Britain's desperate situation as well as Romania's new foreign policy, Bucharest did not even bother looking to England for advice and assistance.[101] Tilea informed the Foreign Office that "he was clear... that the circumstances of this unhappy story did not involve H.M.G. in an implementation of their guarantee."[102] All the British could do was to express their sympathy, stating that "no occupation of territory of a friendly government could be a matter of indifference to H.M.G."[102] Neither England nor the United States recognized the annexation.

Fearing further Soviet aggression, along with the possibility that Hungary might attempt to take advantage of Romania's difficulties and seize Transylvania, Carol continued to try to gain Hitler's favor. In an effort to win the support of the Iron Guard, Carol reorganized the government, giving several cabinet positions to members of the Guard, including Horia Sima, their new leader. Romania

---

[99] *Gerrnan Foreign Policy*, X. 28; J. W. Brügel, "Das Soviet Ultimatum an Rumanien im Juni 1940," *Vierteljahrshefte für Zeitgeschichte*, 4, (1963), 412-413; New York Times, June 25-29, 1940.

[100] Roumanian Minister's Conversation, June 28, 1940, F.O. 371/24968 R6648/9/37; *The Ciano Diaries* 19391943 (ed. Hugh Gibson, Garden City, New Jersey, 1946), 270.

[101] Roumanian Minister's Conversation, *op. cit.*

[102] Roumanian Minister's Conversation, June 28, 1940, F.O. 371/24968.

withdrew from the League of Nations. On 2 July Carol sent a letter to Hitler urging "close cooperation in all fields, guaranteed by political treaties," and requested that he "dispatch a military mission to Bucharest." [103] Measures against the British were also increased. At the beginning of July, Romania renounced her Anglo-French guarantee. Instead of informing the British beforehand, the Romanian Government simply announced its renunciation through the local press. [104] Feeling that nothing could be achieved by giving a reply, the British ignored this discourteous announcement. On 17 July, in a response to a question in Parliament, Under Secretary of State Butler stated that

> His Majesty's Government do not, so far as they themselves are concerned, consider that any further obligation devolves upon them under its terms. [105]

Meanwhile, over thirty English subjects, most of whom worked in the oil industry, were expelled from the country on vague allegations of sabotage. [106] With the onslaught of the Nazi Blitzkrieg in the West, the British Government was unable to do anything to stop Romania from entering the

---

[103] *German Foreign Policy*, X, 91 ; Simion, "Diktat de Vienne," 449.
[104] Foreign Office Minute, July 2, 1940, F.O. 371/24988 R6681/392/37; Traian Bunescu, *Lupta poporului român împotriva dictatului fascist de la Viena*, august 1940 (Bucuresti, 1971), 70,74; *The Times*, London, July 2, 1940.
[105] Foreign Ofice to Hoare, July 19, 1940, F.O.371/94988 R6681/392/37.
[106] Hoare's Memorandum, February 21, 1941, F. O. 371/29975; David J. Dallin, *Soviet Russia's Foreign Policy* 1939-1942 (New Haven, Connecticut, 1942), 321-322. Hoare felt this was done simply to please Hitler.

German camp. One Foreign Office official wrote, "our powers to assist Roumania were nil."[107] At the beginning of July, England began to change her policy towards Romania. A Foreign Office minute of 4 July stated: "We must now regard Roumania as in every way, except fact, a German occupied country and amend our policy accordingly." [108] Another minute declared: "King Carol is already in Hitler's pocket."[109] In retaliation for the seizure of British vessels on the Danube, several Romanian ships were confis- cated in Egypt; Romanian gold in London was blocked, and trade was suspended; the blockade was also applied.[110] At the same time, the British hoped

> to support any element of opposition there may be in
> Roumania with the object of causing as much trouble
> to Hitler as possible in the execution of his policy.[111]

---

[107] Foreign Office Minute, July 4, 1940, F.O. 371/24988 R6681/392/37.

[108] *Ibid.*

[109] Foreign Office Minute, July 2, F.O. 371/24988.

[110] Hoare's Memorandum, February 21, 1941, F.O. 371/29975; Medlicott, *Economic Blockade*, I, 596; Foreign Office to Hoare, July 29, 1940, F.O. 371/24988 R6833/392/37; LeRougetel to Hoare, July 15,1940, F.O. 371/ 24980 R7152/32/37.

[111] Circular letter, September 4, 1940, F.O. 371/24902 R7463/4156/67. On 24 July, Tilea was recalled to Romania. Rather than return home he resigned, strongly condemning the proGerman policy of his government. He remained in England for the remainder of the war. In Tilea's place the Romanian Government appointed Basil Stoica, but London refused to accept a new Minister. Halifax to Hoare, July 26. 1940, F.O. 371/24988 R6833/392/37; *The Times*, London, July 26, August 3, September 12, 1940.

At the end of August, Romania entered a still more severe period of crisis. Public confidence in the government had especially dwindled after Bessarabia and Northern Bucovina were abandoned. People were shocked that the government gave in without a fight. Bucharest wits now called the much boasted about fortifications against Hungary (Carol Line) the - "lmaginescu" line "in most places... nothing more than three strands of barbed wire nailed to trees," an American correspondent claimed.[112] In an attempt to finally settle the perennial territorial dispute between Romania and Hungary, Hitler and Mussolini compelled the Romanian Government to sign the Vienna Decree which gave two-thirds of Transylvania to Hungary.[113] A week later Romania lost Southern Dobrogea to Bulgaria. Since the end of June, one-third of the nation's territory had been surrendered without a shot being fired. Popular outrage was so great that Carol was forced to abdicate and flee the country. [114] Ironically, Carol's dictatorship was replaced by an even more pro-German government under General Ion Antonescu. The British Government refused to recognize the Vienna Award. On 5 September Halifax announced in Parliament that

> we are unable to accept the settlement now announced of the Hungarian-Rumanian dispute over Transylvania since that settlement is the result of a

---

[112] St. John, *Foreign Correspondent*, 118.

[113] For a recent study see Bunescu, *Dictatului fascist de la Viena*. Also Simion, "Diktat de Vienne," 447-472.

[114] Carol abdicated on 6 September 1940. See also *New York Times*, September 5-8, 1940.

dictation by the Axis Powers imposed on Rumania under duress. We do not propose during the war to recognize territorial changes unless these have been evidently and freely agreed between all the parties concerned.[115]

On the other hand, the British approved the transfer of Southern Dobrogea to Bulgaria, which they declared was "reached by means of free and peaceful negotiation and agreement between the interested parties without aggression or compulsion." [116] This was for public consumption; in reality, Romania had little choice. The English, themselves, had occasionally exerted pressure on Bucharest to do this, and with the defection of Romania to the German side, the British were trying to strengthen their position in Bulgaria.[117] The United States did not go along with any of these agreements, following her policy of not recognizing any territorial changes brought about since the war started.[118]

Although Carol's anti-Nazi and pro-Ally son Michael ascended the throne after the abdication, the real head of the state was the honest, outspoken, fiery-tempered General Ion

---

[115] *War and Peace Aims of the United Nations* (ed. Louise W. Holborn, Boston, 1943- 1948), I, 190-191.
[116] *Ibid*.
[117] Minutes on Bucharest Telegram No. 773, July 24, 1940, F.O. 371/24988 R66811 392137; Robert Lee Wolf, The Balkans in Our Time (Cambridge, Massachusetts, 1956), 197; Avramovski, "Neutral Bloc." 134.136.147-148; Gafencu. Last Days, 108.
[118] Cordell Hull, The Memoirs of Cordell Hull (New York, 1948), II, 11 68.

Antonescu.[119] Antonescu (nicknamed Red Dog) headed a coalition government made up of military men, technicians, and members of the Iron Guard.[120] A career officer, after World War he spent several years in London and Paris as Military Attache. Later he rose to become Chief of the Romania General Staff, and in 1938 was apponted Minister of War in the Goga Government. But because of his association with Codreanu as well as his refusal to compromise on crucial defense issues, Carol had him

---

[119] King Michael, son of King Carol and Queen Helen of Greece, was born on 25 October, 1921. As a result of his father's renunciation of the throne in December, 1925, Michael was proclaimed king upon the death of his grandfather King Ferdinand on 20 July, 1927. But because Michael was only five years old, a regency was created. After Carol returned, nine year old Michael was made Crown Prince and Great Voevod of Alba Iulia. When Carol was forced to abdicate on 6 September, 1940. Michael became king again. For the next four years Michael would remain a figure head while General Antonescu ran the country.

[120] The Guard was Antonescu's logical choice for an ally at this time. He needed some popular support, but the Peasants and Liberals refused to participate in his dictatorship. Moreover, he had to have the backing of a party which the Germans would go along with. The coalition government he formed was basically a matter of convenience. It was not long before relations between Antonescu and the Guard became strained. The Guard held six cabinet positions in the new government. The Foreign Minister, Prince Mihai Sturdza, was a Guardist, and the Interior Minister, Constantin Petrovicescu, was closely connected with them. Horia Sima was Vice Premier. The rest of the government was made up of friends on Antonescu.

arrested. When he first came to the attention of the Germans in the thirties, he was viewed as being an able, hard-working Romanian patriot with strong French sympathies. He showed little interest in Germany and did not speak the language. While at times he had expressed sympathy with the lron Guard, politically he favored an authoritarian, conservative government.

Like most Romanians, Antonescu was impressed with the efficiency and strength of the German war machine.[121] With the defeat of France and the apparent hopelessness of Britain, Antonescu came to believe that the future of Europe rested with Germany. Partly through the efforts of Madame Veturia Goga, the widow of the former Premier, and Mihai "lca" Antonescu, a law professor at the University of Bucharest and persona grata in Berlin, the Germans adopted a favorable attitude towards Antonescu.[122] Because Berlin felt he was the one man who could save the country from choas they supported him during the September crisis. Shortly afterwards, fearing further Russian and Hungarian designs on his country the Soviets had begun to utilize their old tactic of accusing the Romanians of starting border

---

[121] Ratay to War Department. February 6. 1941, Military Attache Report No. 2560. See the reports of the American Military Attache for detalls on Antonescu's activities during his first several months in office.
[122] Nagy-Talavera, Green Shirts, 309-310 Mihai Antonescu was a friend, but not related to the Premier.

incidents- Antonescu asked Hitler to send troops to protect the frontiers and help train the Romanian army.[123]

Under Antonescu, England's relations with Romania deteriorated rapidly. In September and October, the Romanians expelled most of the British who had not already left.[124] Bucharest was an important British espionage center, and rumor had it that quite a few of the English living in Romania were involved in espionage. A number of English subjects were kidnapped by the Iron Guard and beaten. On one occasion five were seized by the Guard, tortured, and forced to sign confessions admitting acts of sabotage.[125] The British government protested strongly. On 29 September, Halifax warned the Romanian Charge d'Affairs, M. Radu Florescu, that if their protests were ignored

> His Majestey's Government would be forced to draw the conclusion that the Roumanian Government no longer attached importance to the maintenance of

---

[123] *Kriegstagebuch des Oberkommandos des Wehrmacht* 1940-1945 (ed. Hans Adolf Jacobsen, Frankfurt am Main, 1965), I, 96-99; Ratay to War Department, September 19, 1940, Military Attache Report No. 2553.

[124] Hoare's Memorandum, February 21,1941, F O. 371 /29975.

[125] Hoare to Foreign Office, September 26, 1940, F O. 371/24989 R7719/392/37; Fătu; Spălățelu, *Garda de fier*, 290-291, *New York Times*, September 29, 1940. Two of the Individuals, Mr. Young and Mr Brazier, worked for the Romano-Americana oil company. A third was Captain John Tracy, who was also involved in the oil industry. The other two arrested were Mrs. Tracy and Mr. Anderson.

relations such as normally exist between civilized countries.[126]

Several weeks later the five prisoners were released.[127] London felt the Germans were behind these activities in order to eliminate British influence in Romania.

More serious was the entry of German troops in September and October. The British saw this as a German occupation, and "tantamount to an infringement of Roumanian neutrality."[128] While they knew their protests would have no effect in Bucharest, they still went through the motions.[129] The Romanian Government claimed that the troops were there just to teach the Romanian Army and help evacuate refugees from Bessarabia, and that no more than

---

[126] Halifax to Hoare, September 29, 1940, F.O. 371/24989 R7746/392/37.

[127] LeRougetel's Memorandum, December 30, 1942, F.O. 371/33278; *Pe marginea prăpastiei*, 21-23 Ianuarie 1941 (2v., Bucureşti, 1942), II, 190-193; Hoare's Memorandum, February 21,1941, F.O. 371/29975.

[128] Hoare to Roumanian Foreign Minister September 14, 1940, F.O. 371/24993 R7535/1073/37; Foreign Office Minute, September 10, 1940, F.O. 371/24993 R7537/1073/37; Minute on Bucharest Telegram No. 1251, October 6, 1940, F.O.371/24993 R7561/1073/37; Traian Udrea, "La politique exterieure de la dictature legionnaire Antonescienne (septembre 1940- janvier 1941)," *Revue Romaine d'Historie*, 10 (1971), VI, 978.

[129] Hoare's Memorandum, February 21, 1941, F.O. 371/29975; Hoare to Foreign Office, October 8, 1940, F.O. 371/24993 R7827/1073/37; Ion Popescu-Puţuri, "Les principales caracteristiques du regime politique de Roumanie pendant la dictature militaire-fasciste et l'agression hitlerienne," *La Roumanie pendant la deuxieme guerre mondiale*, 18-19.

three thousand German soldiers were expected in Major Ratay, the American Military Attache in Bucharest, estimated that by the middle of December around thirty thousand Germans were in Romania.[130]

For some time, London and Berlin had been fighting a propaganda war in Romania. Both supplied the people with large amounts of free reading material, as well as engaged in devious activities designed to make the other look foolish. For example, the Germans circulated an anti-British paper called the Paris Noir, which many Romanians at first mistook for the real Paris Soir. The English countered with a film which alternated between Hitler speaking and a pig squealing. At the end of an impressive German military parade in Bucharest, which included a whole motorized division parading by King Michael, suddenly Sir Reginald Hoare sailed by the reviewing stand in his old Rolls Royce with its Union Jack flying and horn blowing "as a brief reminder... that the British were still around." Time, however, was quickly running out for the British.

As a result of the flow of German troops into Romania and the rupture of normal diplomatic activities, on 8 October Hoare was given permission to break off relations at his discretion.[131] Four days later Hoare notified London that he was sending most of the British Legation to Istanbul, but that for the time being he would remain with a skeleton

---

[130] Ratay to War department, February 6, 1941, Report No. 2560.
[131] Foreign Office Minute, October 8,1940, F.O. 371/24993 R7827/1073/37.

staff.[132] After this the British Legation in Bucharest "became little more than an observation and reporting post."[133]

After the middle of December the number of German troops in Romania greatly increased. The American Military Attache reported that by the first of January German soldiers were entering at the rate of ten thousand or forty trains a day, the full capacity of the Romanian railway system. Ratay believed that the Germans were building up an invasion force of between fifteen to thirty divisions.[134] At the same time, the Romanians and the Germans limited travel by diplomatic personnel within the country; contact between Romanians and members of the English Legation was closely watched. [135] At the end of January, Hoare informed London that he doubted if he could continue to function as a worthwhile observation center. [136] Shortly afterwards, feeling that the Legation in Bucharest could no longer serve a useful purpose and that it might even limit their ability to carry out sabotage activities, the Foreign Office ordered Hoare to withdraw his Mission. [137] On 10

---

[132] Hoare to Foreign Office, October 12,1940, F.O. 371/24990 R7900/392/37.

[133] Hoare's Memorandum, February 21,1941, F.O. 371 /29975.

[134] Ratay to War Department, February 6, 1941, Report No. 2560.

[135] LeRougetel's Memorandum, December 30, 1942, F.O. 371/33278; Ratay to War Department, March 10, 1941, Military Attache Report No. 2561.

[136] Foreign Office Memorandum, February 8, 1941, F.O. 371/29993 R9013/80/37.

[137] Foreign Office Memorandum, February 8, 1941, F.O. 371/29993; Minutes on Bucharest Telegram 159 and 160, January 28, 1941, F.O. 371/29990 R607/79/37.

February Hoare officially notified Antonescu that because the Germans were using Romania

> as a military base. for prosecuting the war..without one word of dissent from you... His Majesty's Government... decided to recall me and to withdraw the diplomatic Mission and the Consular Officers under my control.... The United States Minister has been authorized to take charge of British interests in this country.[138]

Although Romania was firmly in the German camp and British policy was based on this, the Foreign Office believed that most Romanians were still basically friendly to the Allies. Shortly after relations were severed, in a lengthy report Hoare wrote:

> The peasant has a deep conviction that the English and the French are his friends. The prejudice against all Germans runs very deep.[139]

On the other hand, he realized that the peasants had little, if any, political power, and that the British could not look to them for much support. "The hearts of most Roumanians will remain on our side," explained Hoare, "but

---

[138] Hoare to Antonescu, February 10, 1941, F.O. 371/29992 R2546/80/37; New York Times, February 11, 15, 1941. As a result of the break of diplomatic relations, the Roumanian Government recalled its Legation and Consulate. Like Tilea, Romanian Charge d'Affaires, M. Radu Florescu, resigned his post and remained in England. *New York Times*. February 12, 15, 1941.

[139] Hoare's Memorandum, February 21, 1941, F.O. 371/29975. See also Arthur Gould Lee, *Crown Against Sickle* (London, N. D.), 59.

we must not expect too much from this, except perhaps in isolated acts against the Germans."[140] Moreover, the British doubted that many Romanians would help them as long as they felt only Germany could protect them from the Soviets. As the noted Romanian economist Virgil Madgearu observed: "It was, of course, the Russian bogy which provided that percentage of tolerance for the presence of Germany in Roumania." [141] The Foreign Office saw the government and the Iron Guard as their real enemies in Romania. LeRougetel described the government as consisting of "generals without any political following and Iron Guard or 'Greenshirt' nominees vowed to a policy of plunder under German auspices." [142] British opinion of Antonescu was also poor. Overall, the Foreign Office saw the controversial conducator as essentially a career soldier whose lack of political understanding and fear of Russia opened the way for a Nazi occupation. "He was Hitler's dupe," LeRougetel claimed.[143]

---

[140] Hoare's Memorandum, February 21, 1941, F.O. 371/29975. See also Churchill to Stalin. November 4, 1941, *Stalins Correspondence with Churchill and Attlee* (ed. Ministry of Foreign Affairs of the U.S.S.R., Moscow, 1957), 31-32; *The Times*, London, October 21,1 941.

[141] Hoare to Foreign Office, October 28, 1940, F.O. 371/24990 R8583/392/37.

[142] LeRougetel's Memorandum, December 30, 1942, F.O. 371/33278.

[143] Ibid. Hoare described Antonescu as "vain, rhetorical and not a strong man." Hoare's Memorandum, February 21, 1941, F.O. 271/29975.

By the end of January, Antonescu, with German support, had been able to crush the unruly Iron Guard and make himself military dictator.[144] One of his major goals was to restore Romania's former frontiers. While Romania refrained from participating in Hitler's attack on Yugoslavia and Greece, Antonescu, a long-time enemy of the Soviets and Communism, had no qualms about joining the German invasion of Russia. On 22 June, several hours after Hitler launched a massive attack on the Soviet Union, Antonescu issued a bombastic proclamation to the Romanian people declaring a "Holy War" against Russia for "the preservation of the civilization of the world," and to recover Bessarabia and Northern Bucovina. [145] Popular feeling supported Antonescu's actions to recover the lost provinces; even the

---

[144] Fătu; Spălățelu, *Garda de Fier*, 346-384. Since the fall, relations between Antonescu and the Guard had been deteriorating. In January Antonescu began to suspend Guardist officials, as well as take other measures designed to weaken them. Seeing their position undermined, on 21 January the Guard revolted. After three days of savage fighting in Bucharest they were crushed by the Romanian Army. Hitler backed Antonescu, and the German economic director for Romania and the Balkans, Dr. Hermann Neubacher, was able to get Sima to issue a cease fire on the morning of the 23rd. Although the exact number who died will never be known, according to official figures over four hundred were killed, including many Jews who were senselessly beaten and tortured to death by members of the Guard. Antonescu was now sole dictator. On 27 January, he formed a new cabinet made up almost entirely of army officers. The Iron Guard was dissolved.

[145] *Foreign Relations 1941*, I, 315; *The Manchester Guardian*, June 23, 1941.

popular leader of the democratic opposition, Iuliu Maniu, supported the war at first. [146] Two days after the war declaration, Maniu told Gunther he looked "forward with great satisfaction to the announcement that all of Bukovina and Bessarabia had been occupied.[147]

---

[146] Lee, Crown, 31 Cretzianu, Lost Opportunity, 69; John A. Lukas, *The Great Powers & Eastern Europe* (New York, 1953), 418; *Foreign Relations* 1941, I, 321. Iuliu Maniu was born in Transylvania in 1873. He studied in Vienna and Budapest, became an attorney and taught law at the Blaj Theological Academy. Before World War I, he was a deputy in the Hungarian Parliament and gained a reputation as an outspoken opponent of Magyar policy in Transylvania. In 1918 he helped to organize the National Assembly of Alba-Iulia which in December of that year proclaimed the union of Transylvania with Romania. Until 1924 he was the president of the National Party of Transylvania, and in 1926, became head of the National Peasant Party. He was premier of Romania from 1928 to 1930 and again from October, 1932 to January, 1933. Maniu was especially noted for his personal probity and strength of character which helped to make him a source of admiration to his followers. Yet some of his actions as Premier raised questions about his effectiveness as a political leader. Both at home and abroad he was probably the most famous Romanian democratic figure.
[147] Gunther to Secretary of State, July 24, 1941, State Department Telegram, No. 689, 871.00/887. Maniu regarded this as taking back provinces which the Russians had stolen from them. Almost from the start, though, he urged Antonescu not to allow the Romanian Army to advance beyond the Dniester. Foreign Relations 1941, I, 314-320; *New York Times*, August 17,1941.

In the meantime, Britain continued her policy of trying to stir up as much trouble as possible for Hitler in Romania. A Foreign Office memorandum of May stated:

> Our main objects in Roumania must for the present be (1) to rouse the Roumanians to passive resistance and even to active sabotage, and (2) to envenom their relations with Hungary. If we can only set Hungary and Roumania at each others throats we can cause the germans real embarrassment.[148]

In trying to carry out these objectives, the British were forced to rely largely on radio broadcasts. Little, if anything, was accomplished. Moreover, some of their broadcasts were so inaccurate and exaggerated that the American Legation reported that the English have been

> losing rather than gaining ground among Rumanians.... Many Rumanians whose pro-British sentiments are unquestioned now state flatly that they refuse any longer to listen to the Rumanian broadcasts from London because they have been revolted by statements such as "the Rumanians have turned their guns on the Germans" and "Ploeşti has been destroyed" or "is in flames" the latter being particularly offensive since it is manifest to all that it is untrue.[149]

London was aware of the problem; but the difficulty was trying to acquire "convincing material" for propaganda

---

[148] Foreign Office Memorandum, May 8, 1941, F. O. 371/29994.
[149] Benton to Secretary of State, September 18, 1941, State Department Telegram, No. 829,871.001897 PS/BH; *The Times*, London, October 21, 1941.

purposes. Too often they had to rely on Russian reports "from which such exaggerated accounts were usually derived."[150] The English had hoped that Maniu would take the lead in organizing subversive activities within Romania, and at the time Hoare left in February, they supplied him with a radio transciever. But Maniu was reluctant to get involved with the type of active subversion London wanted. On the other hand, he did supply intelligence information over his radio.[151] The American Government tried to help the British by broadcasting declarations and speeches by Roosevelt and other government officials claiming that the Allies would win the war. Gunther had the most important of them mimeographed and distributed to Romanian Government officials and other interested persons.[152] With the Axis invasion of the Soviet Union in the summer of 1941, England's relations with Russia and Romania entered a new phase. In spite of her traditional suspicion and distrust of the Soviets, all the more because of Stalin's pro-German policy since 1939, Britain was practically isolated and in desperate need of allies. On the night of 22 June the English Prime Minister, Winston Churchill, a staunch foe of Communism since the days of the October Revolution, broadcasted to the nation his desire to join with Russia against Germany.

---

[150] Foreign Office Memorandum, August 27, 1941, F.O. 371 /29995 R7909/80/37.

[151] Barton Whaley, *Codeword Barbarossa* (Cambridge, Massachussets, 1973), 64-65.

[152] *Foreign Relations* 1941, I, 310-311.

We have but one aim and one single, irrevocable purpose. We are resolved to destroy Hitler and every vestige of the Nazi regime....Any man or state who fights on against Nazidom will have our aid... It follows, therefore, that we shall give whatever help we can to Russia and the Russian people.[153]

When asked by his private secretary if this was not "bowing down in the House of Rimmon," Churchill replied,

> Not at all. I have only one purpose, the destruction of Hitler, and my life is much simplified thereby. If Hitler invaded Hell I would make at least a favourable reference to the Devil in the House of Commons.[154]

Wartime cooperation developed very slowly; traditional distrust by both sides as well as many outstanding problems prevented a firm alliance from being formed. One of the important areas of controversy was Romania. Beginning in September Moscow began to urge the British to declare war on Finland, Hungary, and Romania, since these countries were already at war with the Soviet Union. Churchill was "most reluctant" to do this, and, for a while, the British tried to ignore the issue. In London, the Soviet Ambassador Ivan Maisky kept up the pressure. "Eden sent for me," Cadogan jotted in his diary on 24 October, "he had Maisky with him whining because we hadn't declared war on Finland, Hungary, and Romania." [155] On 4 November, Churchill expressed his opposition in a personal letter to Stalin.

---

[153] Winston Churchill, *The Grand Alliance* (Boston, 1950), 372.
[154] Ibid., 370.
[155] Dilks, *Cadogan*, 410.

Will you... consider whether it is really good business that Great Britain should declare war on Finland, Hungary, and Roumania at this moment?... These countries are full of our friends: they have been overpowered by Hitler and used as a cats-paw. But if fortune turns against that ruffian they might easily come back to our side.[156]

Nevertheless, the Russians would not budge. Four days later an angry Stalin notified the British Prime Minister that the situation had become "intolerable." Stalin hinted that Britain was responsible for the Soviet's request for a declaration of war on these allies of Germany being leaked to the press, and that even the United States was considering this question.

For all that the British Government declares that it takes a negative view of our proposal. What is the explanation? Can it be that the purpose is to demonstrate that there is disagreement between the U.S.S.R. and Great Britain?[157]

Maisky had the unpleasant job of delivering this acerbic letter to Churchill. Upon reading it "he seemed to explode," Maisky related later.[158] Churchill refused to send a reply.

The United States Government, meanwhile, had tried to aid the Soviets by attempting to persuade the Romanians

---

[156] Churchill to Stalin, November 4,1941, *Stalin's Correspondence*, 31-32.

[157] Stalin to Churchill, November 8, 1941 *Stalin's Correspondence*, 33.

[158] Ivan Maisky, *Memoirs of a Soviet Ambassador* (London, 1967), 202.

and Finns to end their military operations.[159] In September, the British Charge d'Affaires, Sir Ronald Campbell, asked Hull if the State Department would increase its efforts to get these two countries to cease hostilities. Hull told Campbell that the Romanian Charge d'Affaires Brutus Coste assured him that Bucharest "would cease active hostilities against the Soviet Government when Odessa had fallen and the former Romanian territory had been regained.[160] When the British asked Hull's advice about the request from Russia to declare war on Romania, however, the Secretary said he "could not express an opinion."[161]

The need for unity among Britain and Russia finally caused Churchill to give in. Moreover, the Germans were at the gates of Moscow, and there was the possibility that Stalin might sign a separate peace. On 28 November, the Foreign Office asked the United States to inform the Romanian Government

> that unless by December 5th they had ceased military operations and had in practice withdrawn from all participation in hostilities against the U.S.S.R., the ally of Great Britain, H.M. Government would have no choice but to declare the existence of a state of war between the two countries.[162]

---

[159] Hull. *Memoirs*, II, 977.

[160] *Foreign Relations* 1941, I, 68-70; Hull, *Memoirs*, II, 977-978. See also *The Trial of the Major War Criminals Before the International Military Tribunal*, V. 38,221 -L, 89.

[161] Hull, *op. cit.*, 980. See also Maisky, *Memoirs*, 200.

[162] Foreign Office Minute, December 6, 1941, F.O. 371/29995 R10352/80/37.

Shortly before Churchill told Eden: "My opinion about the unwisdom of this measure remains unaltered."[163] The Romanian Government remained silent until the day after the ultimatum expired. Romania's reply to the British communication amounted to an attempt to justify her actions, arguing that her policy was "one of legitimate self-defense against... acts of aggression."[164] This note was not received by the Foreign Office until 11 December. Four days earlier, on 7 December, the British had officially declared war on Romania.[165]

Antonescu himself was not basically hostile to the British: the deterioration of relations between the two countries had been largely beyond his control. In response to the British declaration in a radio broadcast on 7 December, he claimed that England declared war without justification.

"We regret," stated Antonescu, "that the suffering and tragedy of the Rumanian people... have been so little understood."[166] On the same day that Britain went to war with Romania the conflict became worldwide as the Japanese attacked Pearl Harbor. Five days later, Romania, as

---

[163] Churchill, *Grand Alliance*, 534.

[164] Halifax to Foreign Office, December 11, 1941, F.O. 371/29995 R10510/80/37.

[165] Foreign Office Minute, December 6, 1941, F.O. 371/29995; Halifax to Foreign Office, December 7, 1941, F. O.371 /29995 R10375/80/37.

[166] Reuter's Communication, December 1941, F.O. 371/29995 R10437/80/37.

an ally of Germany and Japan, was compelled to declare war on the United States.[167]

Since Antonescu came to power, relations between the United States and Romania had remained relatively friendly; overall, Washington viewed Romania as on occupied country and only partially responsible for her actions. The persecution of Jews and the freezing of Romanian assets in the United States were the two main areas of conflict. Anti-Semitic activities flared up again in the summer and fall of 1940. In November, 1940, the anti-Semitic Iron Guard carried out a bloody Jewish pogrom which included the murdering of the Romanian historian, Nicolae Iorga, and the economist, Virgil Madgearu, as well as the massacring of sixty-four political prisoners in the Jilava Prison.[168] These atrocities shocked many Romanians, including Antonescu, and helped to widen the growing split between the Premier and the Guard. In the following January during the Guardist uprising in Bucharest, several hundred more Jews were slaughtered, synagoges were set afire, Jewish shops looted, and in one instance, Jews were herded into a slaughterhouse and dissected as animals.[169] Franklin Gunther kept a close watch on these developments, and without lodging any formal protests, repeatedly

---

[167] On November 23, 1940 Romania joined Germany, Italy, and Japan in the Tripartite Pact, which provided for mutual assistance against new belligerents, except Russia. It was aimed primarily against the United States.

[168] *New York Times*, November 28-29, 1940.

[169] Raul Hilberg, *The Destruction of the European Jews* (Chicago, 1961) 489-490. See also Michel Sturdza, *The Suicide of Europe: Memoirs of Prince Michel Sturdza* (Boston, 1968).

expressed his "strong disapproval."[170] King Michael simply a figurehead and his mother, Queen Helen, were appalled at these senseless killings, and, with the help of Gunther, a few Jewish doctors and other professional people were able to get out of the country, "but their number was a drop in the ocean." For the most part, the United States blamed the Iron Guard for these activities, and not the Romanian Government and General Antonescu.[171] In October, 1940, Washington froze Romania's assets in America which amounted to roughly thirteen million dollars.[172] The United States did this chiefly in order to prevent these funds from falling into the hands of the Germans, although British pressure might have been a further incentive. In spite of repeated protests, the United States refused to release these funds.

The American Legation in Bucharest had a more favorable and sympathetic opinion of Antonescu than the British. In January, 1941, Gunther wrote to the State Department that Antonescu was

> honorable to the highest degree and has always acted in what he sincerely felt was Rumania's best interest. he inherited an appalling situation and has been in desperate straits ever since his accession to power...

[170] *Foreign Relations* 1941, I, 867.
[171] *Foreign Relations* 1940, II, 746-779 passim; *Foreign Relations* 1941, II, 860-879 passim. Arthur Gould Lee, *Helen, Queen Mother of Rumania* (London, 1956), 202.
[172] *Foreign Relations* 1940, II, 780; N. Goldberger; Gheorghe Zaharia, "Le caractere national et international du mouvement de resistance en Roumanie," *La Roumanie pendant la deuxieme guerre mondiale*, 61-62.

Without him the situation would undoubtedly be much worse.[173]

The American Military Attache also had a good opinion of Antonescu. Ratay described him to the War Department as "an honest officer, a strict disciplinarian and idealist," who under the circumstances had no choice but to allow German troops into Romania.[174] On the other hand, he reported that Antonescu was very inexperienced in political affairs. Relations between Washington and Bucharest remained friendly even after the invasion of Russia, although pro-Soviet propaganda by both the English and the Americans hurt their prestige among Romanians.[175]

In reply to a remark by Antonescu that the United States was "condoning and aiding a shamefaced aggressor," Gunther quoted to him the well- known Romanian proverb: "Make a brother of the devil until you get safely over the bridge."[176] Gunther maintained good relations with Antonescu, yet without having any effective influence over him or his friends. During the Summer of 1941, the United States began to establish greater contact with opponents of the Antonescu Government. In the fall, apparently, the State Department secretly gave Maniu forty thousand dollars to

---

[173] *Foreign Relations* 1941, I, 276.
[174] Ratay to War Department, February 6,1941, Report No. 2560.
[175] For a Romanian version see Boris Bălteanu, "Relațiile guvernului S. U. A. cu regimul fascist din România (septembrie 1940 iunie 1942)," *Studii, Revista de istorie*, II, (1958), VI, 77-99.
[176] *Foreign Relations* 1941,325-326.

help him save some of his followers who were awaiting trial.[177]

Gunther was also an old friend of King Michael and the Queen Mother, and frequently visited them.[178] At the same time, the American Government communicated with the English over affairs in Romania, supplying London with political information as well as secret data on bombing Romanian oil shipments.[179] As American-German relations steadily deteriorated during the summer and fall of 1941, Berlin tried to create tension between the United States and Romania. Because of complaints from the Germans, the Romanian Government clamped down on travel and other activities by American diplomatic personnel.[180] It was only

---

[177] Secretary of State to Gunther, November 24, 1941, State Department Telegram, No. 489, 871.00/914A PS/WHA; Gunther to Secretary of State, November 26, 1941, State Department Telegram No. 986, 871.00/916 PS/EUM.
[178] Gunther to Roosevelt, May 16, 1941, PSF, Box 39, Roosevelt Library; Lee, *Crown*, 29.
[179] Naval Attache to Navy Department, October 10, 1941, Box 390, National Archives.
[180] Hillgruber, *Hitler, König Carol und Marschall Antonescu*, 144. See also Gunther to Roosevelt, June 10, 1941, PSF, Box 39, Roosevelt Library. At this time Antonescu's prestige with the American Government somewhat diminished. This was because of the forced evacuation of Jews from Bessarabia and Bucovina to concentration camps in occupied Russia by the Germans and Romanians. Antonescu wanted to remove the Jews from Romania, but he repeatedly told Gunther that he was against the atrocities that were being committed claiming these were done "through error" or by "irresponsible elements." Gunther placed part of the blame for this whole tragic affair on

under strong German pressure that the carrot-haired conductor declared war on the United States.[181] Antonescu's real attitude was reflected in the instructions he gave to the press:

> I am the ally of the Reich against Russia. am neutral between Great Britain and Germany. I am for the Americans against the Japanese.[182]

When the American Charge d'Affaires Benton was about to leave Romania, Foreign Minister Mihai Antonescu went out of his way to tell him that Romania will "never commit any hostile acts against the United States." [183] Bulgaria. Hungary, and Romania all declared war on America on 12 December. Washington refused to take any action for the time being.

Roosevelt notified Hull "that the United States should pay no attention to any of these declarations."[184] In his memories Hull wrote: "We realized that their Governments were puppets of Hitler and had merely jumped when the

---

Antonescu, although he believed that the Germans had insisted that the Romanians carry out these measures. *Foreign Relations* 1941, II, 874, 877, 878; Gunther to Secretary of State, November 15, 1941, State Department Telegram, No. 959, FW 871.00/911.
[181] Gheorghe Barbul, *Memorial Antonesco, le III-e homme de l'axe* (Paris, 1950), 140-141; Bălteanu, "Relațiile guvernului S. U. A. cu regimul fascist," 93-94; Hillgruber, *Hitler, König Carol und Marschall Antonescu*, 144.
[182] Barbul, *op. cit.*, 141 Hillgruber, *op. cit.*, 144.
[183] Cretzianu, *Lost Opportunity*, 73. Since 27 June Mihai Antonescu had been Foreign Minister.
[184] Hull, *Memoirs*, II, 1175.

strings were pulled."[185] On the following day Roosevelt asked Hull to advise Congressional leaders "of this viewpoint so that they would not press for a declaration of war."[186] During the next several months Romania, Hungary, and Bulgaria continued their military assistance to Germany. The United States realized that before long the Soviets would insist, if they had not already, that America declare war against these countries, as they had with the British.

Partly in order to get around this, Washington tried to force them into limiting or ending their military operations against the Soviets. On 24 March the State Department asked Switzerland to inform the Romanians that the United States would declare war unless they "gave prompt evidence... that they would not assist the Axis Powers."[187] Other attempts were made in the following weeks, but all failed.[188]

On 29 May, 1942, the Soviet Foreign Commissar, Vyacheslav Molotov, secretly arrived in Washington for high level talks with Roosevelt. Unwilling to further antagonize the Soviets, on the following day Roosevelt "casually" informed Molotov that we never got around to declaring war on Romania, as it seemed something of a waste of effort. Mr. Molotov said that might be the case, but

---

[185] Ibid., 1114.

[186] Ibid., 1176. Assistant Secretary of State Sumner Welles cabled America's Ambassador in Turkey that these countries "had been obliged to take this action under duress and... that this was contrary to the will of the majority of the people." *Foreign Relations* 1942, 11, 835.

[187] Hull, *Memoirs*, 11, 1176.

[188] Ibid; A. A. Berle, Jr., to Welles, May 18, 1942, State Department memorandum, 871.00/5-1842.

the Romanians were fighting against the Soviets and causing some trouble by helping the Nazi.[189]

Without further discussion Roosevelt asked Senator Connally and Congressman Bloom the probable attitude of their Congressional Committees towards a declaraton of war. "Their thought was that there would be no objection, whereupon the President suggested that appropriate action might take place during the coming week."[190] Roosevelt's reasons for doing this were similar to those which caused Churchill to yield to the Russians six months earlier. Moreover, the Western Powers, in a lengthy conflict with the Soviets which just temporarily ended, had been largely successful in repelling their demands that Bessarabia and Northern Bucovina be recognized as part of Russia. In his message to Congress on the 2nd of June asking that war be declared on Romania, Hungary, and Bulgaria, Roosevelt pointed out that these countries declared war "not upon their own initiative or in response to the wishes of their own people, but as instruments of Hitler." Molotov "has undoubtedly demanded these declarations of war on our part," noted the powerful Republican member of the Senate Foreign Relations Committee Arthur H. Vandenberg in his diary. "It is perfectly logical and appropriate that we shall make them. But it is significant that we do in response to

---

[189] Robert E. Shewood, *Roosevelt and Hopkins* (New York, 1948), 567.
[190] Ibid.

Russian demand."[191] On 5 June the United States declared war on Romania, Hungary, and Bulgaria.

Since the fall of 1939, Romania had abondoned her neutrality and became an ally of Hitler. The threat of Russia finally drove her to seek protection with Germany and later to participate in the invasion of the Soviet Union. On the other hand, by the end of 1941, Russia had become the crucial element in the relations of the Western Powers with Romania. Primarily because of the need for unity with the Soviets, both England and the United States declared war on Romania. While overall Western policy was based upon the goal of defeating Hitler, for the remainder of the war their specific policies towards Romania would be largely determined by their relations with the Soviet Union.

---

[191] *The Private Papers of Senator Vandenberg* (ed. Arthur H. Vandenberg, Jr., Boston, 1952), 31-32. See also Bălteanu "Relațiile guvernului S. U. A. cu regimul fascist," 97.

CHAPTER IV

The Allies and Romanian "Peacefeelers"

During the years 1942-1944, British and American policies towards Romania involved both military and political considerations. The British continued their policy of trying to cause difficulty for the Germans, with the overall aim of persuading Romania to change sides. On the other hand, both of the Western Powers wanted to provide for an independent postwar Romanian state based on the principle of national self-determination; and despite their more immediate military objectives, from the earliest days of the war, their long-range political goals were ever present.

One of the major sources of conflict between the Western Powers and the Soviet Union during the war concerned the latter's territorial ambitions in Eastern Europe. Stalin an adherent of the Old Diplomacy of Machiavelli and Bismarck, from the beginning made no secret of his territorial objectives. In December, 1941, during the first wartime visit of the British Foreign Minister Anthony Eden to Moscow, the Russian dictator insisted that London recognize the western frontiers of the Soviet Union as of June, 1941.[1] So far neither of the Western Allies had recognized any of the territory acquired by the Soviets since the outbreak of the war, including the annexation of Bessarabia and Northern

---

[1] Woodward, *British Foreign Policy*, II, 146.

Bucovina.[2] Stalin also wanted Britain's approval for Russia to maintain air bases in Romania after the war.

Since the outbreak of the war in Europe in 1939, it had been the policy of the United States Government to postpone all questions involving territorial changes until the war ended.[3] American policy was further outlined in the Atlantic Charter in August, 1941.[4] In this lofty statement of war aims, the American and British governments promised to oppose territorial changes that did not accord with the wishes of the people involved and to uphold the rights of all people to freely choose the form of government they desired.

The British Government, however, did not take these promises as seriously as Washington did and believed that in certain instances exceptions might be made.' Britain's attitude worried the State Department. They especially feared that under pressure London might recognize Russia's new borders. It was this fear which caused Hull to quickly send a personal message to Eden just before he left for

---

[2] Russia had also acquired the Baltic States and the eastern half of Poland.

[3] The United States adopted this policy upon the outbreak of the war in Europe even though they themselves did not get involved in the fighting until December, 1941.

[4] Churchill, Grand Alliance, 442. Churchill wrote to Clement Attlee that the Charter was only "an interim and partial statement of war aims designed to assure all countries of our righteous purpose." See also Foreign Office Minute, December 3, 1942, F.O. 371/33257 R8370/22/37.

Moscow reminding him of Washington's territorial views and the Atlantic Charter.[5]

In spite of strong pressure in Moscow, Eden refused to give in. He repeatedly told Stalin that he had no authority to agree to changes of frontiers and that the British Government had agreed with the Americans that such changes should not be decided until after the war.[6] Eden's primary purpose in going to Moscow was to get Stalin to agree to a general military and political treaty providing for collaboration between the two countries during the war and establishing overall principles which would govern the postwar period of reconstruction.[7] An irritated Stalin told the British Foreign Secretary that unless the frontier changes he specified were included in the agreement his government would not be able to sign it. After a week the talks ended with little accomplished. But before leaving, Eden informed the Soviet leader that he would present his proposals to London and Washington for discussion and "would endeavor to obtain a favorable decision."[8]

Stalin's demands angered Churchill. He telegraphed Eden that to concede "would be contrary to all the principles for which we are fighting... and would dishonor our cause." Territorial questions "must be left to the... Peace

---

[5] *Foreign Relations* 1941, I, 194-195; Herbert Feis, *Churchill, Roosevelt, and Stalin* (Princeton, New Jersey, 1967), 25.

[6] *Foreign Relations* 1942, III, 507.

[7] *Ibid.*

[8] *Ibid.*, 509; Feis, Churchill, *Roosevelt, and Stalin*, 28.

Conference."[9] But at the same time, Churchill was painfully aware how London's reluctance to give Russia a free hand in Eastern Europe had led to the Nazi-Soviet Pact. Moreover, he hoped that if the Western Powers could establish close collaboration with the Russians during the war, it would pave the way for good relations in the postwar period. A Foreign Office Memorandum of January pointed out that Britain would "need Russian collaboration after the war as a counter weight to Germany."[10] By February Churchill's initial anger had subsided and he was reluctantly prepared to meet most of Stalin's objectives.

Lord Halifax, now British Ambassador to Washington, was instructed to present these views to the State Department to see if the Department would alter its policy. Hull was apprehensive. Several weeks before, after studying Eden's report from Moscow, he had the Department prepare a lengthy memorandum for Roosevelt which declared:

> If the British Government, with the tacit or expressed approval of this Government, should abandon the principle of no territorial commitments prior to the Peace Conference, it would be placed in a difficult position to resist additional Soviet demands relating to frontiers, territory, or to sphere of influences which would almost certainly follow whenever the Soviet Government would find itself in a favorable bargaining position. There is no doubt that the Soviet Government has tremendous ambitions with regard

---

[9] Churchill, *Grand Alliance*, 695; William H. McNeill, *America, Britain, and Russia, 1941-1946* (London, 1953), 167-168.
[10] Woodward, *British Foreign Policy*, II, 151.

to Europe and that at some time or other the United States and Great Britain will be forced to state that they cannot agree... to all of its demands. It would seem that it is preferable to take a firm attitude now, rather than to retreat and to be compelled to take a firm attitude later when our position had been weakened by the abandonment of... general principles.[11]

A follower of the New Diplomacy of Wilson, Roosevelt's chief reason for opposing Soviet territorial claims was his concern that they would violate the principles of the Atlantic Charter.[12] Like many, he believed that the secret territorial commitments which the Allies made during

World War I was a major reason for the failure of Wilson to carry out his Fourteen Points. In addition, he viewed military victory over the Axis as his principal objective and the wrangling over postwar frontiers as only hindrance to this effort.

Halifax's inquiries received a cold response from the State Department. The British had no doubt that if it ever came to a final showdown between Moscow and Washington they would cast their lot with the latter, but for the present they felt they had to go along with the Russians, and, consequently, began to put pressure on the Americans. At the same time, Roosevelt countered by urging Churchill to resist the Russians.[13] In addition, he sent a personal message to Stalin "strongly urging our point of view," but

---

[11] *Foreign Relations* 1942, III, 510-512.
[12] McNeill, America, Britain. and Russia, 169-170.
[13] Hull, *Memoirs*, II, 1170.

was abruptly told by the Soviets that the problem did not concern the United States."[14] This was how the situation stood at the end of March when Eden notified the Americans that the British Cabinet had agreed to go ahead and negotiate a treaty with the Russians in which most of Stalin's goals would be met. "Great Britain cannot neglect any opportunity offered to establish close and friendly relations with Stalin," Eden declared.[15] In spite of strong opposition from the State Department, Roosevelt now suggested a compromise solution. He proposed a plan whereby the Russians would get the frontiers they desired, but that the inhabitants of these regions would be able to freely leave if they wanted to.[16] The Russians, however, still refused to make any concessions. On 20 May Molotov arrived in London to negotiate the controversial treaty. Hull, who recently returned to work after being ill for two months, had persuaded Roosevelt to stand firm.[17] Shortly after the talks in London began, Roosevelt approved a State Department telegram warning the British that if they signed the treaty in its proposed form the United States "might have to issue a separate statement clearly stating that we did not subscribe to its principles and clauses."[18]

---

[14] *Ibid.*, 1170-1171.
[15] *Foreign Relations* 1942, III, 536; Gaddis Smith, *American Diplomacy During the Second World War, 1941-1945* (New York. 1965), 43.
[16] *Foreign Relations* 1942, III, 538-539; Smith, *American Diplomacy,* 43.
[17] Hull, *Memoirs,* II, 1172.
[18] *Ibid.*

But Roosevelt was worried. He feared that flatly rejecting the Russians could seriously endanger the alliance. In order to avoid this, as well as postpone the question of frontiers, he asked Stalin to send Molotov to Washington to discuss a "very important military proposal." [19] What Roosevelt apparently had in mind was a tacit arrangement whereby the Russians would postpone seeking recognition of their western boundaries in return for the opening of a second front in Europe in 1942.[20] The Russians were clearly more interested in a second front than their future borders.[21] The results were a temporary victory for the West. In London, Molotov signed twenty year pact of mutual assistance which made no mention of frontiers. "I was enormously relieved," wrote the tenacious American Secretary of State. Shortly afterwards in Washington, Roosevelt told Molotov "that we expect the formation of a second front this year." The territorial problem could be discussed later, the President noted.[22] Molotov simply replied "that he and his government had very definite convictions in the opposite direction, but that he had deferred to British preference and to what he understood to be the attitude of the President."[23] Roosevelt also agreed to declare war on Romania, Hungary, and

---

[19] *Foreign Relations, op. cit.*, 543; Feis, *Churchill, Roosevelt, and Stalin*, 61.

[20] Sherwood. *Roosevelt and Hopkins*, 526; Feis, *op, cit*; Smith, *American Diplomacy*, 44.

[21] Woodward, *British Foreign Policy*, II, 249.

[22] *Foreign Relations 1942*, III, 577, 569; Sherwood, *op. cit.*, 563.

[23] Foreign Relations, op. cit., 569.

Bulgaria. The frontier dispute was thus suspended for the time being.

Although England and the United States were officially at war with Romania, both countries kept up communications with opponents of the Antonescu Government.[24] Their main contact was the elderly Maniu, dominant figure in the democratic opposition, and leader of the National Peasant Party. At the same time, Washington and London cooperated in formulating their policies towards Romania; but the British, who traditionally had a greater interest in this part of Europe, took the lead.

Maniu had been at odds with the Antonescu regime since its establishment indeed, having spent most of his political life in opposition, this was his forte. By the beginning of 1942 he was attempting to work out an agreement with the British whereby Romania would eventually change sides. He notified the English that he was thinking about organizing "a well-prepared coup d'etat" against the Antonescu Government, so that "at the right moment. The entire force of the Romanian Army could be turned against the Axis."[25] But Maniu had his price. In return he wanted the Allies to specifically guarantee the future independence of the Romanian state, as well as its prewar

---

[24] During 1942 and 1943, much of the contact with the Romanian opposition was done through British and American intelligence agencies, the Special Operations Executive (SOE), and the Office of Strategic Services (OSS).

[25] Lord Glenconner to P. J. Dixon, January 7, 1942, F.O. 371/33256 R213/22/37. See also Research and Analysis Report No. 1480 Subject Iuliu Maniu, Rumanian Statesman, November 23, 1943, State Department Report, National Archives.

frontiers, including Bessarabia and Northern Bucovina. Moreover, because the Romanians stood little chance alone against the Germans, Maniu was extremely reluctant to take any action until British and American forces landed in the Balkans.[26]

In 1942, the British were in no position to agree to Maniu's terms. The prospects of a Balkan invasion by the Western Powers were slight, and they were fully aware of the importance Russia placed in getting Bessarabia and Northern Bucovina back. To the rumor that summer that the Soviets were backing down and would consent to the holding of a plebiscite in these two areas after the war one Foreign Office official commented: "We have heard nothing to corroborate this... which strikes us as extremely improbable. In any case a plebiscite run by the Soviet Government would be as valuable a guide to opinion as an announcement that the inmates of a German concentration camp had subscribed to a Christmas present for Himmler."[27]

Equally important, the British were reluctant to antagonize the Soviets by taking independent action in a theater in which only Russian troops were fighting. Nevertheless, the English felt they had little to lose by bringing Maniu's peacefeelers to the attention of the Kremlin, and, in the spring of 1942 made several attempts to interest them in the possibility of causing trouble for the Germans in

---

[26] Pearson to Dixon, October 10, 1942, F.O. 371/33257 R6805/22/37.
[27] Dixon to Pearson, August 6, 1942, F.O. 371/33271 R5017/5017/37.

Romania.[28] After a delay of several months Maisky informed the Foreign Office that "the Soviet Government did not for the moment want to take any action."[29]

While the British were not optimistic about starting an anti-Axis movement in Romania at this time, they continued their probing with Maniu. In the fall of 1942, he began to indicate that he might consent to a compromise on Bessarabia and Northern Bucovina. [30] The crux of the problem, however, was Romania's fear of Russia. Above all, Maniu did not want to be left at the mercy of the Russians or have the country invaded by Soviet armies.[31]

By the spring of 1943, the rapidly changing military situation on the Eastern front was forcing the Western Powers to compromise their ideals. With Soviet armies advancing towards Eastern Europe and the Balkans, it was becoming clear that what happened in those areas would be mainly decided by the Kremlin. Any lingering hopes the British had of keeping the Russians out of Bessarabia and Northern Bucovina had been abandoned by now.[32] More

---

[28] The British were especially interested in blocking the flow of oil to Germany at this time. See also Foreign Office Minute, May 9, 1944, F.O. 371/43999 R7287/294/37.

[29] Foreign Office Aide-Memoire, June 5,1942, F.O. 371/33256 R4116/22/37.

[30] Pearson to Dixon, October 10, 1942, F.O. 371/33357 R6805/22/37.

[31] Foreign Office Minute, October 16, 1942, F.O. 371/33257 R6805/22/37; Eden's Brief,March 8, 1943, F.O. 371 /37375 R2305/111/37.

[32] Ibid; Foreign Office Minute, December 3, 1942, F.O. 371/33257 R8370/22/37.

important, the British had concluded that for the time being they would have to follow the policy that Romania was predominantly a Russian area.[33] Eden's brief on Romania for his Washington visit in March, 1943 stated:

> Our policy towards Romania is subordinated to our relations with the Soviet Union and we are... unwilling to accept any commitments or to take any action except with the full cognizance and consent of the Soviet Government.[34]

With the shifting military balance of power on the Eastern front in favor of the Russians, Roosevelt was also coming to realize that concessions would have to be made to Stalin. The second front he promised had not materialized and during Eden's visit he reluctantly agreed to Russia's claim to Bessarabia.[35] Part of this was probably owing to Roosevelt's growing optimism about the Russians, a feeling he shared with many in the United States and Great Britain. Although he had little sympathy for Communism, he was coming to view Stalin as a man he could deal with. "Don't worry. I know how to talk to Stalin," he told his old friend Cardinal Spellman. "He is just another practical man who wants peace and prosperity."[36] Unlike the Fascists, Roosevelt felt the Soviets were not out to conquer the world and that

---

[33] Eden's Brief, *op. cit*; Foreign Office Minute, August 11, 1943, F.O. 371/37386 R7346/111/37.

[34] Eden's Brief, *op. cit*.

[35] *Foreign Relations* 1943, III, 13-14; Feis, *Churchill, Roosevelt, and Stalin*, 123; John Lewis Gaddis, *The United States and the Origins of the Cold War, 1941-1947* (New York, 1972), 135.

[36] Robert Gannon, S. J., *The Cardinal Spellman Story* (New York, 1962), 246.

much of the difficulty between East and West in the past had been simply due to a lack of knowledge. With infinite confidence in his own personal charm he hoped to overcome this barrier through personal tete-a-tetes with the Red dictator. Ironically, Roosevelt himself suffered from a glaring lack of knowledge of the Russians. "I don't understand the Russians", he confided to Frances Perkins, his Secretary of Labor. "I just don't know what makes them tick. I wish I could study them." He asked her to find out all she could about them and tell him from time to time. "I like them and I want to understand them."[37] For the most part, though, Roosevelt left it up to the State Department to handle detailed questions involving Romania and the Balkans. Like the English, the State Department had been receiving peacefeelers from Romania, but so far they had only listened to what the Romanians proposed, without getting involved in any serious discussions.[38] For the time

---

[37] Frances Perkins, *The Roosevelt I Knew* (New York, 1946), 86.
[38] There were several Free Romania Movements in the West. Tilea headed a Free Romania Committee in England, Victor Cornea, who worked in the area of educational exchange in the Romanian Legation in London, led another, and Charles A. Davila, a former Romanian Minister to Washington, headed a third organization in the United States. Neither of these organizations were given any official recognition by the Western governments for a number of reasons. The most important were due to the difficulties this could lead to with the Soviets and because there were no Romanians abroad who commanded widespread support back home. Moreover, the British Government viewed Tilea as being a political opportunist and a nuisance, whose past was too closely

being, the Department cautiously continued to follow the lead of the British.

The Foreign Office had come to the conclusion that the best solution to the Romanian problem would be to persuade the Russians to cooperate with the West in reaching an agreement with Romania. Not only would this pave the way for an insurrection in Romania, but also this seemed to be the best means by which they could restrain Stalin and provide for an independent postwar Romanian state. In March the Russians began to show some interest in Romania for the first time. When the British Ambassador in Moscow, Sir Archibald Clark Kerr, offered to put the Soviets in touch with Maniu, although Molotov rejected the offer as being premature, he suggested that the British continue their contact with the Maniu group.[39] "The Soviet Government," Molotov commented, "consider this group... the only serious opposition in Roumania, and that it is possible that in the

---

associated with King Carol. Divisions among the Romanians abroad also hurt them. London and Washington seemed to make little use of these organizations in dealing with people within Romania. The British Government, however, erected a Romanian bureau in July, 1942, with Major J. P. C. Back as its head. The purpose of the Bureau was "to unify Romanians in England and to provide them as far as possible with useful war work." Eden's Brief, March 8, 1943, F.O. 371/37375; Roumanian Bureau, August 1943, F.O. 371/37382 R7794/ 458137. See also *The Times*, London, June 3, August 21, 1941, January 10, November 18-1 9, 1942, February 11,1943, *New York Times*, February 6. May 6, 1941, January 7-8, 1942.
[39] Clark Kerr to Foreign Office. March 10, 1943, F.O. 371 /37375 R2193/111/37.

course of negotiations a basis may be found for collaboration."[40]

But the chances that Romania would change sides were still slight. Maniu largely clung to his original terms. In August, 1943, he notified the Foreign Office that Romania was "ready to negotiate with the Allies but not with Russia, unless she receives definite guarantees from the Anglo-Saxons."[41] The British were in no position to make such promises. One Foreign Office expert described Maniu's demands as being "exorbitant."[42] London had also been receiving peacefeelers from the shrewd and unscrupulous Mihai Antonescu. Yet, whereas they doubted that he had the backing of the conductor for this, and Mihai himself lacked the support of the army and the people, for the most part, his proposals were not taken seriously. [43] Making the problem more dismal for the British was the Soviet's

---

[40] Clark Kerr to Foreign Office, March 21, 1943, F.O. 371 /37375 R2760/1 11 /37.

[41] Georges Duca to British Embassy Stockholm, August 14, 1943, F.O. 371/37376 R8033/111/37.

[42] Foreign Office Minute, August 25, 1943, F. O. 371/37376 R8033/111/37. Maniu had also gone back to his original demands that Bessarabia and Northern Bucovina be restored to Romania.

[43] Eden's Brief, September 28, 1943, F.O. 371/37386 R10358/111/37. Mihai Antonescu contacted the British via the Turkish Ambassador in Bucharest, the Romanian Legation in Stockholm, Lisbon, and Madrid, and through special emissaries.

demand that the principle of unconditional surrender apply to all of Hitler's satellites.[44]

After the shattering defeat of the Axis Armies at Stalingrad, the Romanian Government began to look for a way out of the war even Antonescu (since July, 1941, Marshal) doubted that the German Armies would be able to hold out against the Russians in the long run."[45] During the winter of 1943 Mihai Antonescu began to explore the possibility of forming a bloc of Axis satellites under the guidance of Italy in order to end hostilities with the Allies.[46] This project, however, collapsed in the following summer with the overthrow of Mussolini and the surrender of Italy. By this time war weariness and defeatism were becoming widespread amongst the Romanian people. Sympathy for the Germans, which was never that strong, was rapidly

---

[44] Foreign Office Minute, August 11,1943, F.O. 371 /37386 R7346/111/37.

[45] Hillgruber, *Hitler, König Carol und Marschall Antonescu*, 167. In 1941 the Romanians sent thirty divisions to fight in the East, more than any other Axis state except Germany. Romanian soldiers played a major role in the conquest of Odessa and the Crimea. After Romanian and German armies conquered the territory between the Dniester and Bug rivers it was placed under Romanian control and named Transnistria. Fifteen Romanian divisions took part in the siege of Stalingrad in the fall of 1942 and suffered heavy losses. After this Romanian troops saw only limited action until the Red Army reached Moldavia in 1944. In total, Romania lost three hundred thousand soldiers fighting the Russians. For the most extensive account see Hillgruber.

[46] Cretzianu, *Lost Opportunity*, 90; F. W. Deakin, *The Brutal Friendship* (New York, 1966), 308-318 passim.

diminishing. On the other hand, few Romanians, even in 1941, were hostile towards the Western Powers, and regarded Antonescu's declarations of war as "pure formalities." As it became clear that the war would be lost more and more people looked to the West for protection from what they dreaded the most the Red Army.

In September, British prospects of starting something in Romania finally began to brighten. The appointment of Alexandre Cretianu, a member of the opposition and close associate of Maniu, Romania's Ambassador to Turkey was a sign that the Peasant leader might be ready to start serious negotiations.[47] More important, on 30 September the British received their first direct peacefeelers from Marshal Antonescu. The British Ambassador in Turkey was notified by Antonescu that Romania would "cooperate with any Anglo-American force entering the Balkans."[48] Above all, declared the Marshal, the Romanians did not want Russia to occupy the country. The Foreign Office decided to approach Moscow again on the possibility of negotiating some kind of joint agreement with Romania.[49]

So far the Russians had refused to commit themselves over Romania. As their armies pushed west they were coming to view Romania as their own private concern, During the early part of October the British proposed that if

---

[47] The British knew that the opposition was in contact with King Michael and that he supported them.
[48] Sir H. Knatchbull-Hugessen to Foreign Office, October 6, 1943, F.O. 371/37366 R9626/111/37.
[49] Eden's Brief, October 6, 1943, F.O. 371/37386 R10359/111/37; Anthony Eden, *The Reckoning* (Boston, 1965), 476.

the Romanians offer to surrender they should send "an authorized emissary to the three principal Allies."[50] The suspicious Russians agreed, but let London know that the terms and method of surrender would require "careful consideration" in light of the recent Italian surrender where "there had been certain shortcomings."[51] Shortly afterwards at the Moscow Conference of Foreign Ministers, the British tried to draw the Russians out further on Romania. In Moscow the Big Three promised that they would keep each other informed of any enemy peacefeelers and officially declare that all peace proposals would have to "take the form of an offer by a duly authorized emissary to sign an unconditional surrender to the principal Allies."[52] In order to accelerate negotiations with the Romanians the British had hoped to replace the principle of unconditional surrender with that of "working their passage home.[53] But at the Conference Molotov insisted on unconditional surrender. The Soviets also flatly rejected British attempts to establish

---

[50] Clark Kerr to Foreign Office, October 9, 1943, F.O. 371/37377 R9931/111/37.

[51] *Ibid*. Stalin was upset with the Italian surrender which was handled by the British and Americans with the Russians having a very limited role.

[52] Foreign Office Minute, May 9, 1944, F.O. 371/43999 R7267/294/37; Feis, *Churchill, Roosevelt and Stalin*, 219. According to this idea surrender terms would not be presented to an enemy until after they had actually surrendered.

[53] Report of War Cabinet Joint Planning Staff, October 16, 1943, F.O. 371/37377 R10391/111/37; Foreign Office Minute, October 21. 1943, F.O. 371/37377 R10391 /111 /37.

contact between them and Maniu.[54] The Foreign Office was becoming increasingly worried that Stalin was merely stalling so he would have a completely free hand in Romania.

On 10 November Maniu notified the British that he desired "to send a special delegate out of Romania for the purpose of discussing arrangements for a political changeover in that country."[55] After consulting Moscow and Washington, the British informed Maniu that the Allies would receive

> his emissary on the understanding that his only function would be to discuss operational details for the overthrow of the present regime... and its replacement by a government prepared to surrender unconditionally.[56]

In agreeing to this reply, the Russians told the English that "they considered it absolutely necessary for a Soviet representative to take part in the negotiations with Maniu's emissary."[57] England's desire to get the Romanians to change sides was further strengthened at this time by the decision of the Western Powers at Teheran to invade France in the following spring.

This decision for a cross-Channel invasion practically ended the possibility that the West would carry out a landing in the Balkans. The British had been the main

---

[54] *Foreign Relations 1943*, I, 205.

[55] *Ibid.*, 507.

[56] Foreign Office Minute, January 7, 1944, F. O. 371/43992 R294/294/37.

[57] *Ibid.*

advocate of a Balkan invasion. In 1943, Churchill supported either capturing the Dodecanese Islands, which he felt would bring Turkey into the war and open the Straits to Allied shipping, or landing several Allied divisions on the Dalmatian Coast and with the help of Yugoslavian partisans tying down some thirty German divisions. Eventually this force would make its way through the Ljubljana gap into Austria and Hungary. But these ideas never got off the ground because American military leaders strongly rejected them, fearing that the shifting of troops and supplies to the Balkans would delay the invasion of France.[58] In any case, British plans did not seem to envision sending troops into Romania, at least not at this stage. At Teheran, Roosevelt, much to the chagrin of the American Chiefs of Staff, mentioned the possibility of an invasion eastwards across Romania which would meet the Red Army coming from Odessa.[59] But nothing developed out of Roosevelt's remark.

British efforts to get the Romanians to change sides proceeded very slowly. In December, in order to accelerate negotiations with Maniu, an SOE team of three English officers with Colonel A.G.G. DeChastellaine in charge, were

---

[58] Churchill continued to raise the idea of an invasion through the Ljubljana gap into Austria and Hungary until the middle of the following summer. Again, nothing became of this.

[59] Sherwood. *Roosevelt and Hopkins*, 780; John A. Lukacs, *The Great Powers and Eastern Europe* (New York, 1953), 556-557. For the Teheran Conference see Feis, *Churchill, Roosevelt, and Stalin*; McNeill, America, Britain, and Russia; Churchill, *Closing the Ring*.

parachuted into Romania. [60] This mission (operation Autonomous) and a similar one of the previous August which had failed, ran into nothing but bad luck. After two abortive attempts to parachute the party into Romania, when they were dropped they landed about eight miles from their planned destination and in few hours were arrested; they spent the next eight months in a Bucharest jail. Meanwhile the Allies had decided to see Maniu's emissary in Cairo; but for several months the most that the British were able to get out of Maniu was that his emissary would be "leaving soon." [61] Moreover, the Foreign Office was worried how long they would be able to keep the suspicious Russians from trying to disrupt the planned negotiations. On several occasions Moscow had hinted that the whole idea was futile.[62] To make matters worse, differences had developed between London and Washington over armistice proposals for Romania.

Although the Romanians had been sending peacefeelers to the Americans, so far the State Department continued to follow the policies and lead of Britain.[63] That the United

---

[60] Foreign Office Minute, May 9, 1944, F.O. 371/43999 R7287/294/37; Sweet-Escott, *Baker Street*, 195; *The Times*, London, January 15, 1944.

[61] British Aide Memoire to State Department, January 17, 1944, F. O. 371/43992 R1850/294/37.

[62] Clark Kerr to Foreign Office, February 15, 1944, F. O. 371/43992 R2467/294/37; Lord Killearn to Foreign Office, March 4, 1944, F. O. 371/43993 R3510/294/37.

[63] There were various ways in which the Romanians contacted the United States Government. With the help of the OSS the Romanians often sent messages to Washington through the

States was not completely in agreement with London first became evident in the winter of 1944 when the two began to discuss proposals for an armistice with Romania. The overall problem was that the State Department was beginning to feel that the time had come to affirm, and so far as possible guarantee, Western political objectives in Romania. "While we recognize the Soviet Union's primary interest," a Department memorandum declared,

> we think that both the United States and Great Britain... should apply to Rumania the general principles underlying our conduct of the war, assuring as far as possible Rumania's continued existence as a state with such territory as would enable it to make its way as an independent country.[64]

In order to help guarantee an independent postwar Romania, they wanted American troops to participate in the occupation and looked forward to a joint formation of

---

American Embassies in Istanbul, Madrid, Stockholm, and Bern. Sometimes individuals in the Romanian Legations in these cities would contact members of the American Embassies directly. For example, the Romanian Charge d'Affaires in Stockholm Georges Duca, the son of the slain Premier, was in direct communications with the American Embassy there. This was also the case with the Fmt Secretary of the Romainian Legation in Madrid. Occasionally a special courier from Romania such as a member of a trade mlssion or a person on a business trip would deliver a special message. However. the same individuals might be in direct contact with the British as well as with the Americans.

[64] *Foreign Relations* 1944, IV, 147.

surrender terms by the Big Three.[65] The State Department also still had lingering hopes that the settlement of Bessarabia and Northern Bucovina could be delayed until after the war.[66]

British feared that these proposals would wreck any chance of getting the Russians to negotiate. In order to get around the problem, the Foreign Office told the Americans that they felt it would be better if the Soviets made "the initial proposals as to what the terms of surrender for Rumania should be."[67] London also urged that the frontier issue "not be raised in any way in connection with... surrender terms." The State Department reluctantly decided to wait. In March, Maniu's emissary, Prince Barbu Stirbey, amidst a blaze of publicity information about the secret mission had leaked out to the press finally arrived in Cairo.[68] Stirbey, an old aristocrat and a former Romanian Premier, had many friends in British circles.[69] On the 17th negotiations began. Representing the Allies were Lord Moyne, the British Minister Resident in Cairo, Lincoln MacVeagh and Nikolai Novikov, the American and Soviet Ambassadors to Egypt. Although the British were not sure what the Romanians would have to offer, they were not optimistic. Stirbey's

---

[65] State Department Memorandum, January 12, 1944, 871.00/1010; *Foreign Relations 1944*, IV, 172.

[66] *Ibid.*, 143-144.

[67] Ibid., 149.

[68] Hillgruber, *Hitler, König Carol und Marschall Antonescu*, 180. See also *New York Times*, March 14-16, 1944.

[69] Alexander Cretzianu, "The Roumanian Armistice Negotiations: Cairo, 1944," *Journal of Central European Affairs*, 3, (1951), 247.

suggestions, however, were much more encouraging than they had expected.[70] He told them that both the Romanian opposition and the Antonescu Government realized that the country would have to surrender, and that before leaving Bucharest he had talked with the Marshal and felt that Antonescu had reached the point where he would turn against the Germans.[71] It was Stirbey's view that a volte face by the government watched over by the opposition offered the best chance of success, but that if Antonescu backed down, Maniu was prepared to overthrow the regime. Before doing so Maniu wanted three assurances: that Romania's independence be maintained, that her territorial rights be respected, and that she be given co-belligerent status. Stirbey pointed out that Romania was especially concerned about getting Transylvania back, and that Maniu was "prepared to give up Bessarabia and the Bucovina with a face-saving bogus plebiscite."[72] He also asked for military assistance and agreed that it would have to come mainly from the Russians. For the past several weeks London had been pressing Moscow to produce armistice terms for Romania.[73] The Foreign Office had concluded that since the

---

[70] Memorandum from State Department to Roosevelt, August 26, 1944, Map Room box 164, Naval Aides Files, Franklin D. Roosevelt Library.

[71] Stirbey was Maniu's emissary, and not Antonescu's. Antonescu though had consented to his mission.

[72] *Foreign Relations 1944*, IV, 150-151 Moyne to Foreign Office, March 17, 1944, F.O. 371/43993 R4272/294/37; Cretzianu, "Rumanian Armistice Negotiations," 246-247.

[73] Lord Killearn to Foreign Office, March 7, 1944, F.O. 371/43993 R3733/294/37.

Red armies would "be the first Allied forces to reach Roumania," Moscow would have to "play the principal part in determining... the armistice terms." [74] With Stirbey's encouraging proposals the English stepped up their efforts to get the Russians to act. Moreover, as the day for the invasion of France approached, the military value of a revolt in Romania became increasingly important. But the Soviets refused to commit themselves. Molotov told the British that their reports showed that Stirbey does not represent Maniu, that he does not have the authority to conduct negotiations with the Allies, and that there is no evidence which indicates that either Maniu or Antonescu would change sides. "It is doubtful whether these conversations can lead to a satisfactory result," the Russian Foreign Minister asserted.[75] One angry Foreign Office official called Molotov's arguments "complete nonsense." "I suspect," wrote Orme Sargent

> they do not wish to commit themselves until their armies are actually on the Roumanian frontier and in a position to invade... and... because they resent our having any say as to the terms which might be offered.[76]

But on 26 March the Kremlin unexpectedly reversed its policy. "Telegram from Moscow showing that Russians now, suddenly, agree to play with Roumanians," noted the

---

[74] Foreign Office to Washington and Moscow, January 14, 1944, F.O. 371/43992 R755/294/37.
[75] Clark Kerr to Foreign Office, March 23, 1944, F.O.371/43994 R4634/294/37.
[76] Sargent's Minute, March 18,1944,F.O.371/43993,R4272/294/137.

surprised Cadogan.[77] Apparently this came about as a result of an urgent message sent to the Romanian Government four days before by General Henry Maitland Wilson, the British Commander in the Mediterranean. On 22 March Stirbey told the Allies in Cairo that he had just been informed by Mihai Antonescu that the Marshal had been invited to Hitler's headquarters where undoubtedly he would be faced with demands for greater Romanian military assistance. Whereas only a few days earlier Hungary had been completely taken over by the Germans it was feared that a similar fate awaited Romania if Antonescu resisted Hitler. In light of this, Mihai Antonescu wanted to know if Romania could count on Allied military assistance.[78]

In order to reach Marshal Antonescu before he left Romania, General Wilson sent an urgent message to Bucharest without first consulting with the Russians. Wilson warned the Marshal not to visit Hitler, and to surrender at once to the three Great Powers. The "nature of peace terms imposed on Rumania," the message stated, "will be largely determined by the extent to which she contributes towards the defeat of Germany."[79] Britain's independent action upset

---

[77] Dilks, *Cadogan*, 614.

[78] *Foreign Relations* 1944, IV, 154-1 55.

[79] *Ibid.*, 157. On the morning of the 22nd Generl Wilson, Lord Moyne, Mr. Harold Macmillan, Lord Killearn, Air Marshal Slessar, Mr Leeper. Mr. Makins, and the three Commander-inchief of the Middle East decided to send a message to Marshal Antonescu immediately. Because of the time factor the message was sent before even London could be consulted. The English officials in Cairo felt their instructions justified such an emergency measure. In the end British and Romanian fears

the Soviets. Fearing that a sudden surrender by Antonescu to all three Allies could weaken their own position to dictate terms to Romania, the Soviets notified London that they wanted to make three additional proposals. These instructed Antonescu to "order Rumanian troops in contact with the Russians to surrender," provided for their subsequent use against the Germans, and specified that "practical problems of mutual military aid" would be handled directly by the Soviet and Romanian High Command.[80]

"The Russian proposals," a worried State Department official wrote, "would leave the matter of the Rumanian surrender exclusively in Russian hands." [81] The State Department had hoped that the armistice terms, as well as the surrender of Romania would be worked out jointly by the Big Three. But before the Department could respond to the Soviet proposal, the American Joint Chiefs of Staff told Hull that

> the detachment of Rumania and other Balkan satellites from the Axis is militarily of the highest importance... In view of this, the Joint Chiefs of Staff are of the opinion that no restrictive political consideration should be advanced that would militate against the early surrender of the Rumanian forces.[82]

---

proved to be exaggerated. Antonescu did visit Hitler, but little of any real importance resulted. Lord Killearn to Foreign Office, March 22, 1944, F.O. 371/43994.
[80] Foreign Relations 1944, *op. cit.*, 159.
[81] *Ibid.*
[82] *Ibid.*, 161.

The Joint Chiefs also noted that leaving Romania's surrender to the Soviets would be "only natural" since their troops were the only ones in the area, and from the military point of view, analogous to the Italian surrender. On 29 March Hull notified the Russians that the United States approved their proposal. In the meantime, the British had informed Moscow that they and the Americans expected to be

> consulted in advance in case the armistice terms which the Russians may propose carry any stipulations or implications extending beyond the accomplishment of the military capitulation.[83]

Moreover, London began urging the Russians to extend political assurances to Romania. Having secured their desire to control Romania's surrender the Russians could be generous. On April, as the Red Army began to cross the Pruth into pre-World War I Moldavia, Molotov issued a communique to the press which declared:

> The Soviet Government... is not pursuing the aims of acquirement of any part of Rumanian territory or change of the existing social regime of Rumania and that the entrance of Soviet troops... is exclusively dictated by the military necessity and the continuing resistance of the enemy troops.[84]

---

[83] *Ibid.*, 168.
[84] *Ibid.*, 165-166.

This statement also announced that Russia would retain her 1940 borders.[85]

Several days later the Soviets informed London and Washington of their detailed armistice plan for Romania. While basically covering the points which the Soviets had already made, it also included a number of new terms. They proposed that Romania pay an indemnity for war damages, and, while renewing their pledge not to occupy Romanian territory, stated that the Red Army "must have unrestricted freedom of movement throughout... if the military situation makes it necessary." They also declared that they considered the "Vienna Award" unjust and were ready to help restore part or all of Transylvania to Romania.[86]

Considering the circumstances, the British were satisfied with the Russian terms. Churchill expressed his "admiration" for Molotov's communique of 2 April. [87] Foreign Office officials told the American Ambassador of their "satisfaction," especially since Romania "would fall into Soviet hands anyway if the Soviet military success continued."[88] The State Department, however, was uneasy.

The State Department was reluctant to compromise its war principles. A Department memorandum written shortly after receiving Moscow's proposals stated:

---

[85] In keeping with the recent British request to be consulted in advance the Soviets gave London and Washington a copy of their proposed statement on the previous day.

[86] Foreign Relations 1944, *op. cit.*, 169-170.

[87] Cretzianu, *Lost Opportunity*, 137.

[88] Winant to Secretary of State, April 3, 1944, State Department Telegram, No. 2694, 740.00119 EW/2421.

The terms are essentially Russian, not allied nor tri-partite; they are frankly based on the practical premise that the war with Rumania is Russia's own business.... For example: The American draft was based on the principle of unconditional surrender, envisaged military occupation and carried detailed provisions regarding occupational organs, demobilization... et cetera.[89]

The Soviet terms also differed on territorial questions, including Transylvania, which as a matter of principle the Department wished to leave until after the war. Principles were not the only reason they were concerned. Officials were becoming increasingly worried with the prospects of the spreading of Communism and the establishment of spheres of influence in Eastern Europe and the Balkans. Furthermore, the feeling was growing that the only way to deal with the Russians was to stand firm. [90] But the Department held back its political views in light of the military significance which the Joint Chiefs of Staff placed on getting Romania to surrender.[91] On 8 April the Soviets were told that the United States consented to their terms.

---

[89] *Foreign Relations 1944*, IV, 172-173.

[90] George Kennan, *Memoirs 1925-1950* (Boston, 1967), 211; Philip E. Mosley, "Central Europe 1941-1947," *Fate of East Central Europe*, 57; *Foreign Relations 1944*, IV, 992-998.

[91] Roosevelt was uneasy about abandonmg the principle of unconditional surrender. In the end he dearded on a compromise. He told Hull that he wanted to retain the idea of unconditional surrender in principle, but was willing to see it ignored in specific cases from time to time!

Regardless of the reluctance of the State Department, the Soviets proposals finally put an end to the troublesome question of Bessarabia and Northern Bucovina between the Allies. The British assumed that the Russians would regard their approval of the terms as recognition of their new frontiers.[92] On 24 April MacVeagh told the Russians that as far as Washington was concerned this question was settled.[93]

The British took the lead in trying to persuade the Romanians to accept the armistice terms. While the Big Three hoped that Antonescu himself would lead the country into the Allied camp, the Russians promised the same terms to Maniu if he could gain control of the government and change sides.[94] But even before the Soviets sent Antonescu and Maniu their detailed armistice plan on 12 April, the several indirect replies which the English had received caused them to fear that the Romanians were not ready to act.[95]

The most discouraging was Marshal Antonescu. At the beginning of April he asked the Allies for assurances that Romania would remain independent, as well as for Soviet armistice terms. Shortly before the Russian terms reached Bucharest, Antonescu sent an urgent message to General Wilson in which he appealed "as an old man to a gallant

---

[92] Sargent's Minute, April 5, 1944, F.O. 371/43984 R5445/116/37.
[93] *Foreign Relations 1944*, IV, 177.
[94] Moyne to Algiers, March 28, 1944, F.O. 371/43995 R4946/294/37.
[95] Cairo to Foreign Office, April 4, 1944. F.O. 371/42997 R5407/294/37; Cairo to Foreign Office, April 5, 1944. F.O.371 43997 R54751294137.

soldier for mercy.'"[96] But Antonescu remained silent on all of the Soviet proposals, not even acknowledging receipt of them. In order to get him to act, at the end of the month the British got the Soviets to consent to an ultimatum which threatened to withdraw the terms unless he accepted. [97] Nevertheless, London received no response from Bucharest.

On 16 April the Allies received a message from Maniu which he had sent before receiving the Soviet terms. He asked that two Western air-borne divisions be sent into Romania, and that no other foreign troops be allowed to enter the country without an express request from the government.[98] Four days later Maniu notified Cairo of his receipt of the Soviet terms. He accepted the armistice generally, but added that he wanted to negotiate further. He also informed the Allies that he was sending a second emissary to Cairo to assist with the negotiations.[99]

The British were frustrated. On 21 April Stirbey was told that the Allies were not prepared to negotiate further and demanded that Maniu either accept or reject the terms.[100] One Foreign Office official wrote: "It is high time that Maniu realized that Romania is a defeated nation and in no position

[96] Foreign Ofice Minute, April 22, 1944, F.O. 371/43999 R6436/294/37.
[97] Cairo to Foreign Office. May 3, 1944, F.O. 371/43999 R7168/294/37.
[98] Cretzianu, *Lost Opportunity*, 139.
[99] Foreign Office Minute, April 22, 1944, F.O. 371/43999 R6436/294/37; Cretzianu, *op. cit.*, 139-140; Gheorghe Zaharia, *"L'insurrection nationale antifasciste d'aout 1944 et son importance, "Revue Roumaine d'Histoire*, 13 (1974), IV, 592.
[100] Cretzianu, *op. cit.*, 139.

to dictate terms."[101] Despite these tactics, because the British had not received a reply from Antonescu they decided that in the future they would have to rely on Maniu.[102] What chiefly was holding Maniu back was his lack of faith in the Soviets, and fear that they would take over the country, regardless of their pledge against occupation. Although the British had just about given up on Antonescu, the Marshal was still very deeply involved in negotiations. Unknown at this time to Whitehall, on 11 April Anotnescu's Minister to Sweden, Frederick Nano, had been secretly told by the Russians that they "would prefer to deal with the present government," and not with the opposition.[103] The next day Nano was presented with similar armistice terms as the Soviets were sending to Romania via Cairo. Nano felt the Russians preferred to deal with Antonescu because they viewed Maniu as being too close to the Western Powers.[104]

------

[101] Foreign Office Minute, April 18, 1944. F.O. 371/43998 R6137/294/37.

[102] Cairo to Foreign Office, May 3, 1944, F.O. 371/43999 R7168/294/37.

[103] Frederick Nano, "The First Soviet Double Cross," *Journal of Central European Affairs*, 12 (1952), 247. Also Ecaterina Cimponeriu, "Criza guvernării antonesciene in lunile care au precedat istoricul act de la 23 august 1944," *Studii, Revista de istorie*, 22 (1969), IV, 642. Nano had also been used by the Antonescu Government as a contact with the English and the Americans.

[104] Nano, *op. cit.*, 256. Another theory is that it would have been easier for the Russians to replace an Antonescu Government than a government under the opposition with one of their own making. From the military point of view whereas Antonescu

162

Believing that Romania's best chance rested in talks with the Soviets through Stockholm, Antonescu had broken off his communications with Cairo.

Developments in the Balkans were moving rapidly, however, and the British could not merely stand by until the Romanians made up their minds. In May the English began to curtail their role in Romania. This was in part because of their discouragement over the failure of Romania to accept the surrender terms, and their feeling that the Russians would stand by their proposals in dealing with Romania in the future. Moreover, London believed that Russia had become convinced that an independent Romania was necessary to keep Hungary in check.[105]

At the same time, on 29 April, Molotov sharply accused the English of working behind their backs through a clandestine "British mission" in Bucharest although ironically the Soviets were the ones doing the double-dealing.[106] This angered and puzzled London. Molotov's alleged British mission consisted of the three agents who had been captured shortly after they parachuted into Romania in the previous December and were subsequently used to help transmit five messages to Cairo. Whereas the English had already told Moscow of their activities, the Foreign Office attributed Molotov's statements to unreasonable suspicion and misunderstanding on his part.

---

had the armed forces at his disposal it would have been better to deal with him.

[105] Foreign Office Minute, July 12, 1944, F.O. 371/44003 R10668/294/37.

[106] Molotov to Churchill, April 29.1944, F.O.371/43999.

Nevertheless, because of Russia's annoyance and suspicion over the incident the Foreign Office decided to "cease taking the initiative in Roumanian affairs" for the present.[107] The main reason, however, that the British were willing to curtail their involvement in Romania was because of the growing Communist threat to Greece. At the beginning of May Eden told Clark Kerr that he was "gravely concerned" about the situation in Greece.[108] In order to prevent a Communist takeover on 5 May Eden suggested to the Russians that they "should temporarily regard Rumanian affairs as mainly their concern... while leaving Greece to us."[109] On the 18th the Russian Ambassador informed the Foreign Office that his government favored the idea, but first wanted the approval of the United States. At the end of the month the British Ambassador Halifax sounded out the State Department on a temporary agreement by which "Russia might have controlling influence in Rumania and Great Britain a controlling influence in Greece."[110] On the 31st in a personal telegram Churchill told Roosevelt that it was the only practical solution. He tried to allay Roosevelt's fears by assuring him that "we do not of course wish to carve up the Balkans into spheres of influence and in agreeing to the

---

[107] Foreign Office to Cairo, May 22, 1944. F.O. 371/44000 R7719/294/37.

[108] Eden to Clark Kerr, May 5, 1944, F.O. 371/44000 R7214/294/37. See also D. F. Fleming, *The Cold War and Its Origins* (2v., Garden City, New York, 1961), I,189.

[109] Winston Churchill, *Triumph and Tragedy* (Boston, 1953), 73; Anthony Eden, *The Reckoning* (Boston. 1965). 533.

[110] *Foreign Relations 1944*, V, 112-113; Feis, *Churchill, Roosevelt. and Stalin*, 339.

arrangement we should make it clear that it applies only to war conditions."[111]

But Roosevelt, and in particular Hull, were apprehensive. They saw this as a step towards the balance of power and sphere of influence doctrine which they believed had had such iniquitous consequences in the past.[112] Although both had already agreed that the Soviets would control military operations in Romania they feared that the type of agreement Churchill proposed would harden into permanent spheres of influence. Replying to the British the State Department explained that in their

> view the proposed arrangement... would lead to the division of that region into spheres of influence, despite the declared intentions to limit the arrangement to war conditions.... It is consequently unwilling to give the approval of this Government."[113]

In spite of the State Department, Churchill continued to try to change Roosevelt's mind. Realizing Roosevelt's concern over postwar spheres the Prime Minister suggested a three month trial period. Finally, without first consulting Hull, Roosevelt reluctantly agreed on condition "that we are not establishing any postwar spheres of influence."[114] Hull,

---

[111] Foreign Relations, *op. cit.*, 114; McNeill, America, Britain, and Russia, 423.

[112] James MacGregor Burns,Roosevelt: *The Soldier of Freedom* (New York, 1970), 483; Julius W. Pratt, *Cordell Hull* (V. Xlll of *the American Secretaries of State and their Diplomacy*, ed. Robert H. Ferrell, New York), 642-643. [113]Foreign Relations 1944, V,120.

[113] *Foreign Relations 1944*, V, 120.

[114] Ibid., 131; Burns, *op. cit.*, 484.

who was away for a few days on vacation, did not learn of this until two weeks later, and then from the British!

Actually coordination of policy between the White House and the State Department during the war years was muddled with the latter often groping for postwar policy guidance while the President chiefly concerned himself with the more immediate military objectives. Administrative disorganization and Roosevelt's penchant for secrecy further compounded the problem. Be this as it may, in the meantime, American doubts had begun to worry the Russians. At the end of June Moscow informed the State Department that the "Soviet Government deems it necessary to subject this matter to additional study."[115] On 15 July Washington told the Soviets that the three month arrangement was only between them and the British and that it "would have neither direct no indirect validity as affecting the interests of this Government." [116] On the same day Stalin notified Churchill that because of the attitude of the American Government he wanted to postpone the whole idea. After this whatever lingering hope Churchill still had of keeping his plan alive soon ended as the Soviets slyly began to encourage the Communist resistance group in Greece.

On 25 May, Maniu's second emissary, the veteran diplomat Constantin Vişoianu, arrived in Cairo. Vişoianu reported that Maniu accepted the armistice terms in principle, and that King Michael and Maniu were determined to act regardless of Antonescu. On the other hand, Vişoianu wanted to acquire better terms, even

---

[115] *Foreign Relations 1944*, V, 129.
[116] *Ibid.*, 131.

bringing up the question of Bessarabia and Northern Bucovina with the English again. [117] The British Acting Counselor in Cairo, Christopher Steel, cabled London that Maniu was "out of touch with realities." [118] Lord Moyne believed that

> Vişoianu arrived with instructions from Maniu to upbraid Stirbey with his supine conduct of the conversations and has apparently taken the line that by bargaining further he could have obtained... improved terms.[119]

The frustrated Moyne concluded his telegram by stating that: "Nothing could illustrate better than the above the impossibility of obtaining any practical results through Maniu."

On 31 May the Soviet Government told Vişoianu that before they would discuss any more questions Maniu would have to state "definitely whether he accepts the armistice considerations."[120]

In agreement with the King, on 10 June Maniu cabled the Allies that he accepted their terms and that the means of implementing them were being planned. He further stated that the opposition was forming a Romanian National

---

[117] Moyne to Foreign Office, May 27, 1944, F.O. 371/44000 R8341/294/37.

[118] *Ibid*.

[119] Moyne to Foreign Office, June 2, 1944, F.O. 371/44000 R8748/294/37.

[120] Moyne to Foreign Office, June 1, 1944, F.O. 371/44000 R8629/294/37.

Democratic Bloc, made up of the National Peasants, Liberals, Social Democratic, and Communist parties.[121]

On 27 and 28 June the Allies received Maniu's detailed plan for implementing the armistice. The plan consisted of a coup d'etat against the Antonescu Government followed by the signing of the armistice. In addition, Maniu wanted the overthrow to coincide with a Soviet offensive during which time the Romanian troops at the front would join with the Red Army.[122]

London was pleased that Maniu seemed ready to act; however, there was one aspect which puzzled the Foreign Office. Maniu asked for an improvement in his armistice terms in light of the additional concessions the Soviets had made to Antonescu.[123]

The British were still in the dark on the Stockholm negotiations, which had resumed on 22 May. On 31 May the

---

[121] Moyne to Foreign Office, June 12, 1944, F.O. 371/44000 R9273/294/37; N. Goldberger; Gheorghe Zaharia, "Le caractere national et international du mouvement de resistance en Roumanie," *La Roumanie pendant la deuxieme guerre mondiale*, 83; Zaharia, "L'insurrection nationale antifasciste," 593; Nicolae Ceaușescu, *Romania on the Way of Completing Socialist Construction* (IV, Bucharest, 1969), 356-357. Mircea Ionniţiu, King Michael's Private Secretary and close friend, told me that Maniu and Constantin Brătianu only agreed to join with the Communist and Socialist parties in forming the Bloc as a result of pressure from the British. The English hoped that this would help to facilitate discussions with the Russians. Letter, Mircea Ionniţiu to the author, December 30, 1974.

[122] Moyne to Foreign Office, June 27, 1944, F.O.371/44002

[123] Moyne to Foreign Office, June 28, 1944, F.O. 371/44002 R12174/294/37.

Russians had made several concessions to Antonescu. The two most important were that if the Germans evacuated Romania within fifteen days after the latter changed sides they could remain neutral, and that the Romanians could establish a region in which no foreign troops would have access.[124] In June, while Maniu was working through Cairo, negotiations were going on in Stockholm with Antonescu. But in the end Antonescu's fear of his long-time enemy prevented him from accepting. The Romanians had too many bitter experiences with the Russians to allow them the luxury of the wishful thinking that permeated the West. Only around the beginning of July did Whitehall find out about these talks, and then apparently without any details as to the additional concessions the Soviets made.[125] Because of Churchill's pending agreement with Stalin over Greece and Romania the English decided not to bring the matter to the attention of the Russians.

The Russians were in no hurry to reply to Maniu. By early August, no longer bound by the agreement with Stalin, the Foreign Office began to press Moscow for some action.[126] On the 4th Vyschinski told Clark Kerr that he "had not much faith" in Maniu's proposals, but that he would have the

---

[124] Nano, "Soviet Double Cross," 252.
[125] Foreign Office Minute, July 10, 1944, F.O. 371/44003 R10668/294/37. The United States also knew nothing about the Stockholm talks up to this time. *Foreign Relations 1944*, IV.
[126] Foreign Office to Cairo, July 28, 1944, F.O. 371/44003 R11407/294/37.

government "examine the matter afresh."[127] The Soviets also failed to respond to Maniu's requests for an answer.[128] Finally on 20 August the Soviets ended the suspense by launching a major offensive into Romania. The time for bargaining was over.

The Red Army offensive in August took the Germans and Romanians by surprise; both had expected the next Soviet attack to come further north. The Romanian front consisted of approximately fifty divisions, half of them Romanian, while the Russians opposed them with almost three times that number.[129] During the first several days of the offensive the Red Army overran most of the German and Romanian fortifications along the Dniester. The Germans at first put up fierce resistance, but many of the Romanians either offered no resistance or deserted.[130] On the 22nd Iaşi, the capital of Moldavia was taken, and two days later, Chişinău the chief city of Bessarabia, fell. By 23 August fifteen German divisions were surrounded.

Hitler believed that Marshal Antonescu would remain loyal to Germany to the end, viewing him, next to Mussolini, as his most trusted ally. The Germans were aware of Romania's peacefeelers, but saw Mihai Antonescu and the opposition as the main culprits.

---

[127] Clark Kerr to Foreign Office, August 5, 1944, F.O. 371/44004 R12220/294/37.

[128] Hillgruber, *Hitler, Konig Carol und Marschall Antonescu*, 198.

[129] Alexander Werth, *Russia at War 1941-1945* (New York, 1964), 901; G. Deborin, *The Second World War* (Moscow, n. d.), 375-376.

[130] Werth, *op. cit.*, 901 ; Heinz Guderian, *Panzer Leader* (New York, 1957). 367.

On 5 August the Marshal visited Hitler for the last time at his headquarters near Rastenberg in East Prussia. The Fuhrer asked Antonescu point-blank if he would remain loyal come what may. Although Antonescu side-stepped the question he left Hitler with the impression that he would. The reports of General Erik Hansen, the head of the German military mission in Romania, and the German Minister in Bucharest, Manfred von Killinger, further strengthened Hitler's belief in Romania's loyalty. As a result during August no precautionary measures were taken by the Germans to guard against a possible change over.

Maniu and the opposition were also taken by surprise by the sudden Soviet attack. It was clear to them that this would be their last chance to act before the Russians overran the country. On the same day as the Red Army offensive began Maniu notified Cairo that the opposition and the King had decided to take over the government. He asked the Allies to help them by bombing certain targets and by sending air-borne troops. The coup was scheduled for 26 August. Cairo did not receive Maniu's message until the 22nd.[131] Upon receiving the telegram the British quickly took the matter up with the Soviet Embassy in Cairo. It was all in vain. Lord Moyne told London they got the "usual results." The Russians informed the English that they had no instructions from Moscow regarding Maniu. In light of the Soviet offensive, Moyne wrote, "it is clear that they never will."[132] Before anything further could be done concerning

---

[131] Moyne to Foreign Office, August 22, 1944, F.O. 371/44005 R13108/294/37.
[132] Moyne to Foreign Office, August 22, 1944, F.O. 371/44005.

Maniu's message the political situation in Romania had changed considerably.

Shortly after the Soviet attack began, Marshal Antonescu rushed to the front. By the 22nd it must have been clear to him that the military situation was hopeless. [133] Making Romania's position even more desperate was Bulgaria's announcement that she was about to join with Russia. On the 22nd Antonescu went back to Bucharest. In the meantime, Mihai Antonescu notified the British through the Turkish Government that the Marshal had consented to an armistice. The Foreign Minister asked for a reply within twenty-four hours and offered to dispatch a delegation to sign the armistice to either Cairo or Moscow.[134] At the same time, a special courier was flown to Stockholm to tell Nano to get in touch with the Russians immediately and accept their terms.[135]

Until the last days of the Antonescu Government the opposition tried to get the Marshal to change sides. Ion Mihalache, the Vice-president of the Peasant Party, saw both Antonescus on 22 August. Gheorghe Brătianu, a leader of the Liberal Party, talked with the Marshal on the morning of the fateful 23rd.[136] The opposition was fearful of Hitler's reaction; estimates of German strength in Romania varied from one hundred thousand to four hundred thousand

---

[133] Hillgruber, *Hitler, Konig Carol und Marschall Antonescu*, 215.
[134] Knatchbull-Hugessen to Foreign Office, August 22, 1944, F.O. 371/44005 R13107/294/37.
[135] Nano, "Soviet Double Cross," 254-255.
[136] Bucharest Report to Foreign Office, September 8, 1944. F.O. 371/44010.

troops.[136] If Antonescu led the volte-face not only would he have the army at his disposal, but through his good relations with Hitler, Romania might be able to lessen the Führer's wrath.

Since the previous August young King Michael had been in secret contact with Maniu and the opposition, but so far his role in their activities had been a limited one. Now twenty-two years old, the husky, shy monarch, who like many young men his age liked fast cars and mechanical things, had little if any influence with Marshal Antonescu, who regarded him as "an ignorant boy." Although he was poorly trained for his position when he became king, the plight of the country under the Marshal gradually forced him to become aware of political realities and to work with the opposition. The time was now quickly approaching when Michael would be given a chance to become a true king of his people. On 21 August, Michael and the opposition leaders had their last meeting, after which some of the latter went into hiding. A crucial aspect of their plan was to have Marshal Antonescu in Bucharest on the 26th so he could be arrested if need be. But on the evening of the 22nd the King found out that the Marshal was planning on returning to the front in two days, and, hence, would be out of reach on the day of the coup. Michael acted swiftly. Unable to find the political leaders, that night the King and several of his trusted intimates decided to invite Antonescu to Casa Nouă (a villa on the grounds of the Royal Palace in Bucharest) on the following day and give him one last chance to change sides. If he refused he would be arrested. It was a very risky move. If Antonescu got wind of it he could easily have had the King arrested and shipped off to Germany.[137]

The next day at noon, one of the King's aide-de-camps telephoned the two Antonescus to ask them to come to Casa Nouă to discuss the war situation. The Marshal and his Foreign Minister arrived around half-past four, completely unaware of what was afoot. After a brief discussion of the military situation Michael proposed an immediate armistice. But the Marshal was still reluctant to act. He told Michael that he wanted guarantees that they would get Transylvania, and even Bessarabia back, as well as give advance warning to the Germans so they would have the opportunity to evacuate their troops from Romania peacefully. When the King replied that it was too late for additional bargaining and suggested that he resign the angry Marshal retorted: 'Who can take Antonescu's place? Do you think shall hand the country to you into the hands of a child!' Rather than argue further Michael excused himself and went into his study. After a brief discussion with several supporters he ordered his palace guardsmen to arrest the two Antonescus. 'In the morning you shall be shot,' cried the dumbfounded

---

[137] Lee, *Crown*, 67. That the reason King Michael decided to act ahead of schedule was because of Antonescu's plans to leave the capital before the 26th was further substantiated in a letter to me from Mircea Ionnițiu, who directly participated in all of the above. Letter, Mircea Ionnițiu to the author, December 30, 1974.

Marshal as he was taken away to a large safe which had housed the royal stamp collection for safekeeping.[138]

There is little doubt that the decision to have Antonescu arrested was made by Michael with the recommendation of his advisors. Later the Communists claimed that the overthrow of the dictatorship was essentially due to the uprising of the people under their leadership.[139]

Actually the tiny Romanian Communist Party only played a minor role prior to 23 August. Before Antonescu's

---

[138] Lee, *Crown*, 67-72. This is the best account of the coup See also Roy M. Melbourne, "Rumania: Nazi Satellite," *Doctoral Thesis University of Pennsylvania*, 1951, 209-21 5. Hillgruber, *Hitler, König Carol und Marschall Antonescu*, 216; Bucharest Report to Foreign Office, September 8, 1944, F.O. 371/44010. Shortly after the two Antonescus were arrested, War Minister Constantin Pantazi, Interior Minister Constantin Vasiliu, and Police Prefect Colonel Elefterescu were induced to come to the palace and were subsequently placed under arrest.

[139] A. Petric; Gh. Țuțui, *L'instauration et la consolidation du regime democratique populaire en Roumanie* (Bucarest, 1964), 13-20; P. Constantinescu-Iaşi, "L'insurrection d'aout 1944," *Revue d'Historie de la Deuxieme Guerre Mondiale*, 18 (1968), 70, 39-55; Nicolae Ceauşescu, *Romania on the Way of Building up the Multilaterally Developed Socialist Society* (3v, Bucharest, 1970), IV, 354-355; Gheorghe Gheorghiu-Dej, *30 Jahre Kampf der Partei unter dem Banner Lenins und Stalins* (Bukarest, 1952), 37-38. For two articles on historiography by the Romanians on this period see Mihai Ruşenescu, Istoriografia Românească privind insurecția antifascistă din august 1944 şi urmările sale," Studii, Revista de istorie, 22 (1969), IV, 717-732; Ioan Chiper, "Istoriografia străină despre insurecția armată din august 1944 în România," *Studii, Revista de istorie*, 22 (1969), IV, 733-759.

overthrow the party was illegal, most of its leaders were in prison, and it had very little popular support. Moreover, the party was divided, and two of its top leaders, Ana Pauker and Vasile Luca, were in Russia during most of the war. Both Pauker and Luca were against the voluntary surrender of Romania, and wanted to see the country occupied by the Red Army so that a Communist government could be more easily installed.[140] But during the summer of 1944, with the more active leadership out of the country, those Communists within Romania joined with the Peasants, Liberals, and Social Democrats in forming the National Democratic Bloc in June. From this time until the coup the Communists within the country cooperated with Maniu and the other party leaders in trying to get Romania to change sides. Yet the Communists only learned of Antonescu's arrest post factum, although afterwards a detachment under Emil Bodnăraş, a leader of the party, was used to guard the overthrown dictator after he was moved from the palace.[141]

A few hours after the coup, the young monarch hastily formed a new coalition government of National Peasants,

---

[140] Ghiţă Ionescu, Communism in Rumania 1944-1962 (London, 1964), 75, 79. See also Valter Roman; Vladimir Zaharescu; Aurel Petri, "Etude sur l'histoire du mouvement de resistance anti fasciste en Roumanie," *La contribution de la Roumanie a la victoire sur le fascisme* (ed. Ion Popescu-Puţuri, Bucarest, 1965), 26.
[141] Lee, *Crown*, 81; Stephen Fischer Galaţi, *The New Rumania: From People's Democracy to Socialist Republic* (Cambridge, Mass., 1967), 22-23; Nagy-Talavera, *Green Shirts*, 337; Hillgruber, *Hitler, König Carol und Marschall Antonescu*, 216, 346. For an opposing view see Constantinescu-Iaşi, "L'insurrection d'aout 1944," 47-48.

Liberals, Socialists, and Communists under General Constantin Sănătescu, the Marshal of the Palace and intimate of the King. [142] At ten that evening Michael announced over the radio the cessation of hostilities against the Allies and the formation of the new government.[143] He also declared that the new government was ready to sign the armistice. Michael's action surprised the Allies and the Germans. Hitler responded quickly, however, and during the next two days German stukas cruelly bombed Bucharest. On 25 August, Romania declared war on Germany.[144] On the same day the Russians issued a statement recalling their earlier communique of 2 April that they had no intention to infringe upon the independence of Romania or change the existing social structure. [145] The next day Molotov let Harriman and Clark Kerr know that his government intended to hold to its earlier armistice terms for Romania.[146]

---

[142] Lee, *Crown*, 75; New York Times, August 24-25, 1944; *The Times*, London, August 24, 1944. The new government was made up chiefly of military officers. Grigore Niculescu-Buzeşti, a confident of Maniu, was made Foreign Secretary, General Aurel Aldea became Minister of Internal Affairs, and the heads of the four parties, Maniu, Constantin Brătianu (Liberal), C. Titel Petrescu (Socialist), and Lucreţiu Pătrăşcanu (Communist) were made ministers without portfolio.

[143] *Foreign Relations 1944*, IV, 191-192.

[144] The Americans gave limited assistance by bombing German airbases in Northern Bucovina.

[145] *Foreign Relations, op. cit.*, 193-194; *The Times*, London, August 26, 1944.

[146] *Foreign Relations 1944*, IV, 196-197.

The change-over of Romania was a major blow to Germany. The Germans were forced to abandon much of the Balkans and pull back their forces to Hungary. By preventing the Germans from retreating over the Danube, the Romanians helped the Soviets trap most of the German Sixth Army.[147]

By the end of August the Russians had spread across much of Romania, entering the oil region of Ploieşti on the 30th and Bucharest on the following day. Part of the credit for liberating Romania should be given to the Romanian Army, which cleared away many regions of German troops before the Red Army arrived. In order to give themselves all the credit, however, the Russians would delay the announcement of the freeing of regions from the Germans until they were occupied by the Red Army, despite the fact that they had already been liberated by the Romanians.[148]

---

[147] Guderian, *Panzer Leader*, 367.

[148] Bucharest Report to Foreign Office, September 8, 1944, F.O. 371/44010; Ioan Scurtu, "La contribution de la Roumanie a la guerre antihitlerienne," *Nouvelles etudes d'histoire* (Academie de la Republique Socialiste de Roumanie, Bucarest, 1970), 351-352. N. Goldberger, "La resistance en Roumanie et les Allies," European Resistance Movements 1939-1945 (New York, 1964), 217-220. Until the early nineteen sixties Soviet historians played down the role of the Romanians in freeing their country and did not even mention the palace coup on the 23rd. Since then the Russians have revised their interpretation and have acknowledged Romania's contribution, but the credit is given to the Romanian Communists. Moreover, from the August coup sixteen Romanian divisions fought on the side of the Allies the fourth largest Allied army. Not only did they help to

Overall, Britain took the lead in trying to get Romania to break with Hitler and join the Allies, and succeeded in getting the Russians to make commitments over her. Although a final understanding still had not been reached between the Romanians and Moscow, the Russians had reaffirmed their intentions of adhering to their earlier armistice terms and promises. But how these would be interpreted and carried out was yet to come.

---

liberate their own territory, but also they helped to drive the Germans out of Hungary and Czechoslovakia. During the final stages of the war Romanian losses against the Germans came to 170,000 men. Only Russia, the United States, and Great Britain lost more. For a detailed account of the Romanian armies fighting on the side of the Allies see Eugen Bantea. Constantin Nicolae; Gheorghe Zaharia,-"*La Roumanie dans la guerre antihitlerienne*, aout 1944 - mai 1945 (Bucarest, 1970).

CHAPTER V

The Establishment of the Groza Government

Shortly after King Michael announced that Romania was changing sides on the night of 23 August, the Allies began making preparations for the completion of the armistice agreement. Although the basic terms had been agreed to, both the Soviets and the British now began to prepare a number of clarifications as well as several additions. On 24 August Clark Kerr was instructed to inform Moscow that the British expected to sign the armistice with the Romanians and to participate in all discussions between the Soviets and the Romanians leading up to its conclusion.[1] As a goodwill gesture, on the following day the British suggested that the armistice agreement be completed and signed in Moscow.[2] Molotov announced Soviet agreement with these proposals on the 26th when he reaffirmed his government's intention to maintain its April terms. In the same statement Molotov unexpectedly reported that he wished to make several additions which were requested by the Romanian Government, one of which implied a reduction in the amount of reparations Romania would have

---

[1] Foreign Office to Moscow, August 24, 1944, F. O. 371/44005.
[2] *Foreign Relations 1944*, IV, 195.

to pay.[3] During the next several days the British and the Russians exchanged armistice drafts which included their proposed changes.

One of the major differences between London and Moscow concerned the amount of influence the Western Powers would have in Romania during the remainder of the war. In spite of the failure of Churchill and Stalin to work out an agreement over Romania and Greece during the previous spring, since 1943 the British had viewed Romania as predominantly a Russian sphere. Although nothing specific had been mentioned in the earlier armistice terms, by the summer of 1944 it was taken for granted by the Western Powers that the supervision of an armistice with Romania would rest chiefly with the Soviets. The functions, if any, that the English and Americans would have in Romania had never been discussed with the Kremlin. Before Romania changed sides the only Russian statement on this question was made in the previous April when Molotov wrote to Churchill that "there could be in Romania... British

---

[3] *Ibid*, 196. The other two alleged concesions were practically meaningless. Basically they were a watered down version of the additional concessions the Soviets had offered to Marshal Antonescu. One granted the Romanians a free zone for their seat of government. But the most important aspect of Russia's earlier concession that no foreign troops would be allowed in this area was not included. The second concerned Romania's right to remain neutral the Germans evacuated peacefully within fifteen days. Since Romania was already at war with Germany, this provision did not apply.

and American representatives on political questions in the same way as we have political representatives in Italy."[4]

The British were determined to have some influence in Romania, and on 28 August Clark Kerr was instructed to propose that "machinery through which the Allied requirements would be transmitted to the Romanian Government" be erected and made part of the armistice accord.[5] The Foreign Office proposed that this body be an inter-Allied Control Commission which would include British representatives. But the Soviets had no intention of relinquishing any control to the West. This was made perfectly clear in the Soviet armistice draft of 31 August. The preamble to the draft simply stated that the terms would be implemented "under the control of the Soviet High Command, hereinafter called 'Allied (Soviet) High Command,' acting on behalf of the Allied Powers." Article sixteen of the same draft further declared:

> A record commission will be established which will undertake the regulation of and control over the execution of present terms under the general direction and instructions of the Allied (Soviet) High Command.[6]

---

[4] Molotov to Churchill, April 10, 1944, F.O. 371/43998. A Red Army general was the Soviet representative on the Allied Control Commission for Italy. In addition the Russians had an official on the Advisory Council for Italy and a special diplomatic representative attached to the Italian Government.
[5] Foreign Office Memorandum, September 2, 1944, F.O. 371/44006.
[6] *Foreign Relations 1944*, IV, 209-212.

Nothing was said about the West having representatives on any commission or with the Romanian Government.

Another issue which upset the British was the inclusion by the Russians of a reparations sum of three hundred million dollars in their armistice draft of 31 August. Not only did the British feel that this amount was probably too high, but also it had been their general policy to leave the determination of specific reparation figures to the peace conference when they could be given thorough consideration. Moreover, in the spring the Soviets had agreed not to ask for a specific reparations figure.[7] At the same time, the English suggested to the Russians that the armistice be more specific in defining war materials and in disposing of enemy and Allied property in order to protect British interests; that Romania be required to repeal discriminating legislation against the Jews; and that she break relations with Japan.[8]

For the most part, the United States supported the British proposals. Both governments kept in close communication over their armistice terms; the British took the lead, however. Since the State Department had been bypassed by the Joint Chiefs in the spring over Romania, its policy had become cautious and restrained. A Romanian delegation under the leadership of Lucretiu Pătrăscanu, a leader of the Romanian Communist Party and member of the Sănătescu Government, and Prince Stirbey arrived in Moscow at the

---

[7] Foreign Office to Moscow, September 7, 1944, F.O. 371/44007; Foreign Office Minute, August 26, 1944, F.O. 371/44005; Hull, *Memoirs*, II, 1461.

[8] Eden to Clark Kerr, September 3, 1944, F.O. 371/44006.

end of August to sign the armistice. The Romanians had hoped to sign the agreement right away, but because of the additional terms and points that needed clarification they were not presented with the armistice until the 10th of September. The British were especially concerned with ironing out their differences with Moscow before the armistice was shown to the Romanians. The worried Romanians could do little but urge the Allies to settle their differences as soon as possible. Meanwhile, negotiations continued in Moscow between Clark Kerr, Harriman, and Molotov. The Russians were especially reluctant to make concessions on Western participation in the execution of the armistice agreement and reparations. By 4 September the Soviets had changed the name of their proposed "record commission" to that of Allied Control Commission for Romania, but pointed out that it would still operate under the Allied (Soviet) High Command. [9] Clark Kerr and Harriman argued that the Soviets were represented on the Allied Control Commission for Italy and had several other representatives in Italy as well, even though the Italian armistice and the instrument for its implementation the Control Commission were chiefly under Western supervision. On 11 September Molotov finally consented to Western representatives sitting on the Control Commission for Romania but for all practical purposes without any power. He informed Clark Kerr that the

> position of the Allied representatives on the Allied
> Control Commission will be determined by the fact
> that the executive functions will belong to the Soviet

---

[9] *Foreign Relations 1944*, IV, 219.

representatives who have efficient executive machinery. The task of the other powers in the Allied Control Commission including the British representatives would be analogous to the position of the Soviet representative on the Allied Control Commission for Italy and would consist in maintaining liaison between their respective governments and the Commission. The British and American representatives will thus be able to obtain all required information about the work of the Commission for their governments.[10]

Moreover, in a conversation with Harriman, Molotov implied that the West could not have any direct political contact with the Romanian Government, but only through the Russians.[11] The English, who were the most adamant in providing for Western participation in Romania, were far from satisfied with Molotov's statements, and Clark Kerr was told to continue pressing for further concessions. The Western Powers were even less successful in getting the Russians to give way on a fixed reparations figure. The tenacious Molotov told Harriman and Clark Kerr that the

amount of reparations the Soviets were asking was extremely modest and that it was necessary in order to satisfy Russian opinion that the armistice terms fix the amount to be paid... for war damages... The Soviet Government considers fixing a definite sum...

---

[10] Clark Kerr to Foreign Office. September 11, 1944, F.O. 371/44008 R14322/294/37.
[11] *Foreign Relations 1944, op. cit.*, 223.

one of the most important provisions of the armistice.[12]

On 4 September Harriman cabled the State Department that "it is clear that the Soviets will not change their position.... I recommend that we concur."[13] Rather than get involved in a major squabble over this question during the next several days both Harriman and Clark Kerr were authorized to agree if the Soviets refused to back down. On 10 September, after Molotov "unequivocally insisted on the inclusion of the fixed amount," the American and British ambassadors gave in.[14] The Russians acquiesced on several of the British proposals for greater clarification in defining and disposing of enemy and Allied property, and agreed that while they did not want to get involved with Japan, they had no objections to Romania severing relations. By the time the Romanians were shown the armistice all of the important differences between the Allies had been settled, with the exception of several Western demands involving the Allied Control Commission.

After finally being presented with the armistice on the night of 10 September, the Romanian delegation met with the Allies twice during the next two evenings to discuss its terms. The Romanians' objections mainly concerned the economic provisions and the extent to which the Allied (Soviet) High Command would control the country. They "protested strongly about the reparations clause," wrote Harriman, "asking that it be made more flexible to meet an

---

[12] Foreign Relations 1944, IV, 219.

[13] Ibid.

[14] Ibid; Feis, *Churchill, Roosevelt, and Stalin*, 415.

eventual inability to pay."[15] The Romanians also sought recognition of Allied or co-belligerency status for the remainder of the war. For the most part, Molotov, who acted as chairman for the Allies, allowed the Romanians to talk at great length, but "did not fairly face or discuss the points they raised and rode over them brusquely whenever he felt that enough time had been spent on a given point."[16] "There was little serious discussion," Harriman pointed out. "Molotov showed no willingness to retract in any way on the reparations question nor to assent to anything which would limit Russian military power in Rumania during the military period."[17] In the end, Molotov gave in on two relatively minor points.[18]

When the Romanians tried to get a specific provision put into the armistice providing for the departure of Russian troops after hostilities with Germany ended, Molotov declined, declaring that this would take place "as soon as the military situation permitted."[19]

The armistice agreement was signed in Moscow at five in the morning on 13 September, although dated the 12th. By

---

[15] *Foreign Relations 1944*, IV, 232.

[16] *Ibid.*, 235.

[17] *Ibid.*, 232.

[18] Molotov agreed that Jewish refugees from Hungary would not be included in the provision which required the Romanian Government to intern Hungarian and German citizens residing in Romania. The second concession related to the addition of language to the effect that the Control Commission would terminate its activities when a peace treaty was concluded.

[19] *Foreign Relations 1944*, IV, 236.

its terms Romania was to assist the Allies by supplying twelve infantry divisions and allow free passage to Soviet troops. She was to pay a reparations sum of three hundred million dollars in goods (oil products, grain, lumber, etc.) over a six year period and restore all property taken from the Allies. [20] War criminals were to be arrested, Fascist organizations disbanded, and the Russians had the right to impose strict censorship. The territorial clauses acknowledged the Soviet annexation of Bessarabia and Northern Bucovina, and annulled the detested Vienna Award which gave Northern Transylvania to Hungary. The armistice was to be supervised by the Allied Control Commission operating under the Allied (Soviet) High Command.[21]

In spite of Molotov's refusal to make concessions, "the Roumanians went away feeling that they had been let off fairly lightly," a British report stated.[22] The State Department was informed that the Romanians felt the "terms were as favorable as they had a right to expect but were greatly

---

[20] In November the Russians demanded that the Romanians deliver the three hundred million dollars worth of goods based on world prices of 1938 instead of 1944. This greatly increased the reparations amount, in some cases doubling the quantity of goods Romania had to deliver.

[21] *A Decade of American Foreign Policy*, Senate Committee on Foreign Relations, 81st Congress, 1st Session (Washington, 1950) 487-491. There were also two protocols attached to the armistice agreement.

[22] Sir A. Clark Shaw to Sargent, September 17, 1944, F.O. 371/44010 R16034/ 294137. See also *New York Times*, September 29, 1944.

concerned about how they would be interpreted and enforced by the Soviet Command."[23] Harriman, however, whose firsthand dealings with the Russians was beginning to cause him to have serious doubts about their intentions, saw little justification for optimism, and predicted that the terms would "give the Soviet Command unlimited control of Rumania's economic life" and "police power for the period of the armistice."[24]

In the meantime, Clark Kerr and Harriman continued to press for further concessions over Western participation in Romania. On 20 September, Vyshinski notified the British and Americans that their representatives on the Control Commission would be allowed only five officials each on their staffs; that their contact with Romanian officials could only be through high ranking Russian members of the Commission; and that they would have to have Soviet permission before making trips into the country. This upset the Foreign Office. "I am sure we ought to react vigorously," declared Orme Sargent.[25] Two days later the British told the Russians that since their representative on the Control Commission was to be denied direct contact with Romanian officials they were going to appoint a separate British political representative with suitable staff who would be independent of the Commission and have complete freedom to communicate with the Romanian Government. The Foreign Office justified this by pointing out that the English representative would be similar to the Soviet diplomatic

---

[23] *Foreign Relations 1944*, IV, 235-236.

[24] *Ibid.*, 236-237.

[25] Foreign Office Minute, September 22, 1944, F.O. 371/44009.

representative in Italy, and that this was in accordance with Molotov's promise to Churchill in April. The British also rejected the Soviet limitation on to size of their staff. At the same time, they informed Moscow that the head of the British section of the Control Commission would be Air Vice Marshal Donald F. Stevenson and that their diplomatic representative would be former Counsellor John LeRougetel, who had considerable experience in Romanian political affairs.[26]

The Foreign Office was prepared to go through with this even without Soviet approval, and on 26 September British officials began arriving in Bucharest. By the end of the month LeRougetel and his staff had arrived. This bulldog stubbornness of the English finally got results. On 1 October LeRougetel was formally instructed to take up his functions as "British Political Representative in Roumania" and "make contact with the Roumanian Government as soon as possible."[27] Shortly afterwards, London received word that Vyschinski accepted their demands.[28]

The State Department supported the British, and although less forceful, presented the Soviets with similar demands. The Americans assumed that the Soviet concessions to the British of 1 October would equally apply to them, but did not want to act until they received "definite

[26] Foreign Office to Moscow, September 22, 1944, F.O. 371/44009; *Foreign Relations 1944*, IV, 239-240.
[27] Foreign Office to Bucharest, October 1, 1944, F.O. 371/44009 R15557/294/37.
[28] Clark Kerr to Foreign Office. October 1, 1944, F.O. 371 /44009 R18670/294/37.

approval" from Moscow. But because of several minor problems involving the United States representatives, as well as Soviet delays in replying to Harriman's notes, the American delegation did not arrive in Bucharest until November. The State Department appointed the Consul General at Istanbul, a Balkan expert, Burton Y. Berry, as their senior political representative. Intelligent and personable Brigadier General Cortlandt Van R. Schuyler, a head of anti-aircraft within the United States, though he knew practically nothing about Romania or Russia, was appointed American military representative on the Control Commission (now that the war was almost over there was a surplus of anti-aircraft officers who needed jobs!).[29]

During this period Romania was in a state of disorganization and uncertainty. The Red Army was received with reserve.[30] As the Red Army moved through

---

[29] Interview with General Cortlandt Van R. Schuyler, March 1, 1975. Burton Y. Berry was born in Fowler, Indiana in 1901. He graduated from Indiana University and entered the foreign service in 1928. He served in Naples, Istanbul, Athens, Teheran, and Cairo. Prior to being appointed to Romania he had served in Istanbul for two years as Consul General. Brigadier General Cortlandt Van R. Schuyler was a career soldier. Graduating from West Point in 1922 he spent more than twenty years in the artillery. He had formerly been commander of the Anti-Aircraft Artillery Training Center at Camp Davis North Carolina.
[30] Bari to Caserta, Italy (Allied Headquarters), September 3, 1944, F.O. 371/44007 R189351294137; Bucharest Report to Foreign Office, September 8, 1944, F.O. 371/44010; OSS Reports 11213, 11282, 11225, from Military Attache, Istanbul, File RG 226, Army Records, National Archives, Washington. The

Romania, London received reports of numerous ugly incidents between civilians and Russian soldiers, especially involving rape, looting, and the wholesale requisitioning of automobiles and horses. Such stories were substantiated by the American OSS detachment under Lieutenant-Commander Frank Wisner which had been flown into Romania at the end of August.[31] Nevertheless, one English observer in Bucharest "thought this was not in most cases worse than that of any other occupying army."[32] Another British report stated that

> everybody is reserved; the bourgeoisie and the middle class are even in a state of panic... Everybody is asking himself what are the real intentions of the Soviets and in what measure the assurances given by the Soviet authorities will be respected.[33]

Communists claimed that the "broad masses of the population" welcomed the Russians "with enthusiasm." Nicolae Ceausescu, Speech delivered at the Jubilee Session of the Grand National Assembly dedicated to the 25th Anniversary of the Homeland's Liberation,form the Fascist Yoke (Bucharest, 1969, 15-16; Ion Popescu-Puturi, L'impotance historique de l'insurrection armee d'aout 1944," *Nouvelles Etudes d'histoire* (Academie de la Republique Socialiste de Roumanie, Bucarest, 1965), 425.

[31] Wisner was responsible for later bringing E. Howard Hunt of Watergate fame into the C.I.A.

[32] SOE Report to Caserta, September 11, 1944, F.O. 371/43987 R14561/230/37; Foreign Office Minute, September 18, 1944, F. 0. 371/43987 R15148/230137.

[33] Bucharest Report to Foreign Office, September 8, 1944, F.O. 371/44010.

By the middle of September, as the bulk of the Red Army pushed north into Transylvania, the number of incidents involving civilians began to diminish. The painful impression the Red Army left on Romanians can be seen by the nickname the people of Bucharest gave to the statue of the unknown Russian soldier the unknown Russian rapist![34] At the same time, Romanian politics was in a state of constant unrest. The political parties began to intrigue against each other and rally support for their side.[35] The National Democratic Bloc formed in the previous June between the National Peasants, Liberals, Social Democrats, and Communist parties was just a temporary union designed to help Romania change sides. It quickly fell apart in September.

Before 1944 the Romanian Communist Party was an insignificant clandestine movement on the fringe of political life. From its inception in 1921 the party remained subservient to the Kremlin.[36] Romanian politicians attacked the party as being anti-Romanian, whose members first loyalty was to Russia; in 1924, the party was outlawed. The Communist main support came from industrial workers, intellectuals, and certain minority groups, especially Jews and Hungarians. While party membership probably never

---

[34] Interview with Nicolae N. Ionnitiu, former Romanian officer and liaison with the OSS in Bucharest, August 3, 1974.

[35] Macmillan to Foreign Office, September 12, 1944, F.O.371/43987 R14561/230/37.

[36] Stephen Fischer-Galați, *Twentieth Century Romania* (New York, 1970), 74; Paul Lendval, Eagles in Cobwebs (Garden City, New York, 1969), 348; Wolf, *Balkans*, 278-280.

exceeded a few thousand, in the elections of 1929 and 1931, under the name of the "Workers' and Peasants' Bloc," they managed to win two percent of the total vote. At the time of the August coup they had barely one thousand members.[37] Furthermore, during the summer of 1944, a power struggle within the party was developing. On the one hand were those Romanian Communists who spent most of the war in Russia. Their two principle figures were Ana Pauker, an intelligent, strong-willed, dedicated Communist (rumor had it that she turned her husband into the Russian secret police for Trotskyite leanings), and Vasile Luca, a Hungarian from Transylvania. They came to be regarded as the "Muscovite" group. The second or "native" group was made up of Communists who spent the war in Romania, often in prison. The better-known names among them were Lucreţiu Pătrăşcanu, a lawyer and intellectual, Gheorghe Gheorghiu-Dej, a former railroad worker, Gheorghe Apostol, Chivu Stoica, and Miron Constantinescu. Although both groups faithfully supported Soviet policies, the Kremlin placed more confidence in the "Muscovite" group, and this wing tended to dominate within the party.[38] Despite such an inauspicious history, in the months succeeding the coup the party surprisingly was able to increase its membership to over one hundred thousand.[39]

---

[37] Fischer-Galaţi, op. cit., 78.

[38] Ionescu, *Communism*, 85, 100, 118; David Floyd, *Rumania: Russia's Dissident Ally* (New York, 1965), 17-20.

[39] Ceausescu, Socialist Society, IV, 361-362. See also Ceauşescu, Anniversary of the Homeland's Liberation, 23; Gheorghe Ţuţui,

The only other two Romanian left wing parties that had any following to speak of were the Social Democrats and the Ploughmen's Front. The Social Democrats commanded a larger following among the working class than the Communists, and during the 1920's and 1930's, their membership rose as high as seventy-five thousand.[40] But in terms of national politics this was insignificant. The problem was that Romania was predominantly a peasant country with a very small industrial working class. [41] The Ploughmen's Front was the only left wing party to have peasant support. Founded in 1933 in Transylvania, it was led by Petru Groza, a wealthy landowner and industrialist, who had been a minister in Marshal Averescu's People's Party cabinet in 1920 and 1926.[42] The Front was a radical

---

"Dezvoltarea Partidului Comunist Român in anii 1944-1948." Anale de Istorie, 6 (1970), 3-5.

[40] Stephen Fischer-Galaţi, "The Party and Political Organization," *Romania* (ed. Stephen Fischer-Galaţi, New York, 1957), 67.

[41] On the eve of World War II, the total number of industrial workers in the Old Kingdom amounted to approximately 800,000. Fischer-Galaţi, *op. cit.*

[42] Petru Groza was born in Transylvania in 1884. His father was an Orthodox priest. In World War I he sewed in the Austro-Hungarian Army. At that time he was a follower of Maniu. In 1919 he joined the People's Party of Marshal Averescu and served in two cabinets, first as Minister for National Minorities and then as Minister of Communications. During the same period he became a rich man. He became involved with the Ploughmen's Front in 1934 as its legal advisor and later became its head. He was especially interested in reforms for the poorer peasants and in improving relations between Romanians and

peasant party made up of peasants dissatisfied with Maniu's party.[43] During the Popular Front years of the Thirties they collaborated with the Communists and strongly denounced Fascism. Yet, before World War II they achieved a widespread following only in Transylvania. One of the party's drawbacks was Groza himself, whose reputation as a lover, tennis player, and master of the sordid joke caused many to view him as not being a serious politician. During the summer of 1944, these two parties worked closely with the Communists. After the armistice both the Social Democrats and the Ploughmen's Front significantly increased their support. Although the left wing parties were still small, British reports in the fall of 1944 saw them as having as much as fifteen percent of the electorate.[44] In October the Social Democrats, Ploughmen's Front, as well as several smaller organizations, joined with the Communist

---

Hungarians in Transylvania. Many saw him, however, as a shallow, flamboyant opportunist. Because of his left wing and pro-Soviet sympathies he was viewed with suspicion by the Antonescu Govern ment. In April, 1944 he was arrested for complicity with the Communists, but was released after serving one month in jail.

[43] In 1944 they advocated extensive agrarian changes such as the confiscation without compensation by the state of all land belonging to those who collaborated with the Germans, as well as all holdings over fifty hectares (one hundred and twenty-three acres) and its subsequent distribution to poorer peasants.

[44] Foreign Office Minute, October 21. 1944, F.O. 371/43988 R17085/230/37; Eden's Memorandum "Roumanian Political Parties," March 5,1945, F.O. 371/48549.

Party in forming the National Democratic Front.[45] In spite of outward appearances, the Communists were the dominant force in the coalition. The leaders of the traditional parties, Iuliu Maniu and the elderly Constantin "Dinu" Bratianu, the third brother of this aristocratic family also closely cooperated.[46] Both feared that the Soviets would interfere in Romanian politics and help the Communists. In order to strengthen their forces for an expected showdown, Maniu and the Communists tried to win over former members of the Iron Guard.[47] More important, Maniu looked to the West for support against the Communists and the Russians, while the Communists counted on the Kremlin aiding them. Even though it was almost impossible to accurately judge the strength of the various parties, British and American reports from Romania unanimously agreed that the National Peasants were the largest. A detailed study of Romanian political parties by the American Legation in Bucharest concluded:

---

[45] The other groups were the Patriots' Union, Socialist Peasant Party, Union of Young Communists, the Union of Romanian Writers, and MADOSZ, the Union of Hungarian Working People. Traian Udrea, "Condiţiile istorice ale formării frontului naţional democratic," *Studii, Revista de istorie,* 17 (1 964), IV, 854.
[46] For a recent in depth study of Maniu and Brătianu by the Romanians see Mihai Fătu, *Sfirsit fara glorie* (Bucuresti, 1972).
[47] LeRougetel to Foreign Office, December 17, 1944, F.O. 371/43989 R21176/230/37; Bari to Caserta, September 11, 1944, F.O. 371/44008 R14435/230/37; Traian Udrea, "L'attitude des principaux partis et organisations politiques a l'egard du developpement democratique de la Roumanie apres le 23 aout 1944," *Revue Roumaine d'Histoire,* 11 (1972), V, 828-829.

Claims regarding the strength of the National Peasants can only be taken from random samplings and the sum total of opinions of observers, since free political elections have not been held in Rumania for ten years. However, all but the most blinded extreme Leftists agree that the National Peasants are the most popular party, and would head the vote in any free election.[48]

In order to avoid further tensions with the Russians, the British tried to have as little contact with Maniu as possible. Long before the August coup the British saw Maniu as trying to gain their backing against the Soviets by turning them against the Russians. In addition, the Peasant leader's delaying tactics before Romania changed sides helped to further lower the Foreign Office's opinion of him. After the armistice the Foreign Office was very cautious in accepting what Maniu and his followers said about the Russians. At the same time, the English closely watched for any Soviet interference in Romanian domestic political affairs. Although the Sănătescu Government was coming under increasing attack from the left, on 7 October, LeRougetel could report from Bucharest that "the Communists here were not supported by any responsible Soviet agency."[49]

By the end of September Churchill had decided to make another bid for a "division of responsibility" in the Balkans with Stalin. With the Red Army pouring through Romania

---

[48] Despatch to State Department, No. 386, June 27, 1945, 871.00/6-2745.
[49] LeRougetel to Foreign Office, October 7, 1944, F.O. 371/44010 R16035/294/37.

and Bulgaria, the Prime Minister was especially determined to save Greece from a Communist takeover. Because Churchill wanted to take the matter up with Stalin personally, at the beginning of October he flew to Moscow. Shortly after alighting in the Russian capital he raised the question with the Soviet leader. Churchill later wrote in his memoirs:

> The moment was apt for business, so said, "Let us settle about our affairs in the Balkans. Your armies are in Rumania and Bulgaria. We have interests, missions, and agents there. Don't let us get a cross-purpose in small ways. So far as Britain and Russia are concerned, how would it do for you to have ninety percent predominance in Rumania, for us to have ninety percent of the say in Greece, and go fifty-fifty about Yugoslavia?" While this was being translated wrote this out on a half sheet of paper.... I pushed this across to Stalin.... There was a slight pause. Then he took his blue pencil and made a large tick upon it, and passed it back to us. It was all settled in no more time than it takes to set down. Of course, we had long and anxiously considered our point, and were only dealing with immediate war-time arrangements. All larger questions were reserved on both sides for what we then hoped would be a peace table when the war was won.[50]

Overall, the so-called "percentage agreement" was the culmination to the policy that Britain had been following since 1943, i.e. Romania was predominantly a Russian

---

[50] Churchill, *Triumph and Tragedy*, 227.

sphere. In order to get a free hand in Greece, Churchill had to reciprocate over Romania. While Churchill hoped that the Russians would adhere to the Romanian armistice and their earlier promises, by this time he felt there was little he could do to stop them if they decided to ignore these conditions. Churchill wanted to be able to act against the Greek Communists without Soviet interference, and for this he was willing to compromise over Romania.

The United States was not a part of this agreement. Because Roosevelt could not go to the Moscow meeting as a result of the upcoming elections, he had Harriman sit in on the discussions, but without the power to make decisions. Several days before the talks Roosevelt cabled Stalin that:

> I choose to consider your forthcoming talks with Mr. Churchill merely as preliminary to a conference of the three of us which can take place... any time after our elections.[51]

The President wanted to make it clear that he would not be bound by any agreement they made. In his instructions to Harriman he told him to bear in mind that there could be "no subject that can anticipate that might be discussed between Stalin and the Prime Minister in which will not be greatly concerned. It is important that I retain complete freedom of action after his conference is over."[52] Two days after Churchill and Stalin concluded their percentage

---

[51] Sherwood, Roosevelt and Hopkins, 834.

[52] *Ibid*. Harriman was not present during the first meeting when the percentage agreement was arranged.

agreement the Prime Minister assured the President that "we shall handle everything so as not to commit you."[53]

During Churchill's visit to Moscow the Sănătescu Government ran into its first serious political crisis. When the government was set up most of the cabinet posts went to army officers, apparently in the expectation that the fighting with the Germans would be more severe than proved to be the case. The traditional parties had considerable influence, much more than the Communists, and with the young King provided much of the direction for the government.[54] In September the parties of the left, especially the Communists, began to strongly criticize the government. They called for agrarian reforms, making a greater contribution to the war effort with a view to recouping Northern Transylvania, workers control in industry, and the purging of war criminals and Fascists from the administration.[55]

The government countered by arguing that all major reforms would have to wait the end of the war. Making the situation much more difficult for the government was the confusion caused by having parts of the country directly under Red Army control, disorganization in the state administrative structure, and the wholesale removal by the

---

[53] Churchill, *Triumph and Tragedy*, 228.

[54] The only Communist member of the government was Lucretiu Pătrăscanu.

[55] Petric; Tutui, *L'instauration regime democratique*, 37; Boris Bălteanu, "Situatia politică a României în preajma instaurării regimului democrat-popular," *Studii, Revista de istorie*, 10, (1957), II, 70.

Russians of supposedly German equipment and hence "war booty."[56]

On 6 October, the Soviet High Command forced the resignation of General Gheorghe Mihail, the Chief of the Romanian General Staff, because of his objections to the Russian order for the disarming of all Romanian military units except the twelve divisions at the front. Three days later General Sergie Vinogradov, the Chief of the Russian Mission and Chairman of the Allied Control Commission, requested that the government arrest forty seven Romanians as war criminals. Included were two cabinet ministers, General Gheorghe Potopeanu, the Minister of the National Economy and General Ion Boiteanu, the Minister of Education. [57] The Soviets justified their action on the slowness with which the government was arresting former officials of the Antonescu regime.[58] The traditional parties saw this as the start of Russian interference in Romanian

---

[56] Seton-Watson, *East European Revolution*, 203. Northern Moldavia and parts of the Banat andTransylvania were under direct Soviet control at this time.

[57] A number of the individuals, including General Potopeanu who had been for short time Military Governor of Transnistria, had served on the Russian front.

[58] One OSS report stated that during the first six weeks after the August coup the government dismissed only eight Romanian officials. The Romanians claimed that the bureaucracy would not be able to function if large scale removals were carried out. It was only under Russian pressure that the government reluctantly began to remove officials who worked with Antonescu. Military Attache to Military Intelligence, M.A. Report No. R-785, February 7, 1945, File No. RG 226.

domestic affairs, and rumors spread that the government would resign.[59]

The political situation became more tense on 13 October when a Peasant Party demonstration in Bucharest ended in a clash with the Communists. In the name of the Allied Control Commission the Russians sent a note to the Romanian Government claiming that the Peasant demonstration "was of a pro-Fascist character directed against... the Soviet Union," and that shouts were heard against the Russians and for the Iron Guard.[60] The Soviets asked the government to punish those who were guilty. The Russians also closed down the large pro-British newspaper Universul and banned a Peasant demonstration scheduled for the 15th. The young Romanian Foreign Minister Grigore Niculescu-Buzeşti, a strong supporter of Maniu but not a member of the Peasant Party, strongly denied to LeRougetel that the demonstration was anti-Soviet, and declared that he, Maniu, and probably the whole government would resign. The "Russian note in effect labelled the National Peasants (and therefore M. Maniu himself) as fascists."[61] Although the British were skeptical about believing what the Romanians told them, later reports from English and American eyewitnesses denied hearing anti-Soviet and pro-Fascist

---

[59] LeRougetel to Foreign Office, October 11, 1944, F.O. 371/43987 R16321/230/37
[60] Circular dispatch, October 16, 1944, F.O. 371/43988 R16571/230/37.
[61] LeRougetel to Foreign Office, October 15, 1944, F.O.371/43988.

cries.[62] During the weeks that followed the demonstration, the recently formed left-wing National Democratic Front clamored for the government's resignation because of its failure to carry out their program, which they steadfastly proclaimed most of the people desired.[63] They threatened to call a general strike unless they were given control of a new government. Despite the percentage agreement the Foreign Office by no means had decided to abandon Romania to the Communists. British policy aimed at maintaining the political status quo. While there was concern over the recent Russian actions in Romania, the Foreign Office was not sure how far Moscow intended to go. The overall feeling was that Russia probably would be satisfied with a friendly government and would not try to install a Communist regime. Moreover, London felt that the Romanians exaggerated Russia's intentions. LeRougetel was instructed that:

> All encouragement should be given to the King and the leaders of the bourgeoisie parties. They should be encouraged to stand on their own feet and not appeal for support from outside against the dangers which they consider menaces them. We on our side will do our best to give them support but we cannot do this if they try to play us off against the Russians.[63]

Air Vice Marshall Donald Stevenson warned Maniu "to do nothing rash... but to let the situation develop, to hold his

---

[62] LeRougetel to Foreign Office, October 18, 1944, F.O. 371/43988 R16780/230/37.
[63] Petric; Ţuţui, *L'instauration regime democratique*, 35-40.

204

horse and ride the race."[64] The Foreign Office advised the Romanians that the best solution would be to form a non-party government. [65] But the Romanians rejected this believing it would antagonize the Soviets. Perhaps the advice of the British had some effect, for Niculescu-Buzesti suggested a compromise solution. He got the government to agree to postpone its resignation while a note was delivered to the Soviet delegation on the Control Commission asking them to reconsider their actions and to investigate the incident further. On 19 October the Russians lifted the ban on the Peasant rally and allowed the Universul to reopen. Two days later the National Democratic Front dropped its threat of calling a general strike.[66] This temporarily ended the crisis. Beginning at this time the removal by the Russians of oil equipment from British and American owned oil companies caused additional friction between the West and Moscow. The Soviets claimed that the equipment was German and therefore could be confiscated and sent to Russia. For the next several months the West repeatedly protested, but to no avail. The English were also disturbed about the failure of the Russians to disarm para-military left-

[64] Foreign Office to Bucharest, October 22,1944, F.O.371/43988 R17085/230/37. See also Arthur Gould Lee, Special Duties (London, 1946), 194-195.

[65] Stevenson to War Office, October 22, 1944, F.O.371/44011 R17085/230/37.

[66] LeRougetel to Foreign Office, October 27, 1944, F.O. 371/43988 R17325/230/37; Foreign Office Minute, October 21,1944, F.O. 371/43988 R17085/230/37.

wing groups, especially the Communist Guard, even though they had ordered other groups to give up their weapons.[67]

The lull in the political fighting hardly lasted a week, and by the end of October, the Communists were again vociferously demanding a new government. Sănătescu, a well-meaning career officer with no prior political experience, was bewildered by the harassment of the left and criticisms of the Russians. On November the shaky government was reshuffled. In the new cabinet ten seats were given to the Peasants and Liberals, and seven to the parties of the National Democratic Front. This was a sizeable gain for the left. Groza became Vice Premier, and Gheorghe Gheorghiu-Dej, Minister of Transportation. The crucial Ministry of the Interior, however, which the Communists had been striving for, went to Nicolae Penescu a member of the Peasant Party. LeRougetel, who was more pessimistic about Soviet intentions in Romania than most British officials, reported to London that Soviet interference in domestic affairs was increasing, and that they had a hand in the formation of the new Sănătescu Government.[68] Making the situation look bleaker for the anti-Communists was the arrival of the dreaded Vyschinski in Bucharest on 8 November "to check up on Romania's execution of the

---

[67] Clark Kerr to Molotov, October 26, 1944, F. O. 371/43988 R18183/230/37, Nicolae Goldberger, "L'instauration et la consolidation du pouvoir populaire en Roumanie," *Nouvelles Etudes d'histoire* (Academie de la Republique Socialiste de Roumanie, Bucarest, 1965), 435.
[68] Foreign Office Minute, November 6,1944, F. O. 371/44012 R14879/230/37, LeRougetel to Foreign Office, November 2, 1944, F. O. 371/44012/230/37.

armistice terms." [69] Vyschinski claimed that the "strained situation" in Romania was chiefly because of "the tendency of certain Romanian political groups to escape from or delay the fulfillment of the armistice terms." [70] Nevertheless, by the middle of November, the Foreign Office was becoming increasingly concerned over Soviet objectives in Romania. But before this matter could be raised with the Russians, Churchill reminded Eden of the percentage agreement. "Considering the way the Russians have so far backed us up over what is happening in Greece," the Prime Minister pointed out,

> we really must not press our hand too far in Roumania. Remember the percentages we wrote out on paper. I think we have had pretty good treatment from Stalin in Greece, much better in fact than we have had from the Americans. It is an awful thing that one cannot have it both ways, but you and I took great responsibility and we cannot overplay our hand in Roumania least of all at a time like this. [71]

The reorganization of the Sănătescu Government had little effect on solving the political crisis. The Communists began removing mayors and prefects by force in a number of areas and placing their own followers in these positions

---

[69] *Foreign Relations 1944*, IV, 257 General Schuyler told me that the Romanians were "frightened to death" of Vyschinski and tried to avoid him whenever possible. Interview with General Schuyler, March 1, 1975.

[70] Churchill to Clark Kerr, November 12, 1944, F.O. 371/43989 R19370/230/37.

[71] Churchill to Eden, November 12, 1944, F.O. 371/44014.

(according to the Communists "appointed by the revolutionary action of the mass of the people").[72] When the new Minister of the Interior tried to stop this, the left unleashed a strong campaign to have him removed. Around the middle of November, the Peasants decided to launch a counteroffensive. Maniu warned LeRougetel that the Russians were giving support to local Communists and that they were sending two more Red Army divisions into the country while reducing the size of Romanian divisions and police force. He also predicted that unless the West helped Romania she "would soon be incorporated into the Soviet Union." [73] Maniu's immediate objective was to force Sănătescu, who he felt was too willing to acquiesce to the activities of the local Communists, to resign and erect a non-party government.[74] LeRougetel, who felt sorry for Maniu,

---

[72] LeRougetel to Foreign Office, November 27, 1944, F. 0. 371/43989 R19567/230/37, OSS Report No. GR-38, November 30, 1944, File No. RG 226; OSS Research and Analysis Branch Report No. 2727, December 6. 1944. See also D. Turcus, "Din lupta condusă de P. C. R. pentru demascarea si scoaterea elementelor fasciste din aparatul de stat institutii si întreprinderi (23 August 1944 - 6 Martie 1945)," *Studii si materiale de istorie contemporană* (Academia Republicii Populare Române, Bucuresti, 1962), 299-331 passim. This had taken place at Constanta, Brasov, Deva, Galati, Timisoara, and in various places in Moldavia. In Constanta, Brasov, and Deva for example, the Communists merely seized power driving the regular officials away. When the Romanian police tried to interfere Russian troops backed the local Communists.
[73] LeRougetel to Foreign Office, *op. cit.*
[74] Berry to Secretary of State, November 28, 1944, 871.00/11-2844; Petric; Tutui *L'instauration regime democratique*, 69.

encouraged him to stand firm against the Communists, as well as agreed with his desire for a non-party government; similar advice was given to King Michael.[75] On 2 December the much harassed government resigned after the Peasants withdrew their support. King Michael, ignoring demands for a government controlled by the left, at first leaned towards a non-party government, but in the end decided to make only several replacements. The major change was the replacement of Sănătescu with another career soldier, General Nicolae Rădescu, who did not belong to any party. Courageous and impulsive, Rădescu had a reputation for speaking bluntly, having been put in a concentration camp for two years by the Germans for protesting against their occupation of Romania. Rădescu also took over the Ministry of the Interior and had his friend, General Ion Niculescu, made War Minister. The National Democratic Front had hoped for the replacement of Penescu with a left-wing candidate and the appointment of General Vasiliu Răscanu as Minister of War.[76] For a while it looked like violence would erupt, and it was only at the last minute that the left backed down and accepted Rădescu. LeRougetel told the

[75] OSS Report No. GR-38, November 30, 1944; LeRougetel to Foreign Office. November 25, 1944, F.O. 371/43989 R19307/230/37; LeRougetel to Foreign Offlce, November 27, 1944, F.O.371/43989 R19567/230/37.
[76] OSS Research and Analysis Branch Report No. 2727, December 6,1944.

Foreign Office that they did this partly out of fear that the King would erect a non-party government.[77]

The new government was viewed by the British as a triumph for the non-Communist forces. Stevenson described it as a "Russian backdown". What was especially pleasing to Whitehall was the acceptance of the new government by the Russians. Vyschinski, who was still in Bucharest, told King Michael that he "was very satisfied with the new Rumanian Government." He also affirmed that the Soviet Government "had no desire to see Rumania a Communistic state," but only wanted "a neighbor which was friendly."[78]

Shortly afterwards Eden wrote to Churchill that he did not share his

> apprehension regarding Roumania's chances of survival as sovereign state, or Soviet intentions to set up a Communist regime... This would be contrary to every statement that the Soviet Government have made in public and in private about their policy, and they must be aware that such a volte-face would endanger the whole of their relations with the Americans and ourselves.[79]

But the American political representative Burton Berry, who had been in Romania for only a few weeks and had taken a back seat to the British, saw the situation differently. He cabled the State Department that English optimism was "unwarranted as all of the basic elements for a clash of

---

[77] LeRougetel to Foreign Office, December 8, 1944,
F.O.371/43989 R28559/230/37.
[78] *Foreign Relations 1944*, IV, 280.
[79] Eden to Churchill, December 8, 1944, F.O. 371/44013.

interests which were present at the beginning of the month are equally present today."[80]

For the next month and a half the political situation in Romania was surprisingly calm. Rădescu has "done his best to co-operate with the Russians in carrying out the terms of the Armistice," a Foreign Office minute stated.[81] At last the country seemed to have a government that satisfied all the political parties. Around the middle of January, however, Ana Pauker and Gheorghiu-Dej went to Moscow. Shortly after they returned London learned that they "have been talking rather wildly to the other Roumanian Communist leaders. In particular they claim to have received Soviet approval for the bringing into power of a Communist Government." [82] The left wing now stepped up their campaign to gain support, while Maniu and other leaders of the traditional parties were denounced as Fascists who opposed the desires of the people.[83] When the Peasants and

---

[80] *Foreign Relations 1944, op. cit.*, 282.

[81] Foreign Office Minute, January 25, 1945, F.O. 371/48547 R1771/28/37.

[82] Foreign Office to Washington, January 29, 1945, F.O. 371/48547 R1771/28/37; The Diary of General Cortlandt Van R. Schuyler (unpublished), 1-10, (in the possession of its author).

[83] The Democratic Front was not as politically united as they hoped their opponents would believe. There was growing friction, especially between the Social Democrats and the Communists. The Social Democrats did not agree with some of the tactics of the Communists, such as the forceful removal of local officials. There was also growing hostility towards Socialist dominated unions by the Communists. But this had not reached the point where the Social Democrats were willing

Liberals attempted to counter their claims, several of their newspapers were closed down, either directly by the Control Commission or through the refusal of the left dominated printers union to allow publication. [84] The Foreign Office was puzzled. "There seems no particular reason why the Soviets should wish to overthrow a Government which is apparently doing all they ask of it," an anxious official remarked.[85]

Up to now one of the chief mysteries for the West was the "extent the Roumanian Communists… enjoyed Russian support."[86] Although there were a number of instances of Soviet interference in Romanian domestic affairs, London and Washington had little evidence to show that they had directly helped the Communists. As far as they could judge, for the most part, the Russians had only given them "some general support."[87] Nevertheless, the Foreign Office was

---

to break away and work with the traditional parties. Berry to Secretary of State, March 15, 1945, 871.00/3-1545. For a different view see Gheorghe Tutui, "Partidul Social-Democrat din România în perioada luptei pentru instaurarea puterii democrat-populare (august 1944 - martie 1945)," *Studii, Revista de istorie*, 27 (1974), III, 343-362.

[84] Berry to Secretary of State, February 8, 1945, 871.00/2-845; Schuyler to Allied Force Headquarters, Caserta, Italy, War Department Message No. M 488, Franklin D. Roosevelt Library.

[85] Foreign Office Minute, January 25, 1945, F.O. 371/48536 R1771/28/37.

[86] Foreign Office Minute, February 11, 1945, F. O. 371/48536 R2961/10/37.

[87] *Ibid*; Schuyler to Allied Headquarters, Caserta, January 15, 1945, War Department Message, No. M. 268.

disturbed with the latest reports from Romania and suggested to Washington that both governments ought to raise this question with the Russians. But before anything further was done, the situation in Romania temporarily died down. This did not last long though, and by 10 February, both Rădescu and King Michael feared that the left was preparing a coup d'etat. [88] Making the situation more ominous was the further reduction of Romanian soldiers and police in the capital and reports that the Russians were sending in N.K.V.D. political troops. From February 4th to the 11th the Big Three held a major conference at the recently war-ravaged Tsarist seaside resort of Yalta, in the Crimea. Although Romania was hardly mentioned at the conference, both Churchill and Roosevelt were worried about Soviet objectives in Eastern Europe and the Balkans.[89] The State Department had drawn up a "Declaration on Liberated Europe" which reaffirmed the principles of the Atlantic Charter, as well as envisioned a European High Commission to help implement these ideas in the occupied and satellite

---

[88] Stevenson to War Office, February 9, 1945, FO. 371/48536 R3059/10/37; Majoribanks to Foreign Office, February 10, 1945, F.O. 371/48548/28/37.

[89] MacGregor Burns, Roosevelt, 564. The Western Powers had planned to raise questions involving the Allied Control Commission and the removal of oil equipment from Romania at the meeting, but because of the lack of time these topics could not be discussed. For detailed accounts of the Yalta Conference see. Feis, *Churchill, Roosevelt, and Stalin*; Woodward, *British Foreign Policy*; Churchill, *Triumph and Tragedy*. For a recent study see, Diane Shaver Clemens, Yalta (New York, 1970).

countries. Roosevelt approved the declaration, but rejected their plans for a European High Commission. The President never went into detail on his reason for rejecting such a commission, other than telling the State Department that he did not want "another commission," and that such matters could be handled by the foreign ministers. [90] Edward Stettinius, Jr., who had recently succeeded Hull as head of the State Department, wrote in his memoirs that he "was greatly disappointed." The British also felt that some kind of enforcement machinery was necessary. [91] The declaration itself was quickly passed by the Big Three with only some minor changes of language. It called for the formation of provisional governments

> broadly representative of all democratic elements in the population and pledged to the earliest possible establishment through free elections of governments responsible to the will of the people.

In order to enforce this, the document stated that

> when, in the opinion of the three governments, conditions... make such actions necessary, they will immediately consult together on the measures necessary to discharge the joint responsibilities set forth in this declaration.[92]

[90] Edward R. Stettinius, Jr.. Roosevelt and the Russians (Garden City, New York, 1949), 88.

[91] Foreign Office Minute, February 16, 1945, F.O.371/48536 R2961/10/37.

[92] Stettinius, Roosevelt, 343-344; McNeill, America, Britain, and Russia, 559.

When the Western Leaders left Yalta they were in an optimistic and cheerful frame of mind. To many it was the "high tide of Allied unity." Unfortunately no sooner had the conference ended than this unity was faced with its first serious confrontation. In Romania the situation continued to deteriorate. The left-wing press, especially the Communist newspaper Scînteia, sharply attacked the Rădescu Government and demanded that it be replaced by one of the National Democratic Front. Rădescu and his supporters were accused of attempting to set up a military dictatorship and provoke a civil war.[93] The Soviet press denounced Rădescu as well. The Russians warned that they could not allow any disorder in Romania which was in the rear of the Red Army and would threaten their lines of communications. I.V. Pavlov, recently appointed Soviet political representative on the Control Commission, complained to Schuyler that unless the Rădescu Government "rid itself of... Fascist elements and show itself willing to meet the desires of the people... the people themselves can be expected to take necessary corrective action."[94] Western representatives began warning their governments that Soviet troops were directly assisting the

---

[93] Petric; Tutui. *L'instauration regime democratique*, 75-78; V.A. Varga, "Din lupta maselor conduse de P. C. R. pentru instaurarea regimului democrat-popular (Ianuarie - 6 Martie 1945)," *Studii si materiale de istorie contemporană* (Academia Republicii Populare Române, Bucuresti, 1962), 355-371.
[94] Schuyler to Allied Headquarters, Caserta, February 16, 1945, War Department Message. No. M. 425.

Communists and in some cases arresting their opponents.[95] The Communist Under Secretary of the Interior, Teohari Georgescu, refused to take orders from Rădescu and even told the Interior Ministry not to pay any attention to the general. Things became more tense on 20 February when fighting broke out between the Communists and the workers at the Malaxa factory in Bucharest; several were killed and wounded on both sides.[96] By this time American and British officials in Romania feared that the Russians were supporting a left wing takeover. "The stage was now fully set up," declared the anxious Schuyler, "for a coup d'etat by the National Democratic Front elements backed by General Vinogradov."[97]

On the evening of 21 February both the British and American representatives on the Control Commission protested to Vinogradov about the threatening situation. Stevenson urged the Russians to lift their ban on a number of Peasant and Liberal party newspapers and to agree to maintain a coalition government until Romania could hold

---

[95] Marjoribanks to Eden, February 28, 1945, F.O. 371/48536 R3652/10/37; Schuyler to Allied Headquarters, Caserta, February 20, 1945, War Department Message, No. M 444.
[96] Berry to Secretary of State, February 22, 1945, 871/0012-2245; Berry to Secretary of State. February 21, 1945, 87/00/2-2145. In the melee Communist labor leader Gheorghe Apostol was seriously wounded.
[97] Schuyler to Allied Headquarters, Message No. M 444; Marjoribanks to Eden,February 23, 1945, F.O. 371/48536 R3652/10/37. LeRougetel was at Bari ill throughout the crisis. James Marjoribanks took over his functions until he returned in March.

free elections. Supported by Stevenson, Schuyler called for "strong Action" by the Allied Control Commission in an effort to avoid a civil war, as well as its issuing of a public statement asserting its responsibility to maintain a coalition government under the terms of the Yalta Declaration on Liberated Europe. Vinogradov "agreed to consider the matter carefully." [98] Even though Schuyler was new to Romania it did not take him long to understand how the Russians operated. That night he wrote in his diary: "I left the meeting convinced that nothing would be done."

As a result of the percentage agreement, the British were in an awkward position. [99] But because this "seemed a particularly flagrant attempt by the Russians to interfere in Roumanian internal affairs," they decided to "take the matter up in Moscow."[100] Kerr was instructed to urge the Soviets to take immediate measures to prevent an armed minority from overthrowing the government by force. In an attempt to keep this within the context of the percentage agreement, Kerr was told to point out that they "fully admit the Soviet Government's predominating interest in Roumania," but that the British Government would be placed in "an impossible position" if the Control Commission, in which Britain was involved, permitted a minority to establish a

---

[98] Schuyler to Allied Headquarters, Caserta, February 22, 1945, War Department Message, No. M 460.
[99] Churchill was the first to make use of the agreement. In December he used British troops to prevent the Communists from seizing control in Greece. For Churchill's own account, see *Triumph and Tragedy*, Chapters 18 and 19.
[100] Eden to Churchill, March 5, 1945, FO. 371/48537.

government which "under no circumstances" could they approve. [101] The State Department notified Harriman to support the British. This angered the Russians, who were bent on having things their own way in Romania. Molotov replied by claiming that their information was "not in accordance with the facts," and that the blame rested with the Radescu Government which was run by Fascists, "encouraging violence," and shooting "peaceful citizens."[102]

On 24 February the crisis in Romania reached a climax. Around five in the afternoon, as a large National Democratic Front demonstration moved towards the Ministry of the Interior, shots rang out from somewhere in the crowd. Romanian soldiers on the roof of the Interior building reacted with several bursts of machine gun fire over the heads of the demonstrators, although some bullets might have been fired into the crowd. Firing was also heard from nearby side streets, but whether from soldiers or demonstrators was never determined. When it was over, several people were killed and a dozen or more wounded.[103]

---

[101] Foreign Office to Clark Kerr, February 23, 1945, F.O. 371/48536 R3653/10/37. See also Eden, *The Reckoning*, 604-605.
[102] Clark Kerr to Foreign Office, February 25, 1945, F.O. 371/48537 R3739/10/37.
[103] It is very difficult to determine what actually happened that day. The Communists placed the entire blame on the Romanian soldiers who they claimed killed five and wounded about eighteen, or as Ceausescu later related "tens of citizens" were killed. Petric; Tutui, *L'instauration regime democratique*, 79. See also Ceausescu, *Socialist Society*, IV, 1957. Western reports stated that there were two separate demonstrations, the first one at five near the Interior building and the second around

That evening General Rădescu, who had been living under the constant threat of a coup for the past several weeks as well as the fear that the opposition was trying to kidnap him, lost his temper and denounced the Communist leaders over the radio.[104] The Russians now sharply criticized him, and Molotov notified the West that the Control Commission would have to act "to bring about order in the country."

---

eight that evening. Although there were eight to ten American officers and enlisted men watching the earlier demonstration Western accounts vary. Who fired the first shot is unknown. Some accounts stated that it came from a slightly drunken Russian officer, while another related that the gun of a sentry accidentally went off. This touched off firing by soldiers on top of the Interior building (according to Schuyler some of the demonstrators were attempting to tear down the fence around the building), but it cannot be said for certain whether they actually hit anyone. General Rădescu later informed the Americans that the autopsies revealed that most of the bullets came from Russian weapons and not German which the Romanian soldiers were still using. The Communists never mentioned a second incident. According to Western reports this involved several hundred National Peasants who were fired on by unidentified assailants while passing by the palace. Two or three of the demonstrators were killed and a dozen wounded. Their version asserted that the Communists falsified the first shooting in the press and prevented the latter from being reported. Schuyler's Diary, 65-69; Stevenson to War Office, March 2, 1945, F.O. 371/48549 R4289/28/37; Foreign Relations 1945, V, 480; Interview with Nicolae N. Ionnitiu, August 3, 1974; Robert Bishop, E. S. Crayfield, *Russia Astride the Balkans* (New York, 1948), 166-167.

[104] Marjoribanks to Foreign Office, February 24, 1945, F.O. 371/48537 R3781/10/37.

On the evening of the 27th the frightful Vyschinski unexpectedly arrived in Bucharest. Without wasting any time he went straight to the palace to see the King, and, in part reading from a prepared statement "insisted" that Rădescu be replaced and a government "truly representative of the democratic forces of the country" be formed.[105] The shaken young ruler replied that for days he had been considering possible solutions to end the crisis, but that as a constitutional monarch he would have to follow specified legal procedures in making any governmental changes. To Michael's statement that a new government would have to conform to the Yalta Declaration, Vyschinski bluntly remarked that there was nothing in the Declaration about Rădescu. On the following afternoon Vyschinski returned to the palace to find out what steps had been taken to remove Rădescu. When King Michael told him that he had begun consulting with party leaders about choosing a successor, Vyschinski shouted that he was not satisfied, and pulling out his watch, gave him until six that evening to announce his firing. The intimidated King had no choice but to consent. As Vyschinski left the room he banged the door so hard that he cracked the plaster in the wall.[106]

The Western Powers continued to protest to the Russians both in Moscow and Bucharest. The British believed that the Communists with Russian support had been preparing to

---

[105] Marjoribanks to Foreign Office, February 28, 1945, F.O. 371/48536 R3989/28/37.
[106] Marjoribanks to Foreign Office, February 28, 1945, F.O. 371/48536 R4045/10/37; *Foreign Relations* 1945, V, 487; Schuyler's Diary, 59-60.

take over the government by force but that partly because of Allied intervention in Moscow on the 23rd, the Russians changed plans resulting in Vyschinski's sudden visit. [107] Vychinski's appearance caused London to shift tactics. The Foreign Office advised Bucharest that

> it seems... improbable that the Russians will now be prepared to acquiesce in the continuance of General Rădescu in office. It should therefore be our policy to try to bring about the formation of a new coagovernment, if necessary under a neutral Prime Minister, representative of all parties in accordance with a fair estimate of their present strength.[108]

Similar instructions were sent to Clark Kerr. It was the United States, however, which now began to take the lead. On the same night that Vyschinski arrived in Bucharest, Harriman was authorized to tell the Soviets that

> Allied responsibilities under the Atlantic Charter, obligations implied in the Rumanian armistice and decisions taken at the Crimean Conference... permit no escape from the responsibility of... ensuring the continuity of a broadly representative governmental regime in Rumania.

Harriman was also informed to point out that a "National Democratic Front or other exclusive party government would be unacceptable," and that all parties

---

[107] Marjoribanks to Foreign Office, February 28, 1945, F.O. 371/48537 R4043/10/37; Stevenson to War Office, March 2,1945, F.O.371/48549 R4289/28/37.
[108] Foreign Office to Bucharest. February 28,1945, F.O.371/48537 R3796/10/37.

and special groups should be disarmed. If the situation became worse he was to request "full consultation among the three principle Allies as contemplated in the Crimea Declaration on Liberated Europe."[109] The next day Berry was instructed to make similar representations to Vyschinski and to try to get him to "take no decisive action" until the situation could be discussed in Moscow.[110]

But Western protests were unable to do much to stop Vyschinski. After his meeting with the King on the afternoon of the 28th, the latter turned to the elderly Prince Stirbey to form a government. But this never got off the ground as the National Democratic Front refused to participate in any government not under their control.[111] On 1 March, shortly after Stirbey informed the King of the hopelessness of his task, Vyschinski sent word that Petru Groza "was the Soviet choice." After consulting with party leaders, King Michael grudgingly gave Groza permission to form a government as long as it was "broadly representative of all democratic elements in all parties."[112] The Soviets choice of Groza, and not a Communist or even an all Communist government, might have been a concession by Moscow [113] Nevertheless the West failed to see any substantial difference. When Vyschinski first made himself

[109] *Foreign Relations 1945*, V, 482-485.
[110] *Ibid.*, 485.
[111] Berry to Secretary of State, March 1, 1945, State Department Telegram, No. 148, 740.00119 CONTROL (Rumania) /3-145.
[112] *Foreign Relations 1945*, V, 493.
[113] Fischer-Galati, New Romania, 28-29. See also *Foreign Relations, op. cit.*, 492.

available to Western representatives on March, to Berry's request that a representative government be maintained he replied that "the important point was not representation upon a quantity but a quality basis."[114] To the protests of the British political representative, however, an angry Vyschinski retorted: "The Soviet Government had not intervened in Greece. In this country the U.S.S.R. expected to be supported rather than thwarted by the British."[115]

The British finally reached the point where they had to either back down over Romania or give full support to the United States who was now calling for full consultation among the Allies in light of the Yalta Declaration. Churchill was very hesitant about protesting further "considering the informal arrangement about Greece and the strict manner in which it was kept by U. J."[116] Prospects of an upcoming confrontation with Stalin over Poland, and the fear that the Russians might invoke the Yalta Declaration over Greece were also on Churchill's mind.[117] Yet as Eden viewed the situation "the alternative... is to part company with the Americans and go back on the Yalta Declaration on the very first occasion on which it should be brought into play."[118]

---

[114] *Ibid.*, 489.

[115] Marjoribanks to Foreign Office, March 1, 1945, F.O. 371/48537 R4062/10/37.

[116] Roosevelt and Churchill among themselves nicknamed Stalin Uncle Joe.

[117] Churchill to Eden, March 4, 1945, F.O. 371/48537; Lord Moran, *Churchill Taken from the Diaries of Lord Moran* (Boston, 1966), 250.

[118] Eden to Churchill. March 5, 1945, F.O. 371/48537; Foreign Office Minute, March 1, 1945, F.O.371/48537 R4061/10/37.

This settled it; London decided to give full support to the United States. In recent years a considerable debate has developed among historians as to whether the United States Government was responsible for honoring the terms of the percentage agreement. Without going into the various arguments as to which side is correct, unpublished British documents show that London took it for granted that the agreement in no way committed the United States. This was in accordance with Roosevelt's view, as already shown, that the agreement was not binding upon Washington. Schuyler was not aware that such as agreement even existed.[119]

Vyschinski's action caused the Americans to step up their protests. Harriman was notified to "point out to Molotov personally the importance which this Government attaches to an immediate exchange of views."[120] But the Soviets rejected this. The Russians argued that "the only consultation required of the Soviet Government" was for their representative on the Control Commission "to keep the Allies informed of the situation in accordance with... the Armistice agreement." Molotov justified Soviet intervention by claiming that it "is absolutely clear that such a situation in the rear of the Soviet Army could not be tolerated and must be eliminated by the forming of a government... which will be able to maintain order."[121] The State Department rejected these arguments and further instructed the American

---

[119] Interview with General Schuyler, March 1, 1975. For an opposing view see, Gar Alperovitz, Atomic Diplomacy: Hiroshima and Potsdam (New York, 1965), 133-138.
[120] *Foreign Relations 1945*, V, 495.
[121] *Ibid.*, 495-497.

Ambassador "to take whatever steps were appropriate to impress upon the Soviets the urgency which the American Government attaches to its proposal for... joint action."[122]

The Western Powers, especially the United States, put little stock in Soviet arguments and claims.[123] Yet Soviet arguments were not without some foundation. The Romanian officer corp was deeply divided, and one general was caught plotting to turn his troops against the Russians.[124] Furthermore, the British had some evidence which indicated that certain Romanian officials had been conspiring with the Germans. There was nothing to show that the Rădescu Government was involved though, and those suspected of being implicated were removed.[125] But these seemed insignificant considering the firm military control the Red Army had. Moreover, as far as Western

---

[122] *Ibid.*, 501.

[123] The State Department told Harriman for "his own information" that they found "it impossible to accept Molotov's argument that the Soviet Government's unilateral intervention in the Rumanian political crisis is justified by the Rumanian Government's 'inability to maintain order,' since the Soviet Government itself is in large measure responsible for the difficult situation in which the Rădescu Government found itself." Foreign Relations, *op. cit.*, 497.

[124] Hillgruber, *Hitler, Konig Carol und Marschall Antonescu*, 229-230; Seton-Watson, *East European Revolution*, 206. Hillgruber's information comes from conversations he had with German officials. The General who was caught was Aurel Avramescu, the commander of the fourth Romanian Army.

[125] Foreign Office Minute, April 2, 1945, F.O. 371/48540.

officials could tell, most of the unrest had been directly provoked by the Communists.

By the beginning of March, Bucharest was an armed camp. Between six and ten thousand Romanian soldiers had been sent home or to the front, while Russian troops and tanks patrolled the streets. For several days Groza tried unsuccessfully to form a new government. He was un- able to gain the support of the Peasants and Liberals, which was not surprising considering that they certainly did not want a government controlled by the left, and besides, he would not offer them any seats. His first proposed cabinet was rejected by the King on 3 March. But when King Michael began to consider taking away Groza's mandate Vyschinski sent word that the Soviet Government would consider this "a hostile act." "From that time," Michael told Berry, "he had to decide whether to get out or stay."[126] Two days later Vyschinski notified the King that unless Groza was accepted he "could not be responsible for the continuance of Rumania as an independent state," while promising him a "great improvement" in relations if he consented.[127] Groza also warned him that he had full Russian backing for a coup d'etat. Finally, on the afternoon of the 6th, the King wearily gave in. He later explained to Berry that

> if he abdicated it would be hailed in some quarters...
> as a magnificent gesture for a principle but the
> Rumanian people would be no better off. If he

[126] *Foreign Relations 1945*, V, 503.
[127] *Ibid.*

stayed and "ate some humble pie" he might be able to do something for his people.[128]

The new Groza Government was controlled by the National Democratic Front, which possessed fourteen of the eighteen seats. The Communists held the important Ministry of the Interior, along with that of Justice, War, and the National Economy. The remaining four seats went to Liberals and Peasants who had previously broken away from the main body of those parties.[129] At the insistence of Vyschinski, Carol's former Premier Gheorghe Tatarescu, once an ardent anti-Communist and now a supporter of the Soviet Union, became Vice-premier and Foreign Minister.[130] A dismayed Foreign Office official described the government as a "stooge" for Moscow.[131]

---

[128] *Ibid.*, 503-504; Schuler's Diary, 54-81 passim. Some of the Konig's close advisors, such as Visoianu and Saver Radulescu, as well as Maniu, urged him to abdicate. Dimitrie Negel, the Marshal of the Court, and Bratianu felt he should stay. Queen Helen wanted a regency.

[129] There were three dissident Peasants in the government, as well as Tatarescu, who represented the dissident Liberals.

[130] In the summer of 1944 the Russians considered bringing former King Carol back to form a puppet government. Tatarescu, who apparently had been involved in discussions with the Russians during the war, might have had a hand in this. It was from the war years that Soviet confidence in him can be dated. Eden's Memorandum, March 5, 1945, FO. 371/46549. See also Alice-Leone Moats, *Lupescu* (New York, 1955), 201-202.

[131] Winant to Secretary of State, March 8, 1945, State Department Telegram, No. 2385, 871.0013-845; Fischer-Galati. *Twentieth Century*, 96. The Romanian Communist version of the

The Russians hoped that the West would accept their fait accompli. The day after Groza became Prime Minister, Molotov wrote to Harriman that he presumed his "questions" had lost their "keenness by this time... inasmuch as the government crisis has been overcome by the formation of the new government."[132] But the crisis was far from over for the United States, especially the State Department. On 8 March, Churchill explained to Roosevelt how his hands were tied, but assured him that he would give him "every support" [133] Roosevelt's hope that representative governments would be maintained by the Soviets in Eastern Europe until free elections could be held suffered a serious blow. And coming so soon after Yalta made it all the more discouraging.[134] He told James Byrnes, then director of the Office of War Mobilization, that "he had grave misgivings about the future."[135] But because the Polish question was reaching a climax and Romania was under the sole control of the Red Army, the disillusioned President

---

February crisis was basically similar to that of the Russians. The Romanians claimed that the establishment of the Groza Government was due to pressure put on the government and King by the majority of the people. Petric; Tutui, *L'instauration regime democratique*, 81-83; I. Scurtu, Pozitia P.C.R. fata de partidele 'istorice' In timpul guvernului Radescu," *Seria Stiinte sociale. Istorie* (Analele Universitatii Bucuresti, 1966), XV, 183-184; Deborin, Second World War, 404.

[132] *Foreign Relations 1945*, V, 502.

[133] *Ibid.*, 506

[134] Sherwood, *Roosevelt and Hopkins*, 869-870; James Forrestal, *The Forrestal Diaries* (ed. Walter Millis, New York, 1951), 35.

[135] James Byrnes, *Speaking Frankly* (New York, 1947), 53.

was hesitant about making Romania "a test case" of East-West relations. For the time being he decided to have Harriman continue to press for tripartite discussions, but not to take the question up with Stalin personally.[136]

The State Department, however, was much more willing to make Romania a test case. On 14 March Harriman practically demanded that high level talks be held in Moscow, to be followed by the erection of a joint Allied committee to apply the policies and procedures agreed upon in the Soviet capital. The Soviets rejected this, claiming that this would emasculate the authority of the Allied Control Commission and that the armistice and Control Commission had the final authority on all questions involving Romania.[137] In response, the Americans argued that the Declaration on Liberated Europe was the supreme document governing Allied policy towards Romania's form of government and that Romanian politics were beyond the authority of the Commission. The Russians ignored this. Both Harriman and the State Department were determined not to back down. The American Ambassador felt that to acquiesce would "be interpreted as weakness on our part," and "would tend to give the impression... we have written off the Declaration as a dead letter."[138] Within Romania the Americans tried to have as little contact with the Groza Government as possible in order to show their disapproval.

---

[136] Byrnes, *Speaking Frankly*, 53; *Foreign Relations 1945*, V, 504510. See also Admiral William D. Leahy, *I Was There*, (New York, 1950), 336.
[137] Foreign Relations. op. cit., 510-511, 516-517.
[138] *Foreign Relations 1945*, V, 521. See also Forrestal, *Diaries*, 40.

On the other hand, by the middle of March the Foreign Office was beginning to have second thoughts about strongly backing the United States. Foreign Office officials took the view that the Russians were going to maintain the Groza Government for the time being regardless of Allied protests and that the West should modify its policy.[139] Moreover, they felt that normal contact should be maintained with the new government.[140] Yet, in the end Churchill and Eden continued to support American policy.[141]

By the end of March Roosevelt was still troubled over Romania. As a result of the State Department's failure to get the Russians to agree to joint talks the President sent a personal letter to Stalin.

> I frankly cannot understand why the recent development in Roumania should be regarded as not falling within the terms of that Agreement [Declaration on Liberated Europe]. I hope you will

---

[139] In order to help win popular support for the Groza Government on 9 March, the Russians agreed to the establishment of Romanian administrative control in Northern Transylvania.

[140] Foreign Office Minute, March 21, 1945, F. O. 371/48539 R5270/10/37; Foreign Office Minute, March 14, 1945, F. O. 371/48538 R4975/10/37; Foreign Office Minute, March 15, 1945, F. O. 371/48550 R4920/28/37.

[141] By the beignning of March both the English and the Americans began to have informal contact with the Groza Government.

find time personally to examine the correspondence between our Governments on this subject.[142]

Less than two weeks later, before anything further was done, Roosevelt died suddenly from a massive brain hemorrhage. The growing split between East and West over Romania would now be up to Harry S. Truman to resolve.

Romania had provided one of the first serious disagreements between the Western Powers and Russia. Once again she was becoming a trouble spot over which relations between the large powers revolved. It was the United States which now began to take the lead, and in the process, abandon her traditional policy of isolationism towards South Eastern Europe.

---

[142] Roosevelt to Stalin, April 1, 1945, *Stalin's Correspondence with Roosevelt and Truman 1941-1945* (ed. Ministry of Foreign Affairs of the U.S.S.R.. Moscow. 1957). 201.

CHAPTER VI

Last Attempt to Establish Democratic Government in Romania

When Harry S. Truman became President he had no intention of reversing the policies and goals of his popular predecessor. During the war Truman fully supported Roosevelt's foreign policy; however, he had little experience in foreign affairs.[1] The cocky Missourian had made a name for himself as chairman of a special Senate committee investigating defense expenditures. He had never been a close friend of Roosevelt's, being added to the Democratic ticket in the election of 1944 solely for his vote getting ability, and after becoming Vice President was not even informed of important diplomatic developments.[2]

The new President desired to maintain Roosevelt's policy of cooperation with the Soviets, as well as strongly believed that it was his job to strictly abide by the agreements that had been made between the powers.[3] Yet, because of his lack

---

[1] Harry S. Truman, *Year of Decision* (Garden City, New York, 1955), 12; Gaddis, Cold War, 198.

[2] Jonathan Daniels, *The Man from Independence* (New York, 1950), 259; Cabell Phillips, *The Truman Presidency* (Baltimore, Maryland, 1966). 52; Smith, *American Diplomacy*, 153.

[3] Truman, *op cit.*, 214; Daniels, *op. cit.*, 270; Herbert Druks, *Harry S. Truman and the Russians* 1945-1953 (New York, 1966), 31-32.

of experience from the start he relied more on the State Department than Roosevelt. In addition, his strong belief that keeping ones word was essential in international affairs furthered his cooperation with them.

By the spring of 1945 many in Washington had become alarmed over Soviet actions in Eastern Europe. Shortly after Roosevelt's death, in a number of private conversations Harriman warned the new President of Soviet ambitions and urged him to take a hard line. Important officials such as General John Deane, the Secretary of the Navy James Forrestal, Bernard Baruch, as well as Roosevelt's close friend and ad- visor Admiral William D. Leahy also began calling for a tough line in order to make the Soviets live up to their commitments.[4] The Acting Secretary of State Joseph C. Grew believed

> that the only language understood by the Kremlin is the language of strength, force and power; ... friendly appeasement in any form is regarded as a clear sign of weakness and an invitation to further demands or encroachments.

Grew had even come to the grim conclusion that a "future war with Soviet Russia is as certain as anything in this world can be certain."[5]

One of the first problems Truman had to face was what to do about Romania. At the end of April Schuyler flew back

---

[4] Gaddis, Cold War, 201-202; Stimson Diary, April 3, 1945, V, 51, Yale University Library, New Haven; Alfred Steinberg, *The Man from Missouri* (New York, 1962), 241.
[5] Joseph C. Grew, *Turbulent Era, A Diplomatic Record of Forty Years 1904-1945* (Boston, 1952), II, 1445-1447.

to Washington in an attempt to get the government to do more about Romania, and through the efforts of Grew, on 2 May was able to see the President personally. The American Representative informed him of the recent developments in that country, while pointing out that both Romania and Bulgaria "were test cases." If "the Soviets were able to get away with their program... they would be encouraged to try the same game in every other country in Europe as far as they could penetrate."[6] Truman was "greatly moved" by Schuyler's description of the way the Russians installed a puppet government, and suggested that we remove our officials. It would be better "to pull out than be kicked around" he remarked. But Grew explained that this would "have a bad effect in Romania and generally lead to a weakening of our case."[7] Upon arriving back in Romania Schuyler told LeRougetel that the President "felt strongly on the Romanian crisis," and, consequently "there would be a stiffening of attitude on America's part towards Russia.[8]

The State Department's attempt in March to change the situation in Romania by calling upon the Soviets to agree to high level talks and the erection of a tripartite commission had accomplished nothing. By the middle of April, however, the dispute over Poland was reaching a crucial stage, so for the time being the State Department held back further protests over Romania.[9] During this period the Department

---

[6] Grew, *Turbulent Era*, II, 1454-1 455; Schuyler's Diary, 149-150.

[7] LeRougetel to Foreign Office, May ' 26, 1945, F. 0. 371146541.

[8] *Ibid*; Woodward. *British Foreign Policy*, III, 589590.

[9] *Foreign Relations 1945*, IV, 202. At the Yalta Conference the Big Three had agreed to reorganize the government of Poland with

mapped out its future goals. Their two chief objectives became the creation of a "truly tripartite Allied Control Commission... in which representatives of the three Allied Nations have approximately equal powers," and the "broadening of the ... Groza Government to include proportionately representative participation by all political parties."[10] With the ending of the war in Europe they hoped that the Russians would be willing to make concessions. At the same time, the State Department became increasingly worried over Soviet economic activities in Romania. At the beginning of May Grew informed the President that by accomplishing their political objectives they would help obtain "equality of economic opportunity" and "safeguards for American interests."

In the previous January Moscow had notified the British and the Americans that they would not remove any more oil equipment from Western firms in Romania, even though

---

the Communist Lublin Poles forming the nucleus of the new government. Stalin also gave Roosevelt the impression that elections would be held within a month. During the spring, however, controversy arose over the interpretation and implementation of this agreement. Truman and Churchill now pressed Stalin to create a more representative Polish government. Another related issue concerned the fixing of the western borders of Poland. An arrangement on the composition of the Polish government was finally worked out, with Stalin getting his way as a result of the Hopkins visit to Moscow in May. The Soviets later got the West to give in on the territorial issue as well.

[10] *Foreign Relations 1945*, IV, 543.

they still contended that such material was legal war booty.[11] The Western Powers were far from satisfied and protested that the Soviets should return the equipment already removed. But their objections had no effect. In February Harriman suggested pressuring the Russians into meeting our demands by threatening to curtail the future delivery of petroleum products under Lend Lease. Washington, however, decided to postpone any action along the lines Harriman suggested for the present.[12] In April the Russians confiscated more English equipment. Making the situation more ominous was the new left-wing government in Romania which had in the past advocated the nationalization of industry. By the end of the spring the British and the Americans had become deeply concerned over the future of Western economic relations with Romania. They feared that the Russians were deliberately trying to wreck the Romanian economy in order to tie the country economically to the Soviet Union, as well as monopolize her foreign trade.[13] Lending substance to this were reports of an agreement signed on 8 May between the Groza government and the Russians providing for extensive economic cooperation. [14] Under its terms joint Soviet-Romanian

---

[11] *Foreign Relations 1945*, V, 647.

[12] *Ibid.*, 649-1350.

[13] *The Conference of Berlin* (2 v., Washington, 1945), Foreign Relations, I, 370, 373, 396.

[14] Roberts, *Rumania*, 320; John Michael Montias, *Economic Development in Communist Rumania*, (Cambridge, Massachusetts, 1967), 19-21; "Economia Romaniei in perioada revolutiei populare," *Istoria economiei nationale a României* (Institutul de Stiințe Economice "V. I. Lenin," Bucuresti, 1964), III 34.

companies (SOVROM) were to be formed for the operation of key Romanian industries and the latter's foreign trade was to be almost exclusively with Russia and countries under her control. [15] At the same time, the Russians constantly increased their demands under the economic provisions of the Armistice agreement causing "ruinous inflation," and disrupting "the entire economy." [16] "Under these conditions," the State Department believed, "it will

----

[15] During the next several years joint Soviet-Romanian companies were formed for 15 all major branches of production. For example, in July and August 1945 joint companies for the control of Romanian oil (Sovrompetrol), timber (Sovromlemn), and transportation (Sovromtransport) were erected. Although these companies were to be set up and run on an equal basis, Romania contributed most of the assets while management was in the hands of the Russians. In this way the Soviets were able to further control and exploit the Romanian economy. The Russians also subtracted from Romania's share of the profits what she owed in armistice payments. Ionescu, *Communism*, 112-113.

[16] *The Conference of Berlin*, I, 370, 373. These Soviet demands were in addition to the specific reparation figure in the Armistice which covered compensation for damages done by the Romanian Army in Russia. They came under articles ten and twelve. The first provided for the upkeep of the Red Army while on Romanian soil, and the latter obliged Romania to return all goods and materials taken from the Soviet Union. Under these two articles Romania's reparations payment more than doubled. Mr. Willard Thorp. American economic representative at the Paris Peace Conference in 1946, estimated that the total cost of reparations to Romania by September 1946 amounted to over one billion dollars. Emile Ciurea, Le Traité de Paix avec la Roumanie (Paris, 1954), 126-127.

probably be impossible for American interests to engage in trade with Romania or carry on business in that country."[17]

On 27 May Stalin notified Truman that "the Soviet Government considers it right and timely to reestablish right now diplomatic relations" with Finland, Bulgaria, and Romania.[18] Harriman agreed with Stalin. He felt that the West would

> find it difficult to get the Russians to agree to any real tripartite basis for action in the Control Commissions for the coming period and that we can therefore be no worse and possibly better off by handling as many questions as possible directly with the governments concerned.[19]

The British went along with Harriman, and also proposed that peace treaties should be concluded with these countries as soon as possible. But Truman and the State Department disagreed. On 2 June the President cabled Stalin that he was ready to exchange representatives with Finland, but not with Bulgaria and Romania. "I have been disturbed," he noted, "to find governments which do not accord to all democratic elements of the people and rights of free expression, and which in their system of administration are, in my opinion, neither representative of or responsive to the will of the people."[20] Stalin answered with the argument that the United States had already resumed relations with Italy where the possibilities for the growth of democracy were no

---

[17] *Conference of Berlin*, I, 373.
[18] *Foreign Relations* 1945, V, 547-548.
[19] *Ibid.*, 548.
[20] *Ibid.*, 550.

greater than in Romania and Bulgaria.[21] Truman refused to back down, but got the Red dictator to agree to discuss the problem at their upcoming conference at Potsdam.

In the meantime, the State Department began mapping out their strategy for the Potsdam Conference. [22] They decided to try to force the Russians to make political and economic concessions by refusing to resume diplomatic relations with Romania and Bulgaria. As a further lever they hoped to use public opinion, as well as the threat of curtailing economic aid, especially post war credits. The successful completion of the atomic bomb project was by no means overlooked either. [23] The State Department also believed that to sign peace treaties with the present unrepresentative governments in those countries would only serve to strengthen their position and prestige. The British, however, saw things differently. "Our proposal," the Foreign Office explained,

> is... based upon the assumption that there is no
> immediate chance of persuading the Russians to

---

[21] *Ibid.*, 554-555.

[22] For a thorough examination of the Potsdam Conference see, Feis, *Between War and Peace* (Princeton, New Jersey, 1960). Other works that should be consulted are Woodward, *British Foreign Policy* and Churchill, *Triumph and Tragedy*. For a very critical study of Truman see, Gar Alperovitz, *Atomic Diplomacy: Hiroshima and Potsdam* (New York, 1965).

[23] American officials hoped that their possession of the bomb would make the Soviets more manageable, and that they might be able to secure political concessions from them in return for turning the bomb over to an international agency. See Gaddis, *Cold War*, 244-246.

agree to the formation of more representative Governments. If this is so we must accept the lesser evil of giving some temporary encouragement to the Government now in power in order to secure the withdrawal of the Red Army and thus create conditions in which there is at least some hope of the emergence of democratic government.[24]

But their arguments failed to convince Washington. The State Department doubted that the Russians would allow themselves to be maneuvered out of position in those countries just because they agreed to remove all or most of their troops; and they concluded that the only way was to force the Russians to make concessions now while it might not be too late. At the beginning of July Winant reaffirmed Washington's views, adding that "we intend to press strongly" for our proposals at Potsdam.[25] In the end the English acquiesced, reluctantly notifying the Americans that they would "come along behind" even though they saw little hope for success.[26]

A week before the conference opened American hopes for a greater role in the Control Commission were strengthened when the Soviets announced their plan to revise the procedures for that body in Hungary. The most important proposal promised that directives from the. Commission would be issued only "after... agreement... has

---

[24] Foreign Office to Bucharest, June 15, 1945, F.O. 371/48554 R10240/28/37; *Conference of Berlin*, I, 360.
[25] *Conference of Berlin*, I, 400.
[26] *Ibid.*, 41 7, 320; Woodward, *British Foreign Policy*, 1, 587-595 passim.

been reached" with the Western representatives. The other revisions provided that regular meetings would be held at least once every ten days, that Western representatives would be able to participate in staff conferences and commissions, and that they would be allowed to travel freely throughout the country.[27] A few days later Schuyler was told of similar provisions for the Control Commission in Romania, but instead of providing for "agreement" among the representatives on the Commission before directives were issued, the Soviets only stated that there would be "previous discussion." Overall the State Department was very pleased with these proposals. Grew wrote to the Department's Acting Representative in Bucharest Roy Melbourne that they constitute a "definite improvement," and hoped that they could get the Soviets to extend the provisions requiring "agreement" among the three representatives to Romania.[28] The crucial point, however, was whether the Soviets would execute them in good faith. As Melbourne skeptically pointed out:

> Both General Schuyler and I agree, after an examination of the points, that virtually every difficulty encountered by the American representation upon the ACC since its beginning to date could have occurred during that time with the... points in force, if, as has been the case until now,

---

[27] *Foreign Relations* 1945, IV, 834-835; Herbert Feis, *Between War and Peace*, 190-191.

[28] *Conference of Berlin*, 11, 726-720. Berry went back to Washington for consultation on 18 June and did not return to Bucharest until the end of August.

goodwill on the part of the Soviet Executive of the ACC was lacking.[29]

In order to prevent the Russians form interpreting the execution of the Armistice as they pleased, the State Department began drawing up additional proposals which would help clarify and enlarge those of the soviets.[30]

On 17 July the last of the major conferences of the war began in the palace of the Hohenzollern dynasty in Potsdam. Romania was one of the important topics. At the opening of the conference the Americans presented a proposal stating that the Yalta Declaration had not been carried out in Romania and Bulgaria and called for the reorganization of their governments. After this was accomplished "diplomatic recognition" would "be accorded and peace treaties concluded." The proposal also suggested that the three Allies should assist the "interim governments in the holding of free and unfettered elections."[31] But from the start the Russians strongly objected. Stalin was hoping to get the West to recognize these governments now, and accept his fait accompli once and for all. He tried to accomplish this by bargaining over their desires to modify the Italian Armistice, as well as their efforts to pave the way for a peace treaty

---

[29] *Conference of Berlin*, op. cit., 690.

[30] *Ibid.*, 703-707; Feis, War and Peace, 191. One of the key provisions of the American draft was that agreement among the Allied representatives would have to be reached not only on the orders which the Commissions would be able to give, but also on the questions that they would discuss at their meetings, Conference of Berlin, op. cit., 706; *Foreign Relations 1945*, IV, 843-844.

[31] Byrnes, *Speaking Frankly*, 73; Druks, *Truman and the Russians*,51

with Italy and her entry into the United Nations. He repeatedly stated that Italy should not be granted more favors than countries under Soviet occupation. Truman stubbornly argued that his only objection was that these governments were not democratic, and that he would "not recognize them... until they are reorganized."[32] To this the Russians insisted that the governments of Romania and Bulgaria were just as democratic and "closer to the people" than Italy. In a heated debate on the 24th of July Churchill said that freedom had reemerged in Italy, but that the British mission in Bucharest "had been penned with closeness approaching internment." "An iron fence, he charged, had come down around them." "All fairy tales," Stalin shot back. [33] Whereas neither side would back down, in the end an attempt to hide their differences from the world was made by the publication of a somewhat ambiguous protocol which assigned the Allied Foreign Ministers the task of preparing peace treaties "with recognized Governments" in Romania, Bulgaria, Italy, etc. [34] The protocol further called for the Allies to "examine... in the near future... the establishment of diplomatic relations" with these states.[35]

Other Allied efforts to get the Russians to make concessions fared little better. American hopes to get the Soviets to agree to provisions which would insure that the

---

[32] Conference of Berlin, 11, 371.

[33] Truman, Year of Decisions, 384-385.

[34] Conference of Berlin, op. cit., 1492; Druks, Truman and the Russians, 64.

[35] Conference of Berlin, op. cit., 1492; Deborin, Second World War, 478.

Control Commissions become truly tripartite ended in failure; the Soviets would not budge further from the concessions they had made on the eve of the conference. The published protocol merely announced that the "revision of procedures... will... now be undertaken... accepting as a basis... the Soviet Government's proposals for Hungary."[36] Western efforts to get the Soviets to agree to Allied observation of elections in Romania and Bulgaria, as well as Greece and Italy also failed. The Soviets contended that this would be offensive and unnecessary and that there was no reason to fear that elections would not be free.[37] The Russians, however, promised to ease their restrictions on the entry of Western newspapermen into Romania and Bulgaria. On the question of recovering confiscated oil equipment all that the Russians would consent to was the erection of two commissions, one Anglo-Soviet and one American-Soviet, to look into the matter. Attempts to influence Soviet economic policies in Romania by threatening to restrict American aid had no effect either. With the exception of the possibility of more influence on the Control Commission, and the Soviet's promise to allow the entry of the Western press, concerning Romania the Americans and the British left Potsdam empty handed. On his way home the frustrated American President startled his companions by calling Stalin "an S.O.B." "Force is the only thing the Russians understand," he later wrote in his memoirs.[38]

---

[36] Conference of Berlin, op. cit, 1494.

[37] *Ibid.*, 228, 152.

[38] Truman, *Year of Decisions*, 41 2. See also Steinberg, Man from Missouri, 259, 276. Phillips, *Truman Presidency*, 100.

Meanwhile, the political situation in Romania remained tense. Relations between the Groza Government and the King were bad, as the government tried to pressure him into signing bills which could be used to eliminate their political rivals. Michael told the jovial Berry, who had become very friendly with the pro-Western boy monarch that the Communists were trying to force him to perform unconstitutional acts in order to build up evidence which they could later use in ruining his reputation.[39] The Office of Strategic Services reported that even though the National Democratic Front was in power, the King still leaned on the traditional party leaders for advice.[40] During the spring and summer the Communists continued to build up their strength by filling the administration with their own supporters, either legally or by force, while giving special emphasis to police and judicial posts.[41] On the other hand,

---

[39] *Foreign Relations* 1945, V, 537-538.

[40] OSS Report No. GR-464, April 15, 1945, File No. RG 226.

[41] In May Schuyler sent a memorandum to President Truman summarizing some of the recent political developments in Romania. "During the past month the Rumanian Communist party has been employing every available means to insure a continuation of its newly-acquired dominant position in Rumanian politics. Measures taken include appointment of communist prefects in all Judetes (counties), appointment of communists to important judicial posts, promulgation of laws authorizing the death sentence for political prisoners and for those convicted of membership in a "pro-fascist" organization and the formation of a "voluntary civilian" police force which is making mass arrests of persons with allegedly "fascist" connections." *Foreign Relations 1945*, V. 541.

the new government apparently accepted without question Russia's extensive economic demands. These in addition to the damage done to the economy by the war and the economic disorganization brought about by the government's agrarian reform hurt the economy severely. In the summer Western officials feared Romania was on the brink of a depression.

With the country under the occupation of a million Red Army troops, King Michael felt his only chance of changing the political situation rested upon help from the West. Since the coming to power of the leftists, the King and the leaders of the traditional parties had been urging the West, especially the United States, to implement the principles of the Atlantic Charter and the Yalta Declaration.[42] The State Department assured them that they were doing their best to accomplish this, but as Berry put it, "the encouragement that comes from words expressed in Bucharest at a time when action is desired in Moscow forms but a fragile bulwark for resisting the pressure of powerful groups."[43] As a result of the failure of the United States to alter the situation, in March some Romanians, including Maniu, began speculating about taking some kind of direct action. In April and May they tried to contact Western representatives in Romania about the possibility of having Michael ask for Groza's resignation, or even the carrying out of a coup like

---

[42] *Ibid.*, 541 -542.
[43] *Foreign Relations 1945*, V, 539.

the one of the previous August.[44] Both LeRougetel and Berry strongly warned the Romanians against any such action, and refused to discuss these matters further for fear that the ever suspicious Russians would think that they were involved. One Foreign Office minute stated: "We must keep absolutely clear of this sort of thing.... Maniu is beyond hope and the King is running a risk by having any contact with him."[45] Berry warned Washington that this sort of action would be "inviting disaster."[46] The State Department was especially fearful that this would lead to bloodshed and the forceful elimination of the opposition.

In June Maniu hinted to Schuyler that he was ready to persuade the King to dismiss Groza if he could receive Anglo-American support. But Schuyler refused to get involved and pointed out that any local action might have "serious consequences for Rumania." Disappointed, Maniu let him know that "without definite assurances of Anglo American support" he would not act.[47] At the same time, the indefatigable Maniu secretly began talking to C. Titel Petrescu, the head of the Socialist Party, about the possibility of the latter breaking with the government. [48] While the

---

[44] LeRougetel to Foreign Office, April 23, 1945. F.O. 371/48541; Foreign Relations. *op. cit.*, 539-540; Schuyler's Diary, 120, 157-158, 165, 168, 170-171.

[45] Foreign Office Minute, May 25, 1945, F.O. 371/48554 R9002/28/37.

[46] Foreign Relations, *op. cit.*, 539.

[47] *Ibid.*, 554; Schuyler's Diary, 181.

[48] Berry to Secretary of State. June 14, 1945, State Department Telegram, No.430, 871.0016-1445. Other leading officials in the Socialist Party were Ilie Dumitriu, Ilie Mirescu, A. Dumitriu,

Allies were meeting at Potsdam the Peasant and Liberal parties initiated a limited campaign of open opposition to the government to make it clear to the Allies that all was not well in Romania and that there was an active opposition. Their stated objectives were to replace the present government with one more representative and to hold free elections.[49] It was not until after the Potsdam Conference ended, however, that the United States began to get involved in any of this.

The opponents of the Groza Government realized that time was running out for them, and that they would have to act soon if they were to have any chance to change the

---

Lotar Rădăceanu, and Ștefan Voitec. As the split between the Socialists and Communists grew, Rădăceanu and Voitec became the leaders of the collaborationist wing of the party.
[49] Melbourne to Secretary of State, July 26, 1945, State Department Dispatch, No. 430, 871.0017-2645. This campaign consisted of Maniu and Brătianu addressing student rallies, communications being sent by students to Stalin, Churchill, and Truman, and several demonstrations in Bucharest. On 18 July National Peasant students held a street rally in which they condemned Groza. But two days later when the National Liberal Youth Organization tried to hold a similar demonstration the police broke it up resulting in arrests and injuries. On 22 July a combined force of Romanian police and Soviet N.K.V.D. troops broke up a meeting of the National Liberal Youth. Over forty people were arrested. A Peasant Party luncheon was also disrupted by the police, and more arrests were made. Details and the speeches by Maniu and Bratianu are to be found in Melbourne to Secretary of State, July 26, 1945, State Department Despatch, NO. 430, 871.0017-2645.

situation. The Communists continued to entrench themselves in the administration and had already begun to arrest their political rivals. Members of the opposition parties, especially their leaders, were simply branded as Fascists and enemies of the people and hauled off to concentration camps. At the beginning of August Melbourne reported to the State Department that the opposition "considers this month to be its last great opportunity... Unless significant governmental changes are made shortly by Allied agreement... all hope... will be irretrievably lost."[50]

On 2 August as the Potsdam Conference ended the Allies announced that they would sign peace treaties only "with recognized democratic governments" in several ex-enemy states including Romania. For the desperate Romanian opposition this provided them with the hope that they would be able to replace the Groza Government, as well as the encouragement that the West might be planning to alter its policy. They now began to strongly urge the Western representatives, especially the Americans, to give them active support. Their overall plan was to get the King to dismiss the present cabinet as not being a "recognized democratic government" according to the Potsdam Declaration. The crucial problem, however, was whether the Americans and the British would back them. Without such support the opposition, and especially the King, would not act. One week after the conference ended Melbourne notified Washington:

> All opposition leaders are awaiting as a vital and urgent factor for Rumania's independence an official

---

[50] *Foreign Relations 1945*, V, 563-564.

Allied interpretation that the Groza Government under the Potsdam Declaration is not considered a "recognized democratic government." From available evidence the King would request the resignation of the... cabinet if he were certain this was the case.[51]

Since the spring the United States had stayed clear of this type of direct action; but with the failure at Potsdam the State Department decided to give the Romanians the encouragement they were longing for. On 11 August the State Department instructed Melbourne that he should let the opposition leaders know

> that it is not our purpose to discourage them in their attempts to secure freedom of expression for all democratic groups or to present their case to the Rumanian people and to world opinion for a more representative Government. Without replying directly to questions which may be put to you concerning your Government's attitude toward a particular plan of action you may let it be known in general terms that this Government hopes to see established in Rumania, through the efforts of the Rumanians themselves, and if necessary with the assistance of the three Allied Governments as provided in the Crimea Declaration... a more representative regime, and that the U. S. Govt. looks forward to the establishment of diplomatic relations

[51] Melbourne to Secretary of State, August 9, 1945, State Department Telegram, No. 539. 671.00/8-945.

with a Rumanian Government in which all important democratic parties are represented.[52]

Melbourne was also told to refer to the President's speech of 9 August in which he reaffirmed his determination to carry out the Yalta Declaration and not to allow Romania to be the sphere of influence of any one power.[53]

The Groza Government, meanwhile, had been claiming that under the Potsdam Declaration they constituted a recognizable democratic regime. The announcement by the Kremlin on 6 August of the resumption of diplomatic relations strengthened their contention. Melbourne, however, in a personal interview with the King on 14 August made it perfectly clear that this was not the view of the United States Government. He also informed Michael that

> my government hoped, through purely Rumanian efforts, to see a more representative regime established here with which it could resume diplomatic relations. With the timing and method of any possible efforts completely in Rumanian hands, it was hoped that any eventual changes would include all important democratic parties.

Melbourne reported back to the State Department that Michael

> expressed gratification at the American position and stated his personal intention to follow constitutional lines.... He further asked me to present the American

---

[52] *Foreign Relation* 1945, V, 565-566.
[53] Holborn, War and Peace Aims, 11, 353-354; Foreign Relations, op. cit., 566.

views to the responsible opposition leaders, that they might request audiences of him to discuss eventual... tactics. This request thus coincides with the fact that these leaders have been in virtual daily contact with this mission for further clarification of the Potsdam Declaration and the President's speech.[54]

The Foreign Office was startled by this sudden reversal of policy. "The Americans are intervening vigorously in Romanian internal affairs," wrote one official. "In fact they have begun a full-scale plot against one of the Russians favorite puppets."[55]

During the next several days the leaders of the traditional parties and the King quietly discussed possible plans to remove the government. Melbourne was kept closely informed about what went on (Berry's visit to Washington had been prolonged so he would be out of Romania during this time, and, hence lesson the involvement of the United States in the eyes of the Russians). [56] One problem involved the attitude of the Socialist leader Titel Petrescu. A nineteenth century middle-of-the-road Socialist, Petrescu's hopes for a lasting partnership with the Communists had been as unrealistic as the Victorian elegance he surrounded himself with. He was now closely working with Maniu and the opposition and

---

[54] *Ibid.*, 566-567.

[55] Foreign Office Minute, August 16, 1945, F. 0. 371148557.

[56] Melbourne to Secretary of State, August 18, 1945, State Department Telegram, No. 559, 871.0018-1845; Melbourne to Secretary of State, August 17, 1945, Telegram No. 558, 871.0018-1 745; Interview with General Schuyler, March 1, 1975.

strongly supported a change of government. The opposition would have preferred the Socialists to resign from the cabinet thereby forcing the king to step in, but Petrescu had not reached the point where he was ready to openly break with the National Democratic Front. Another question was whether Groza would resign when requested by the King. It seemed doubtful that he would unless told to do so by the Russians.[57] At the same time, Schuyler received a copy of the latest American proposals for the Control Commission, which basically amounted to an enlarged version of the one that the Soviets had already rejected at Potsdam. Apparently Washington had been planning to present these proposals to the Russians to coincide with the dismissal of the Groza Government.

On the night of 18 August the King's personal secretary and friend since childhood, Mircea Ionniţiu, informed Melbourne of the plan Michael intended to use. In order to minimize the possibility of bloodshed the King would strictly follow constitutional procedures. The next morning he would call a meeting with Groza where he would tell him that he was considering the replacement of the government because of the refusal of the Western Powers to recognize it. Following this he would hold inter- views with the leaders of the Peasant, Liberal, Socialist, and Communist parties, and after receiving the formal approval of all but the Communists for a governmental change, he would ask for

---

[57] Melbourne to Secretary of State, August 15, 1945, State Department Telegram No. 554, 871.0018-1545; Melbourne to Secretary of State, August 19, 1945, State Department Telegram No. 563, 871.0018-1945.

the cabinet's resignation. Because it was expected that Groza would refuse he would then publicly proclaim that the government was illegal and call upon the Court of Cassation and the army to take the necessary steps to remove it. If additional assistance was needed he would request help from the Allies to assist him in forming a representative government under the Yalta Declaration.[58] On the following morning the King met with Groza as planned. Surprisingly, from all indications neither the government nor the Russians had wind of what was going on. Nevertheless, Groza did not appear shaken by the King's statement, and confidently claimed that

> his government actually was never stronger and had entire Soviet support. He added that the question of American recognition of his government was of little significance and that the Soviet Union would eventually secure Anglo-American agreement to a peace treaty.[59]

He also tried to convince the King that he had been misinformed about the views of the Americans towards his government.

Groza's "unshaken confidence" began to cause King Michael and his advisers to have second thoughts about going through with their plan. Moreover, the King had just received word from the British that they "did not wish to

---

[58] Melbourne to Secretary of State, August 18, 1945, State Department Telegram No. 561 871.0018-1 845; *Foreign Relations 1945*, V, 579-580.
[59] Melbourne to Secretary of State, August 19, 1945, State Department Telegram No. 563.

give any advice or encouragement... since they would be unable to protect the King and opposition leaders from the consequences. [60] Since the United States had become involved in the plan to replace Groza, Melbourne had been keeping LeRougetel informed of his instructions, but the State Department made no attempt to coordinate their actions with the British and simply went ahead on their own. At the same time, London warned LeRougetel not to get involved. The English saw little hope for success and feared that the whole thing could easily lead to violence. The Americans "seem... to have gone dangerously far on this occasion," commented one Foreign Office official.[61]

But the Americans were not about to back down at this late date. On the afternoon of the 19th, Michael's secretary told Melbourne about that morning's developments. Realizing that the Romanians were beginning to have some doubts, Melbourne reaffirmed his "instructions in detail." He further stated that "the president's speech of August 9... clearly indicated our intentions to attain a position of equality with the Russians," and "added for the King's information only that General Schuyler had been instructed to negotiate on a truly equal tripartite basis for revised ACC."[62] Later in the afternoon Melbourne assured Dr. Savel Radulescu, one of Michael's advisors, that regardless of the British, America's attitude had not changed and that he did

---

[60] *Ibid.*

[61] Foreign Office Minute, August 16. 1945, F.O. 371/48557 R13745/28/37.

[62] Meloourne to Secretary of State, August 19, 1945, State Department Telegram, No. 563.

not see any reason for harm coming to the King.[63] The royal emissary informed Melbourne that Michael was ready to go through with the plan. In light of the British attitude, however, the King decided not to publicly announce that the government was illegal and call upon the military to remove it, but to appeal directly to the Allies to assist him in forming a new government.[64]

It was almost one year before that the beleaguered monarch had found himself in an equally difficult situation; that time he gambled and won. He was hoping his luck had not run out. The next day, after getting the approval of Maniu, Bratianu, and Titel Petrescu, Michael formally asked for Groza's resignation. As expected he refused, and Michael sent notes to the Allies asking for their assistance.[65]

Caught off guard, the Russians were surprised and angry with Michael's action. Their immediate response was to try to get the King to withdraw his request for Groza's resignation and cancel his appeal to the Allies.[66] General Susaikov, who had replaced Vinogradov during the February - crisis according to Schuyler, Susaikov was humorless, unsympathetic, - and as "tough as nails" belittled the importance of reaching agreement with the Western Powers and urged him to consider the "consequences carefully." On the day after Michael asked for the

---

[63] *Ibid.*

[64] *Ibid*; *Foreign Relations 1945*, V, 579-580.

[65] *Foreign Relations 1945*, V, 574-575; Petric: Țuțui, *L'instauration régime démocratique*, 100-101 Lee, *Crown*, 122-1 23.

[66] *Foreign Relations, op. cit.*, 578, 601.

government's resignation Susaikov urged him to make a public declaration stating:

> That external pressure upon the King and external interference on... the Rumanian Government would find an unfavorable echo in Rumanian public opinion; that Rumanian general elections would take place soon and the people will express their free will for the government of their choice; and that the King had no criticism against the Groza regime.[67]

But the King stood firm, reiterating his appeal for the Allies to help him form a new government. The Soviets and the Romanian Communists now stepped up their threats. Michael's secretary told Melbourne that "every conceivable pressure... has been centered upon the King and his mother with scarcely veiled threats as to their impending fates and those of their advisers." It was even rumored that King Carol might be restored.[68]

In response to Michael's request for assistance, on 23 August the Americans notified Moscow and London that they were ready "to consult... on the measures necessary to discharge the responsibilities set forth in the Yalta

---

[67] *Ibid.*, 585.

[68] *Ibid*. The Americans and British learned that King Carol, Magda Lupescu, and Ernest Urdăreanu, had acquired Portuguese visas and were supposed to sail from Rio de Janiero to Lisbon on 28 August. In order to prevent this, both Western Governments requested Portugal to cancel their visas. The Portugese Government complied, cancelling the visas and ordering the captain of the Serpo Pinto not to allow them to embark. *Foreign Relations. op. cit.*, 597-598.

Declaration" at the earliest time convenient.[69] In Bucharest, Schuyler had intended to take up the revision of the Control Commission with the Russians at their scheduled meeting for 20 August, but Susaikov cancelled it claiming he was ill. Schuyler now urgently requested a special meeting with the Russians to discuss the latest crisis. At the same time, he advised the opposition leaders that they "should take extra precautions to remain calm, avoiding all demonstrations, and any pretexts that might be seized upon by the NDF or the Red Army to intervene.[70] The British supported the United States, but saw little hope of Moscow agreeing to consultations before the planned Foreign Ministers meeting in London in September. The Foreign Office was especially annoyed over the failure of the Americans to coordinate their actions with them, and let them know that they hoped to be consulted in the future.[71]

On 23 August Susaikov agreed to meet with Schuyler and LeRougetel. Beyond agreeing to the meeting though, the upset Soviet official refused to make any concessions. After silently listening to Schuyler's request that the Control Commission prevent any violence locally while talks were pending among their governments, Susaikov accused the Western representatives of solely initiating the crisis and made it clear that the Soviet Government was "definitely

---

[69] *Ibid.*, 582; *New York Times*, August 23, 1945.

[70] *Foreign Relations 1945, op.cit.*, 583.

[71] Winant to Secretary of State, August 22, 1945, State Department Tele ram, No. 8537, 740.00119 CONTROL (RUMANIA) 6-2245; Foreign Office Minute, September 4, 1945, F. O. 371 /48557 R14930/28/37.

opposed" to the resignation of the present cabinet. In the meantime, the Russians continued to intimidate Michael, who since the crisis began had been refusing to sign decrees or make any public appearances, as he largely isolated himself in the Kyselef Palace. The Soviets were especially angry with Michael's intention to boycott the planned celebration for 23 August the anniversary of the coup. So far the controlled press in Romania had not published anything about the crisis. On the morning of the 23rd Susaikov, after awakening Michael at six to request an immediate audience, boldly warned him and his advisors that "there will be tears." But the young monarch refused to give in and avoided the celebration. Threats were also made on the Romanian Socialists. Petrescu informed the Americans that Socialist cabinet ministers were under "tremendous Communist pressure," and were being labeled traitors. Although Petrescu still refused to leave the government, he openly supported the King and authorized the publication abroad of a resolution of the party's executive committee to this effect.[72]

For the rest of the month the situation in Romania remained tense. There were some discussions behind the scenes between members of the traditional parties and the government, but nothing concrete developed.[73] In order to minimize the possibility of forceful Soviet counter- measures,

---

[72] *Foreign Relations 1945*, V, 593; Melbourne to Secretary of State, August 24, 1945, State Department Telegram, No. 596, 871.001&2445.
[73] Melbourne to Secretary of State, August 25, 1945, State Department Telegram, NO. 607, 871.0018-2545.

as well as give ground to their suspicion that the West caused the crisis, Melbourne was ordered to avoid contact with opposition leaders and, in general, to adopt a reserved attitude.[74]

But time was on the side of the Soviets. By September Romanians were beginning to fear that the Russians were giving the West the same old run-around as in the previous March. One Foreign Office official described proposals suggested by opposition leaders on the formation of a new cabinet as "a purely academic exercise." "Groza is there and there is no reason whatever to believe that he will not stay." Finally on 3 September Moscow answered the American note of 23 August requesting consultation between the Big Three. Much of the note consisted of changes that the West instigated the crisis by pressuring the King into submission, while claiming that there was no reason for consultation because the Groza Government enjoyed "the confidence and support of wide circles" of the population, and that the Soviet Government "considers inadmissible in principle interference in the internal affairs of Rumania." On the other hand, the Russians said that if the West insisted on discussions they were ready as long as they "take place sometime after the completion... of the coming session of the Council of Foreign Ministers in London."[75]

---

[74] *Foreign Relations 1945*, V, 594. Romanian historians have largely ignored the constitutional crisis. A few pages on it can be found in Gheorge Ţuţui, "La position de la monarchie dans la vie politique de la Roumanie (août 1944 novembre 1946), *Revue Roumaine d'Histoire*, 11 (1 972), VI, 960-965.
[75] *Foreign Relations 1945*, V, 603-604.

The State Department was not ready to give up so easily. On 6 September Harriman was instructed to simply tell the Russians that the United States "proposes to rise" the issue of Romania's form of government at the upcoming conference in London. The Foreign Office reluctantly agreed to continue to follow Washington's lead. The Director of European Affairs in the State Department pointed out to the British the importance of "publicity" in combating the Russians.

> Our two governments must continue to insist that the Groza Government is not a representative one, and bring all their influence to bear on the Soviet Government to persuade them that constitutional procedures must be restored in Rumania if a serious divergence between the attitudes of the three great powers was not to be revealed.[76]

Moreover, the Truman Administration was holding back on a request from Stalin for a six billion dollar loan in the hopes of obtaining political concessions in Eastern Europe.[77] At the last minute, as the London meeting opened Vyschinski informed Harriman that "he was sure" the Romanian question "would be talked over at the... conference."[78]

The London Foreign Ministers Conference began on 11 September. James Byrnes, who had been appointed Secretary of State in the previous July, headed the American delegation. In his memoirs Byrnes aptly described the

---

[76] Washington to Foreign Office, September 7, 1945, F.O. 371/18557 R15238/28/37.
[77] Gaddis. *Cold War*, 260-261.
[78] *Foreign Relations 1945, op. cit.*, 617.

conference as "a test of strength" between East and West. Byrnes hoped to reach agreement with the Russians on a number of questions involving Eastern Europe, including the reorganization of the Romanian Government, as well as help pave the way for establishing diplomatic relations and the signing of a peace treaty. But the attitude of the Russians was even more rigid than at Potsdam. Byrnes argued that the United States only wanted to see "a government both friendly" to the Soviet Union and representative of all democratic elements" established in Romania. The Russians, though, kept "insisting" that they wanted "a government hostile to the Soviet Union," and that the Groza Government enjoyed "the support of the overwhelming majority of the population." "The Rumanian Government," Molotov asserted, "is liked by the Rumanian population but not by the American Government. What should be done? Should we overthrow it because it is not liked by the United States Government and set up a government that would be unfriendly to the Soviet Union?"[79] At one point Molotov

---

[79] Byrnes, *Speaking Frankly*, 99-101. In October a Moscow radio broadcast announced why they thought the Groza Government was so representative. "The present Rumanian Government enjoys the broadest support of the people.... *Trade Unions* affiliated to the GENERAL LABOUR CONFEDERATION, which unreservedly supports Groza's Government, have a membership of 1,300,000. The Ploughman's Front... numbers 1,500,000 peasants. The *Communist* Party, *Social Democratic* Party and the organizations of the *National-Tsaranist* Party... count together no fewer than 340,000 members. The Union of Patriots... contains 100,000 members. The *National Defence Organization* has over 300,000. The organization of *Progressive*

charged that the other members were "conducting an offensive" against him on Romania.[80] After three weeks of futile wrangling the conference ended in failure; the Foreign Ministers could not even agree on a public communiqué to hide the growing rift.

The failure of the meeting left Byrnes surprised and disappointed. In private he bitterly accused the Russians of duplicity and welching on their agreement. Added to this was the inability of the Americans in Bucharest to get the Soviets to agree to any of their proposals for the Control Commission. World opinion, economics, and "atomic

---

Youth unites 120,000 who have reached voting age. The organization of *anti-Fascist Women* comprises 300,000. Finally, the *Hungarian People's Union* counts 500.000 members. It is obvious that the present Government enjoys the support of the overwhelming majority of voters." One Foreign Office official commented that "the interesting point is that this majority is only obtained by gross exaggeration (particularly the figures for the Ploughmen's Front) and by a perfectly obvious system of counting every supporter two or three times. If we needed confirmation that the Government is not representative this gives it." "The Anti- Fascist Women." noted another English official, "also seems to number almost as many as the Communist, Social Democrats and National-Peasant dissidents combined." Monitoring report of the British Broadcasting Corporation and Foreign Office Minutes, F.O. 371/48560 R16884/28/37. For additional figures see Ceausescu, *Socialist Society*, IV, 590-591.

[80] Byrnes, *Speaking Frankly*, 101. See also Richard D. Byrnes. "James F. Byrnes," *An Uncertain Tradition: American Secretaries of State in the Twentieth Century* (ed. Norman A. Graebner, New York, 1961), 235231 Druks, *Truman and the Russians*, 84.

diplomacy" had failed to force the Kremlin into making concessions. Reviewing the recent crisis in Romania a report from the British Embassy in Moscow concluded:

> The Americans here have... been inclined to overestimate the effect upon Soviet policy in the Balkans of the atomic bomb and of other recent international developments favorable to the Western democracies. They were in particular encouraged by our joint victory over the postponement of the Bulgarian elections to expect similar Russian retreats elsewhere and first of all in Rumania.[81]

Even the oil commissions agreed to at Potsdam through which the West hoped that they could get back some of their oil equipment failed miser- ably to get anywhere with the Russians.

America's failure was reflected in the growing discouragement among the Romanian opposition. The King continued to refuse to sign decrees in spite of constant pressure and threats. On the other hand, the Groza Government was becoming increasingly confident and cocky. During the London Conference political jockeying among government members and the opposition continued, and there were indications that the Russians might support a government headed by Pătrăşcanu, Tatarescu, or even the renegade National Peasant leader Dr. Nicolae Lupu. But with the failure of the London Conference, this died down. Berry cabled Washington that the government was "making political capital" out of the failure of the West to take any

---

[81] Roberts to Foreign Office, September 9, 1945. F.O. 371/48557 R15279/28/37.

action against them. [82] Arrests of political opponents continued unabated, and in October a "Christian Socialist Party" was formed for former members of the Iron Guard who agreed to collaborate with the Communists.[83] Moreover, the American Legation in Bucharest received reports that several hundred former Iron Guardists who had fled to Germany after Romania surrendered were being sent back by the Russians to act as "shock troops."[84] Whereas the press remained under tight censorship there was little the West could do to influence the general population; it was not until the beginning of September that the government even allowed mention of the crisis in the press. Other than through the Western representatives in Romania the only way they could get their views across was over BBC broadcasts and the Voice of America. It was becoming apparent that the Russians could keep the Groza Government in power as long as they desired, and there was little the West or the opposition could do about it.

The first serious violence since the crisis began in August broke out in Bucharest on 8 November, the feast of St. Michael, the King's name day. In spite of the emerging police state, a surprisingly large crowd of between ten and fifteen thousand showed up in the palace square to acclaim

---

[82] *Foreign Relations 1945*, V, 621.

[83] Bucharest to Secretary of State, November 5, 1945, State Department Despatch, No. 593, 871.00/11-545; Berry to Secretary of State, November 19, 1945, State Department Despatch, No. 61 3, 871.00/11-1945.

[84] Bucharest to Secretary of State, November 5, 1945, State Department Despatch. No. 593. 871.00/11-545.

the King and express their dissatisfaction with the government, a considerable embarrassment for the latter. In retaliation, around ten or eleven in the morning trucks loaded with workers armed with clubs arrived and tried to disperse the demonstrators by striking them as they passed by. They angry crowd struck back by overturning and burning several trucks. Shortly afterwards gendarmes from the Interior Ministry building began firing into the crowd, and about one hundred fifty persons were arrested. In the early afternoon the Russian trained Tudor Vladimirescu Division arrived and cleared the square. For the rest of the afternoon demonstrators continued to mill about in the surrounding streets. At one point as a group approached the square, Romanian soldiers opened fire killing two and wounding several others; with the arrival of a Russian three star general, apparently Susaikov, the firing ceased. By nightfall thirteen people were dead and almost one hundred wounded.[85] In an attempt to use the incident for their own

---

[85] LeRougetel to Foreign Office, November 8, 1945, F. 0. 371/48562 R18993/28/37; LeRougetel to Foreign Office, November 12, 1945, F. 0. 371148562 R19175/28/37; Foreign Office Report, November 16, 1945, F.O. 371/48542 R19564/28/37; Roberts, *Rumania*, 302-303. For an opposing view see Gh. Ţuţui, "Infrîngerea de către forţele revoluţionare a acţiunilor anti-democratice şi antiguvernamentale intreprinse de partidele politice reacţionare si de monarhie (august 1945-ianuarie 1946)," *Studii, Revista de istorie*, 20 (1967), VI, 1110-1112. General Ionescu, Groza's Under Secretary of State for Air, and his wife were both wounded by accident by a NKVD patrol. Later Susaikov apologized for the incident and presented the General with six bottles of Russian champagne.

advantage the next day the government-controlled press put the entire blame on the "Fascist" leaders of the traditional parties, as well as announced that it would take severe measures against these people. Western representatives strongly urged Susaikov to set up a special committee to investigate the events of the 8th, but to no avail.

With the failure of the London Conference there was little the West could do to help Romania, at least for the time being. In an attempt to find some way out of the impasse, in October Byrnes sent the well-known liberal editor of the Louisville Courier Journal Mark Ethridge to the Balkans on a fact-finding mission. Byrnes described this as a "new approach" for the purpose of reappraising the situation, and said that he had chosen a man not connected with the government so that the investigation could be conducted "with an open mind."[86] Actually the Secretary was beginning to have second thoughts about the hard line he had followed at London and began considering a compromise solution. The Soviets, meanwhile, had hinted on several occasions that they might be willing to make several changes in the Groza Government in return for diplomatic recognition.[87] Finally, rather than allow the stalemate in the Balkans to drag on, the day after Thanksgiving Byrnes sent a message to the Russians asking for a meeting of the Foreign Ministers to take place in Moscow sometime before Christmas.

---

[86] *Foreign Relations 1945*, IV, 346-347; Foreign Relations 1945, V, 622; Byrnes, *Speaking Frankly*, 107.
[87] LeRougetel to Foreign Office. November 22, 1945, F. 0. 371/48607 R19859/28/37; Berry to Secretary of State, November 17, 1945, State Department Telegram, No. 895, 871.00/11-1745.

The British were also becoming increasingly reluctant to follow Washington's hard line policy. A Foreign Office minute at the beginning of December stated:

> It is already perfectly clear that the Russians are prepared to have a serious public row with us as a result of their support of the Groza Government. Whether or not they are prepared to risk more than this I do not know, but it seems... perfectly clear that we cannot go any further.[88]

On 7 December Orme Sargent explained to Winant that the Foreign Office was considering ways to end the "stalemate," and that "his own thinking was as follows:

> It might be well for the British and U. S. to approach the Russians and get Russian assistance in "diluting" the existing government and then through "nagging"... get additional concessions for foreign journalists and pledges for a greater degree of individual freedom. Having accomplished that, recognition might be extended and then the way would be open to proceed with the very important work of negotiating peace treaties. Until peace treaties were negotiated and signed... plans for normal relations could hardly be developed... and... little hope of Soviet troop withdrawals taking place.[89]

Adding to the need for a solution to the Romanian crisis was the growing fear that the Russians and the government were getting ready to take drastic measures, including

---

[88] Foreign Office Minute, December 4, 1945, F. 0. 371/48607 R20250/2795/37.
[89] *Foreign Relations 1945*, IV, 405-406.

rumors that the government was debating whether to outlaw the Peasant and Liberal parties. Plans were also afoot to have regency set up, and ex-King Carol was still trying to make his way back into Europe with the aid of the Russians and Romanian communists. [90] A weary King Michael informed Berry: "We have reached the hour of twelve. We are on the eve of the creation of a general condition dangerous to our country and to the Crown."[91]

Byrnes arrived in the Russian capital in the middle of December for the Foreign Ministers meeting which he requested. His main goal was to resolve the deadlock over Romania and Bulgaria. The much heralded Etheridge mission, which was to provide the basis for American proposals at the conference, had been presented to the Secretary of State on 7 December. But the report simply confirmed what American representatives had been reporting to Washington all along. [92] Byrnes initial

---

[90] LeRougetel to Foreign Office, December 8, 1945, F. 0. 371148542; Marjoribanks to Foreign Office, December 8, 1945, F. 0. 371/48542; Sargent's minute, December 18, 1945, F. 0. 371/48542; Marjoribanks to Foreign Office, December 18, 1945, F. 0. 371/48546; *New York Times*, December 9, 1945. Even though King Carol had an unlimited diplomatic visa for France, the French Government would not let him enter France or Monaco.
[91] Berry to Secretary of State, December 8, 1945. State Department Telegram, No. 961, 871.00/12-845.
[92] The Ethridge report was never published. Until a few years ago it was listed as "classified information" by the United States Government. Some of his views are given in his joint essay with C. E. Black, "Negotiating on the Balkans, 1945-1947," in

discussions with Molotov were as fruitless as those in London in September. As a result he decided to take the matter up with Stalin personally. After a brief exchange in which Byrnes told Stalin that he would be compelled to publish the Ethridge report if agreement could not be reached, and the Generalissimo replying that in that case he would have to send the Soviet journalist Ilya Ehrenburg to Romania to publish his views, Stalin suggested that "it might be possible to make some changes in the Government there which would satisfy Mr. Byrnes and Mr. Bevin." Byrnes, who was determined to work out some kind of a compromise jumped at the chance. After further discussion it was decided that a commission, composed of Harriman, Clark Kerr, and Vyschinski, would be sent to Bucharest to work out with the Romanian Government the inclusion of two additional ministers, one from each of the two traditional parties. Stalin, however, let Byrnes know that these could not be Maniu, Bratianu, or Lupu.[93] In further talks the ministers agreed that after the Romanian Government was reorganized "free and unfettered elections" would be "held as soon as possible on the basis of universal suffrage and secret ballot." It was also decided that all "democratic and anti-Fascist parties should have the right to take part in these elections," and that the Romanian Government "should give assurances concerning the grant of freedom of the press, speech, religion, and association." In return Byrnes and Bevin promised that after the Romanian

Raymond Dennett and Joseph E. Johnson (eds.), *Negotiating with the Russians.*
[93] *Foreign Relations 1945,* II, 754-756.

Cabinet was reorganized and had given assurances that they would faithfully execute these stipulations, their governments would recognize the Groza Government.[94]

The Moscow Agreement was the final step for the Soviets in getting the West to recognize their dominance of Romania. If the agreement was to be carried out as written it would have represented a major triumph for Washington and London, but few, if any, by this time in the State Department and Foreign Office were so naive. The accord essentially provided the West with a face-saving exit from a very tense situation in which there seemed to be no other way out and was becoming ever-increasingly more tragic. For all practical purposes, the Moscow Agreement, not the elections in the following fall as some historians have claimed, marked the end of Western hopes to create a democratic Romania.

Although Byrnes felt he had achieved a significant victory in settling a problem which had been seriously straining East-West relations for over two years, the reaction to the Moscow Agreement indicated that the Cold War was almost in full swing. Byrnes quickly found himself under attack from the press, Republican leaders, and even some members of his own administration. The American Mission in Bucharest regarded the agreement as a "sell-out" and threatened to resign en masse. [95] Soviet expert George Kennan described it as "some fig leaves of democratic

---

[94] *Ibid.*, 821-822; George Curry, James F. Byrnes (V. XIV of *The American Secretaries of State and Their Diplomacy*, ed. Robert H. Ferrell, New York), 169-183 passim.
[95] Sulzberger, *Row of Candles*, 292.

procedure to hide the nakedness of Stalinist dictatorship."[96] Even Truman himself was upset. Tied down with domestic matters he had given his independent minded Secretary of State a free hand in foreign affairs; furthermore Byrnes had kept the President in the dark on the accord until it was announced. Truman wrote that as he went through the conference papers "it became abundantly clear... that the successes of the... conference were unreal."[97] Having just read the Ethridge report, in a stern letter to Byrnes, the President expressed his frustration:

> It is full of information on Rumania and Bulgaria which confirms our previous information on those police states. I am not going to agree to the recognition of those governments unless they are radically changed.... I do not think we should play compromise any longer... I am tired of babying the soviets.[98]

He "lost his nerve in Moscow," Truman believed.[99]

---

[96] George Kennan, *Memoirs* 1925-1950, (New York, 1967), 299.

[97] Truman, *Year of Decisions*, 550. At Moscow Stalin promised to add two opposition members to the Communist controlled Bulgarian Government. Instead of creating a commission to implement this as in Romania, Stalin saw to it that the Russians handled this alone. In the end, however, the Bulgarian Government was never enlarged.

[98] Truman, *op. cit.*, 551-552. In his memoirs Truman claimed he read the letter to Byrnes personally in the Oval Room of the White House. Byrnes, however, denied ever hearing or reading it.

[99] Daniels, *Man from Independence*, 309-31 0; Druks, *Truman and the Russians*, 91.

The Allied commission charged with implementing the Moscow decision met with King Michael on 1 January. The British, who were receiving reports that the traditional parties were working to have the government reorganized on a wider basis than provided for in the accord, urged Michael to abide by the agreement.[100] The King had little choice in the matter. After several days of discussions it was decided that Emil Hatieganu, a National Peasant, and Mihai Romniceanu, a Liberal, would enter the government as ministers without portfolio. On 8 January the Groza Government solemnly promised to faithfully carry out the stipulations of the Moscow Agreement. In spite of this, American officials in Bucharest saw little hope of this being done. As previously agreed to, in February the United States and Great Britain recognized the Romanian Government.[101]

The Moscow accord gave a temporary lease on life to the traditional parties. A disheartened Maniu told Berry that the agreement was

> a great personal disappointment but that he had accepted... because he understood that the American and British Governments would exert pressure upon

---

[100] Bevin's Instructions to LeRougetel, January 1, 1946, F. 0. 371148564 R216321 28137; Bucharest to Foreign Office, December 30, 1945, F. 0. 371148564 R21632/28/37; Lee, *Crown,*134
[101] Curry, Byrnes, 199. See also Tutui, "Infringerea de catre fortele revolutionare a actiunilor antidemocratice si antiguvernamentale intreprinse de partidele politice reactionare si de monarhie," 11 13.

the Groza Government to make good its commitments.[102]

For the next several months the government allowed a certain degree of political freedom to the opposition. The traditional parties were permitted to reopen a number of newspapers, their two representatives in the government participated in some Cabinet discussions, and political meetings were held. But by the spring it was rapidly becoming politics as usual for the Groza regime. Political violence was increasing, opposition meetings were disrupted, censorship of the opposition press was growing again, and the government continued to ignore its promise not to press its lawsuits against Peasants and Liberals accused of being responsible for the demonstrations on November.[103] Furthermore, the government 8 had done little to prepare for elections which the West had hoped would take place in April or May. On 21 April Washington and London appealed to the Russians to join with them in a three power approach to the Romanian Government. The Soviets rejected this, simply claiming that they saw "no ground" for such an approach. Despite this on 27 May the United States and Britain protested directly to the Romanian government for its failure to live up to the Moscow Agreement. But the Romanian reply gave little satisfaction either. "A weak defensive document filled with sophistries and second rate falsehoods," was how Berry described it.[104]

---

[102] *Foreign Relations 1946*, VI, 583.

[103] *Ibid.*, 582-585.

[104] *Ibid.*, 598; Department of State Bulletin, U.S. Department of State, June 16, 1946 (Washington), 1048.

Following this there was another exchange of notes, but the results were similar.

In July the government drafted a new electoral law designed to allow them to return an assembly of their choice. At first the King was reluctant to sign it, and Maniu threatened not to put up any candidates; he also urged Michael to provoke a new international crisis.[105] There was little the United States could do. By now the State Department believed that protesting to Moscow would be useless, and merely informed Berry that the best course would be for the Romanians to settle it among themselves. There was little doubt among the King and the opposition that the government would win the election under the law. In a private conversation one Communist Cabinet member told Michael "that in a free election the Government could not obtain 20% of the votes, whereas the Government expected to have 80% of the votes."[106] Michael was able to get the government to eliminate some of the most objectionable features of the bill, but when he pressed Pătrăşcanu for additional concessions the latter responded candidly: "If the Government gives more it will be giving the nation to the historical parties - that it can never do. We have given all we can."[107] Michael finally signed the bill. He told Maniu that if he fought a "rear guard action" there was "always hope" of the story someday having a "happy ending." In order to further insure a government victory the Communists insisted that all the left-wing parties run on a

---

[105] *Foreign Relations 1946*, op. cit., 61 2.61 6.
[106] *Foreign Relations 1946*, VI, 614.
[107] *Ibid.*, 61 6.

common electoral list.[108] They had been trying for some time to get the Socialists to join with them in a common list, but Petrescu stuck to his guns and was able to get the party conference in December to vote against this. However, in March the Communists were able to split the party, one group under the former anticommunist Lotar Radaceanu agreeing to their proposal.[109] The rest under Petrescu tried to form an Independent Socialist Party which joined with the Peasants and Liberals in opposition to the government.

The long awaited Peace Conference with Germany's allies began in July, 1946. As far as the West was concerned, most of the important issues with Romania had been settled already one way or the other. The final treaty generally followed the lines of the 1944 Armistice. The United States and Britain hoped that after the peace treaty the Russians would remove their troops from Romania, but the final clause gave Moscow the right to keep "such armed forces as it may need for the maintenance of the lines of communications of the Red Army with the Soviet zone... in Austria."[110] The West was successful in getting stipulations promising nondiscriminatory treatment in matters of trade. Their proposals for the free navigation of the Danube for all states, however, were rejected by the Russians, and in the

---

[108] A. Petric; Gh. Țuțui, *L'unification du mouvement ouvrier de Roumanie* (Bucarest, 1967), 83-89.
[109] D.G.R. Serbanesco, *Ciel rouge sur la Roumanie*, (Paris, 1952), 76-81. See also C. Barbu; V. Gh. Ionescu, "Contributia comitetelor de Front unic muncitoresc in anii 1944-1947 la realizarea unității clasei muncitoare din România," *Studii, Revista de istorie*, 20 (1 967), I, 136-137.
[110] *Foreign Relations 1946*, op. cit., 618.

end they had to settle for an agreement providing for the holding of an international conference to deal with this issue after the present conference ended.[111] Romania's frontiers were to be those of 1 January, 1941, with the exception of Transylvania which was restored to that of January, 1938. The treaty was signed on 10 February, 1 947.[112]

While the Peace Conference was meeting, on 19 November elections were finally held in Romania. By various means the government was able to suppress attempts by the opposition to campaign. In August Groza told Berry that

> when the Anglo-Americans agreed to the Moscow decision they were thinking in terms of free elections such as were held in England or America, whereas the Russians were thinking in terms of free elections such as were held in Russia. In view of the presence of the Russian Army in Rumania, the coming elections would likely be held according to the Russian interpretation of free and unfettered.[113]

On 28 October the United States and Britain sent protest notes to the Groza Government on its campaign tactics. The

---

[111] The Danube problem was not finally solved until the Belgrade Conference of 1948. At that time the Soviet Union was able to get a resolution approved which allowed only riparion states to sit on the Danubian Commission. This meant that Russia would be able to largely control the Danube in the future while Western influence would be eliminated.
[112] Byrnes, *Speaking Frankly*, 123-1 55 passim; John Campbell, The United States in World Affairs 1945-1947 (New York, 1947), 117-137 passim. See also Ciurea, *Le Traite de Paix*.
[113] *Foreign Relations 1946*, IV, 621.

Romanians merely replied that because they had not received a similar protest from the Soviet Union, a co-author of the Moscow Agreement, they regretted to be "unable to retain or discuss" these notes.[114] Whereas the results of the elections were a foregone conclusion, on several occasions the leaders of the traditional parties considered withdrawing their candidates in protest. But Berry advised them against this feeling that this would only make the situation worse. The electoral results surprised no one. "A complete fake," commented on Foreign Office official. The government claimed almost five million votes, while the Peasants received only eight hundred thousand and the Liberals less than three hundred thousand. A frustrated and disgusted Berry summarized his views by stating that the government

> carried through the elections in the same spirit as it prepared for the - elections in utter disregard for promises given and for elementary decency. In fact the Government established a new low level for Balkan elections.

At the same time, Berry asked to be transferred out of Romania.[115]

---

[114] *Ibid.*, 646-647.
[115] *Ibid.*, 655-657; Roberts, Rumania, 304-305. For opposing views see Fischer-Galați. *Twentieth Century*, 104-106; V. Liveanu, "Particularités de la stratégie politique du Parti Communiste Roumain entre 1944-1948" Etudes d'histoire contemporaine de la Roumanie (eds. Miron Constantinescu, "and Others." Bucarest, 1971), 201-202, 207-208. The Communist claim that the election was the freest in the history of Romania. Petric; Țuțui, L'instauration régime démocratique. 106.

Washington issued a press release denouncing the elections, and, at first, intended to protest to Moscow. A proposal was sent to the British asking them to support a note to the Russians calling for new elections in Romania because of the failure of that country to fulfill the Moscow Agreement. Whitehall, however, did not favor this feeling that the Soviets would simply give them the same old run-around. Consequently, Washington decided to drop the issue. Several days before the new Romanian Parliament was to meet, Michael told Berry that he was considering postponing its opening.

> Do you want me to explode a bomb now like did on August 20 last year?... My friends tell me that there is no place for kings in the Soviet system 1 and this is the last clear-cut issue upon which can make a stand....If you can tell me now that your Government will give me more than moral I support if I go out on a limb again will think very seriously about doing so.[116]

But Berry could not give him any encouragement.

American hopes of getting the Russians to slacken their political control over Romania in return for economic concessions accomplished nothing. By 1947 Soviet control over Romania's economy was firmer than ever. The long range hope of the United States was that with the establishment of normal relations and the signing of the peace treaty the position of Russia would gradually weaken, and Romania would reverse her political policies and look

---

[116] *Foreign Relations 1946*, IV, 666-667; Tutui, "La position de la monarchie," 967-968.

more to the West for trade. For the time being, however, the United States was against giving economic aid directly to the Groza Government. Several times during 1946 the Romanians asked Washington for a loan so they could purchase American wheat. In December Gheorghiu-Dej, the Minister of National Economy, told Berry he would like to head an official delegation to visit the United States in the hopes of acquiring wheat and improving economic relations.[117] But other commitments as well as the political situation caused the State Department to reject this. Byrnes explained to Berry that if the Groza Government was successful in acquiring wheat they "would claim the credit," and if not, they would put the blame on the United States. At the request of General Schuyler, during the winter and spring of 1947, when a severe famine hit Moldavia, the United States provided substantial quantities of food and seventy-six thousand tons of wheat. This, though, was done on humanitarian grounds.[118]

In the spring of 1947, the government began mass arrests in an attempt to completely destroy the opposition. In July, Maniu and the remaining leaders of the Peasant Party were imprisoned; shortly after- wards both the Peasant and the Liberal parties were outlawed.[119] In November Maniu and

---

[117] *Foreign Relations 1946, op. cit.*, 669-672.

[118] Statement of the President of 17 February 1947 and other related documents, Truman Papers, File No. 426, Harry S. Truman Library, Independence, Missouri; Interview with General Schuyler, March 1. 1975.

[119] Petric; Țuțui, L'instauration régime démocratique, 129. On 6 May 1948 Petrescu was arrested and imprisoned without a trial.

his followers were brought to trial on charges of conspiring against the safety of the state. In a trial that was typical of the totalitarian mockery of justice, the seventy-four year old Maniu received a sentence of life imprisonment, and the others prison terms varying from five years to life.[120] At the same time, Tatarescu, now no longer needed as window dressing, and his supporters were removed from their posts.[121] There was nothing the West could do but issue verbal protests. Although the Americans and the British knew that their protests would not influence the policy of the Romanian Government they felt that they helped to encourage and stiffen local opposition.[122]

The last obstacle to complete control of Romania by the Communists was finally removed in December 1947. On 12 November Michael went to London for the royal wedding of Princess Elizabeth and Prince Philip.[123]

---

[120] Elizabeth Barker, *Truce in the Balkans* (London, 1948), 79. For the proceedings of the trial see *The Trial of the Former National Peasant Party Leaders Maniu*, Mihalache, Penescu, Niculescu-Buzeşti and Others (Bucharest, 1947).

[121] R. R. Betts, Central and South East Europe (London, 1948), 16; Liveanu, Stratégie politique, 20&209; V. Teodorescu, "Aspecte ale folosirii parlamentului de către forţele democratice conduse de Partidul Comunist Român (decembrie 1946 decembrie 1947)," Studii şi materiale de istorie contemporană (Academia Republicii Populare Române, Bucureşti, 1962), 424.

[122] *Foreign Relations 1947*, IV, 491.

[123] It was during his trip abroad that Michael became engaged to his future wife Princess Anne of Bourbon-Parma.

The Communists were hoping that the King would not return; furthermore, Western reports showed that they had been plotting again with King Carol who was now staying in Portugal. In London King Michael told the American Ambassador Lewis Douglas that he was thinking of not returning and asked for his advice. By this time the United States had come to the conclusion that the now powerless King could do little by going back and was fearful that he might be physically harmed. Douglas pointed out that although he alone must make the final decision "because of the unconcealed Communist domination of his country," the United States felt his return "would serve no useful purpose." In spite of several American notes which repeated the same advice, hoping for a miracle, King Michael returned in December. On the 30th of that month, however, the Communists themselves decided to end this phase of Romanian history. With the Kyself Palace surrounded by Communist soldiers and secret police, Groza mockingly warned the King that he must abdicate or else! Realizing that to stay would probably mean a bloody civil war that he could not win, Michael accepted the inevitable. On the same day the Romanian People's Republic was declared.[124] The

---

[124] For a recent article by the Romanians see Aron Petric, "Proclamarea republicii populare române si semnificatia sa istorică," *Studii, Revista de istorie*, 25 (1972). VI, 1143-1157. Also Liveanu, *Stratégie politique*, 210; Teodorescu, "Aspecte ale folosirii parlamentului," 426.

last Romanian King made his way out of the country into exile several days later.[125]

In 1945 Romania proved to be a serious cause of controversy between the West and her totalitarian rivals. In those crucial months of the spring and summer of 1945, when the Cold War hung in the balance, neither side was willing to back down. Romania became the first postwar test case of East-West relations, with the United States even getting involved in an unsuccessful plot to overthrow a Communist dominated government.

---

[125] With King Michael on the last royal train were his mother Queen Helen, the Marshal of the Palace Dimitrie Negel, the King's private secretary Mircea Ionnițiu, and his brother Nicolae Ionnițiu, two aide-de-camps General Petre Lazăr and Major Jacques Vergotti, as well as several other court officials, and the Queen's lady in waiting.

Conclusion

In some ways the biggest headaches for the large nations are the smaller ones more often than not these are the ones the powerful nations wind up fighting over. Sandwiched between Germans and Slavs, as well as occupying a strategic position along the crossroads of Europe and Asia, it was almost inevitable that Romania should play a pivotal role amongst the powers during the era of the Second World War. In striking contrast to their prior involvement in Romania which mainly concerned economics, during this period Britain and the United States tried to maintain an independent and friendly Romanian state. First with the German threat to Romania, and later during the Russian occupation, the Western Powers saw Romania's independence as affecting their own security. There were three phases in the development of the policies of the West towards Romania: from 1938 to the spring of 1940, the war years, and from the coup of August 1944 to the abdication of King Michael.

During the first period Britain became committed to defend the independence of Romania and several other states in Eastern Europe.

This was a complete reversal of England's traditional policy of nonintervention in that part of the Continent. It was Tilea's famous "ultimatum" which finally led the British to give guarantees to Romania, Poland, and Greece against a German attack.

In the second phase Britain and America tried to persuade Romania to turn against Germany and join the Allies, as well as to provide for an independent and democratic postwar Romanian state. By the summer of 1943 it had become evident that most of the Balkans would fall within the military sphere of the Red Army, and that what happened to Romania in the future would be largely decided by the Kremlin. Hopeful, but not certain, that Moscow would live up to her promise to carry out the principles of the Atlantic Charter and not try to dominate Southeastern Europe, Britain took the lead in getting the Soviets to make specific commitments to ensure an independent postwar Romania. Both the Antonescu Government and the opposition hoped to switch sides; however, they were very skeptical of Russian promises, and it was not until after the military situation made further resistance almost impossible that Romania finally joined the Allies. Nevertheless, the Military changeover of Romania significantly aided the Allies by forcing the Germans to abandon much of the Balkans.

The final phase involved London's and Washington's attempts to get the Soviets to live up to their promises. In March 1945, only three weeks after the conclusion of the Yalta conference, the Russians manifested their real intentions towards Romania by forcing a Communist-controlled minority government on the country. This led to one of the first serious differences between the Soviets and the West.

In spite of the strong position of the Soviets in Romania, the United States and England refused to acquiesce. What made the situation in Romania all the more disturbing were Western fears that the Russians had plans to establish Communism wherever they could. But the Soviets stood firm. In the summer of 1945 Romania became the first postwar test case of East-West relations.

Frustrated over their failures to get the Russians to make concessions, the United States became directly involved in an attempt by the Romanians to overthrow the Groza Government. Yet this only made the situation worse. The end result was a constitutional crisis which brought the government to a standstill for the rest of the year and further widened the growing split between the West and Moscow. In part because of Romania, by the end of 1945 the harmony and optimism of the Big Three at Yalta had been largely destroyed. Although in the end Washington and London failed to establish an independent and democratic Romanian state, perhaps the greatest tragedy was the harm this conflict caused to East-West relations.

Bibliography

Primary Sources

Archives and Manuscript Collections

Great Britain, Foreign Office Documents, 1940-1 945, Public Record Office, London.

GREW, JOSEPH C., Papers, Houghton Library, Harvard University.

HOPKINS, HARRY L., Papers, Franklin D. Roosevelt Library, Hyde Park, New York.

HULL, CORDELL., Papers, Library of Congress, Washington.

MOFFAT, JAY PIERREPONT, Papers Houghton Library, Harvard University.

OSS Reports, Department of the Army, National Archives, Washington.

RATAY, J. P., Reports, Department of the Army, National Archives, Washington.

ROOSEVELT, FRANKLIN D., Papers, Franklin D. Roosevelt Library, Hyde Park, New York.

SCHUYLER, GENERAL CORTLANDT VAN R., Diary, in the possession of its author.

STEINHARDT, LAURENCE A., Library of Congress, Washington.

STIMSON, HENRY L., Diary, Sterling Library, Yale Univesity.

TRUMAN, HARRY S., Papers, Truman Library, Independence, Missouri.

United States Department of State Documents, 1938-1 945, National Archives, Washington.

United States Department of the Army Documents, 1938-1 945, National Archives, Washington.

Public Documents

Die Geheimakten des franzosischen Generalstabes. V. VI of *Deutsches Weissbuch des Auswartigen Amtes,* Berlin, 1941.

Documents of British Foreign Policy 1919-1939. Third Series, London, 1949-1 954.

Documents on German Foreign Policy 1918-1945. Series D, Washington, 1949-

Documents on the Events Preceding the Outbreak of the War. German Library of Information, New York, 1940.

KLOCHKO, V. F., and others., eds., *New Documents on the History of Munich.* Prague, 1958.

Ministry of Foreign Affairs of the U.S.S.R., eds. *Stalin's Correspondence with Churchill and Attlee 1941-1945.* Moscow, 1957.

_____, *Stalin's Correspondence with Roosevelt and Truman 1941-1945.* Moscow, 1957.

Paris Peace Conference 1946: Selected Documents, Washington, 1948.

Parliamentary Debates. Fifth series, Commons, V. 345 (1939).

SONTAG, RAYMOND JAMES; BEDDIE, JAMES STUART., eds., Nazi-Soviet Relations 1939-1941. Washington, 1948.

The Trial of the Former National Peasant Party Leaders Maniu, Mihalache, Penescu, Niculescu-Buzesti and Others. Bucharest, 1947.

U. S. Department of State. *Foreign Relations of the United States: Annual Volumes 1920-1947.* Washington, 1943-1972.

_____, *Foreign Relations of the United States: The Conference at Cairo and Teheran 1943.* Washington, 1961.

_____, *Foreign Relations of the United States: The Conference of Berlin (The Potsdam Conference) 1945.* 2 V., Washington, 1960.

_____, *Foreign Relations of the United States: The Conferences of Malta and Yalta, 1945.* Washington, 1955.

_____, *Peace and War, United States Foreign Policy 1931-1941.* Washington, 1943.

_____, *Postwar Foreign Policy Preparation 1939-1945.* Washington, 1950.

Diaries, Letters, Memoirs, and Published Documents

AMERY, L. S., *My Political Life*. 3 V., London, 1 949-1 955, III.

ANTONESCU, GENERAL ION, *Către Români*. ed. Dan Zaharia, Bucuresti, 1941.

BECK, COLONEL JOZEF, Final Report. New York, 1957.

BERNDT, A.1; LIEBRANDT, G., *Archiv fur Aussenpolitik und Landerkunde*. Berlin, 1944.

BONNET, GEORGES, Dans la tourmente 1938-1948. Paris, 1971.

_____, Fin d'une Europe. Geneve, 1948.

BULLITT, ORVILLE, ed., *For the President Personal and Secret: Correspondence between Roosevelt and Bullitt*. Boston, 1972.

BYRNES, JAMES, All in One Lifetime. New York, 1958.

_____, *Speaking Frankly*. New York, 1947.

CARLYLE, MARGARET, ed., Documents on International Affairs 1939-1946. 2 V., London, 1954, II.

CEAUSESCU, NICOLAE, Romania on the Way of Building up the Multilaterally Developed Socialist Society. 3 V., Bucharest, 1970.

_____, *Romania on the Way of Completing Socialist Construction*. 5 V., Bucharest, 1969.

_____, *Speech Delivered at the Jubilee Session of the Grand National Assembly Dedicated to the 25th Anniversary of the Homeland's Liberation from the Fascist Yoke*. Bucharest, 1969.

CHURCHILL, WINSTON S., *Closing the Ring*. Boston, 1954.

_____, *The Grand Alliance*. Boston, 1950.

_____, *Triumph and Tragedy*. Boston, 1953.

CODREANU, CORNELIU Z., *Eiserne Garde*. Berlin, 1939.

CRETZIANU, ALEXANDRE, *The Lost Opportunity*. London, 1957.

CURTIS, MONICA, ed., *Documents on International Affairs 1938*. 2 V., London, I.

DEANE, JOHN R., The Strange Alliance. New York, 1947.

DEUTSCH, ROBERT, ed., *Nicolae Titulescu Discursuri*. Bucuresti, 1967.

DILKS, DAVID, ed., *The Diaries of Sir Alexander Cadogan*. New York, 1971.

DOMARUS, MAX, ed., *Hitter: Reden und Proklamationen 1932-1945*. 4 V., Munchen, 1961-1965, III, IV.

EDEN, ANTHONY, *Facing the Dictators*. Boston, 1962.

_____, *The Reckoning*. Boston, 1965.

FORRESTAL, JAMES, *The Forrestal Diaries*. ed., Walter Millis, New York, 1951

GAFENCU, GRIGORE, *Last Days of Europe*. New Haven, Connecticut, 1958.

_____, *Prelude to the Russian Campaign*. London, 1945.

GAMELIN, GENERAL MAURICE, *Servir*. 3 V., Paris, 1947, 111.

GEORGE, DAVID LLOYD, *The Truth About the Peace Treaties*. 2 V., London, 1938, 11.

GHEORGHIU-DEJ, GHEORGHE, *Rechenschaftsbericht des Zentralkomitees an den I1 Parteitag der Rumanischen Arbeiterpartei*. Berlin, 1956.

_____, *Dreizig Jahre Kampf der Partei unter dem Banner Lenins und Stalins*. Bukarest, 1952.

GIBSON, HUGH, ed., *The Ciano Diaries 1939-1943*. Garden City, New York, 1946.

GREW, JOSEPH, *Turbulent Era, A Diplomatic Record of Forty Years 1904-1945*. 2 V., Boston, 1952, II.

GUDERIAN, GENERAL HEINZ, *Panzer Leader*. New York, 1957.

HALIFAX, LORD, *Fullness of Days*. New York, 1957.

HART, B. H. LIDDELL, *The Liddell Hart Memoirs*. 2 V., New York, 1965, II.

HARVEY, OLIVER, *The Diplomatic Diaries of Oliver Harvey 1937-1940*. ed. John Harvey, London, 1970.

HENDERSON, SIR NEVILLE, *Failure of a Mission*. New York, 1940.

HOLBORN, LOUISE, ed., *War and Peace Aims of the United Nations 1943-1 945*. 2 V., Boston, 1943-1 948.

HULL, CORDELL, Memoires. 2 V., New York, 1948.

International Military Tribunal, *The Trial of the Major War Criminals*. 42 V., Nuremberg, 1949, XXV.

ISREAL, FRED L., ed., *The War Diary of Breckinridge Long 1939-1944*. Lincoln, Nebraska, 1966.

JACOBSEN, HANS A., ed., *Kriegstagebuch des Oberkommandos der Wehr macht 1940-1945*. Frankfurt am Main, 1965.

JEDRZEJEWICZ, WACLAW, ed., *Diplomat in Paris 1936-1939: Papers and Memoirs of Juliusz Lukasiewicz Ambassador of Poland*. New York, 1970.

KENNAN, GEORGE F., *Memoirs 1925-1950*. Boston, 1967.

LEAHY, ADMIRAL WILLIAM D., *I Was There*. New York, 1950.

LEITH-ROSS, SIR FREDERICK, *Money Talks*. London, 1968.

LIPSKI, JOZEF, *Diplomat in Berlin 1933-1939*. New York, 1 968.

LITVINOV, MAXIM, *Notes for a Journal*. New York, 1955.

MACLEOD, COLONEL RODERICK; KELLY, DENIS, *The Ironside Diaries 1937*. London, 1962.

MAISKY, IVAN, *Memoirs of a Soviet Ambassador*. London, 1967.

MCKENZIE, VERNON, *Through Turbulent Years*. New York, 1938.

MIKOLJCZYK, STANISLAV, *The Patern of Soviet Domination*. London, 1 948.

MINNEY, R. J., ed., *The Private Papers of Hore-Belisha*. London, 1960.

NEUBACHER, HERMANN, *Sonderauftrag Sudost 1940-1945*. Gottingen, 1956.

Pe marginea pripastiei. 21-23 Ianuarie 1941. 2 V., Bucuresti, 1942, II.

PERKINS, FRANCES, *The Roosevelt I Knew*. New York, 1946.

PĂTRĂȘCANU, LUCRETIU, Sous trois dictatures. Paris, 1946.

ROTHSTEIN, ANDREW, ed., *Soviet Foreign Policy During the Patriotic War: Documents and Materials*. London, 1946.

ST. JOHN, ROBERT, *Foreign Correspondent*. Garden City, New York, 1957.

SLESSOR, SIR JOHN, The Central Blue: *The Autobiography of Sir John Slessor, Marshal of the RAF*. New York, 1957.

STEITINIUS, EDWARD R. JR., *Roosevelt and the Russians: The Yalta Conference.* Garden City, New York, 1949.

STIMSON, HARRY L; BUNDY, McGEORGE, *On Active Service in Peace and War.* New York, 1948.

STOICA, VASILE, *America pentru Cauza Romanească.* Bucharest, 1926.

STURDZA, MICHEL, *The Suicide of Europe: Memoirs of Prince Michel Sturdza.* Boston, 1968.

SULZBERGER, C. L., *A Long Row of Candles.* New York, 1969.

SWEET-ESCOTT, BICKHAM, *Baker Street Irregular.* London, 1965.

THARAUD, JEROME ET JEAN, *L'envoye de l'Archange.* Paris, 1939.

TRUMAN, HARRY S., *Memoirs.* 2V., New York, 1955-1 956.

VANDENBERG, ARTHUR H., JR., ed., *The Private Papers of Senator Vandenberg.* Boston, 1952.

WEYGAND, MAXINE, *Memoirs.* 3 V., Paris, 1950-1 957, III.

Other Sources

FLORESCU, RADU, SR., Correspondence.

IONNITIU, MIRCEA, Correspondence.

IONNITIU, NICOLAE, Personal interviews.

MELBOURNE, ROY M., Correspondence.

SCHUYLER, GENERAL CORTLANDT VAN R., Personal interview.

Secondary Sources

Books

ADAM, COLIN, *Life of Lord Lloyd.* London, 1948.

ALPEROVITZ, GAR, *Atomic Diplomacy: Hiroshima and Potsdam.* New York, 1965.

ASTER, SIDNEY, *1939.* New York, 1973.

AVARAMOVSKI, Z., "Attempts to Form a Neutral Bloc in the Balkans (September-December 1939)," *Studia Balcanica.* 4, Sofia, 1971.

BANTEA, EUGENE; NICOLAE, CONSTANTIN; ZAHARIA, GHEORGHE, *La Roumanie dans la guerre antihitlerienne, aout 1944-mai 1945*, Bucarest, 1970.

BARBUL, GHEORGHE, *Memorial Antonesco, le Ill-e homme de I'axe.* Paris, 1950.

BARKER, A. J., *The Civilizing Mission: A History of the Italo-Ethiopean War of 1935-1936.* New York, 1968.

BARKER, ELIZABETH, *Truce in the Balkans.* London, 1948.

BASCH, ANTONIN, *The Danube Basin and German Economic Sphere.* New York, 1943.

BETS, R. R., *Central and South East Europe, 1945-1948.* Liverpool, 1950.

BUNESCU, TRAIAN, *Lupta poporului român impotriva dictatului fascist de la Viena, august 1940.* Bucuresti, 1 971.

BURNS, JAMES MACGREGOR, *Roosevelt: The Soldier of Freedom.* New York, 1970.

BUTLER, J. R. M., *"Grand Strategy," History of the Second World War:United Kingdom Military Series.* Ed. J. R. M. Butler, London, 1957, II.

CAMPBELL, JOHN C., *The United States in World Affairs 1945-1947.* New York, 1947.

CELOVSKY, BORIS, *Das Munchener Abkommen 1938.* Stuttgart, 1958.

CHARLE, KLAUS, *Die Eiserne Garde.* Berlin-Wien, 1939.

CIENCIALA, ANNA M., *Poland and the Western Powers, 1938-1 939.* Toronto, 1968.

CIORANESCO, GEORGE, and others, *Aspects des Relations Russo-Roumaines.* Paris, 1967.

CIUREA, EMILE C., *Le Traite de Paix avec la Roumanie.* Paris, 1 954.

293

CONSTANTINESCU, MIRON, and others, *Etudes d'histoire contemporaine de la Roumanie*. Bucarest, 1971.

CONSTANTINESCU, MIRON; PASCU, STEFAN, eds., *Unification of the Roumanian National State: The Union of Transylvania with Old Romania*. Bucharest, 1971.

DAICOVICIU, C; CONSTANTINESCU, MIRON, *La desagregation de la monarchie Austro-Hongroise 1900-1918*. Bucarest, 1965.

DALLIN, DAVID J., *Soviet Russia 's Foreign Policy 1939-1942*. New Haven, Connecticut, 1942.

DANIELS, JONATHEN, *The Man From Independence*. New York, 1950.

DEAKIN, F. W., *The Brutal Friendship*. New York, 1966.

DEBORIN, G., *The Second World War*. Moscow, n.d.

DENNETT, RAYMOND; JOHNSON, JOSEPH ed., *Negotiating with the Russians*. Boston, 1951.

DRUKS, HERBERT, Harry S. *Truman and the Russians 1945-1953*. New York, 1966.

EASTERMAN, A. L., King Carol, *Hitler and Lupescu*. London, 1942.

FATU, MIHAI; SPALATELU, ION, *Garda de fier, organizaţie teroristă de tip fascist*. Bucureşti, 1971.

FATU, MIHAI, *Sfirsit fara glorie*. Bucuresti, 1972.

FEILING, KEITH, *The Life of Neville Chamberlain*. London, 1946.

FEIS, HERBERT, *Between War and Peace. The Potsdam Conference*. Princeton, New Jersey, 1960.

_____, Churchill, Roosevelt, and Stalin. Princeton, New Jersey, 1957.

FISCHERGALATI, STEPHEN, ed., *The New Rumania: From People's Democracy to Socialist Republic*. Cambridge, Massachusetts, 1967.

_____, *The Socialist Republic of Rumania*. Baltimore, Maryland, 1969.

_____, *Twentieth Century Rumania*. New York, 1970.

FLEMING, D. F., *The Cold War*. 2 V., Garden City, New York, 1961,l.

FLOYD, DAVID, *Rumania: Russia's Dissident Ally*.New York, 1965.

GADDIS, JOHN LEWIS, *The United States and the Origins of the Cold War 1941-1947*. New York, 1972.

GANNON, ROBERT I.,S. J., *The Cardinal Spellman Story*. Garden City, New York, 1962.

GILBERT, MARTIN; GOT, RICHARD, *The Appeasers*. Boston, 1963.

GOLDBERGER, NICOLAE, "La resistance en Roumanie et les Allies," *European Resistance Movements 1939-1 945*. New York, 1964.

_____, "L'instauration et la consolidation du pouvoir populaire en Roumanie," *Nouvelles etudes d'histoire*. Bucarest, 1965.

GRAEBNER, NORMAN A., ed., *An Uncertain Tradition: American Secretaries of State in the Twentieth Century*. New York, 1961.

HARRIS, BRICE, JR., *The United States and the Italo-Ethiopean Crisis*. Stanford, California, 1964.

HILBERG, RAUL, *The Destruction of the European Jews*. Chicago, 1967.

HILLGRUBER, ANDREAS, *Hitler, Konig Carol und Marschall Antonescu*. Wiesbaden, 1954.

IONESCU, GHITA, *Communism in Rumania*. London, 1964.

Istoria economiei nationale a Romaniei. 3 V., Bucuresti, 1964, III.

JACOBSEN, HANS-ADOLF, *Nationalistische Aussenpolitik* 1933-1938. Frankfurt am Main, 1968.

JARAUSCH, KONRAD H., *The Four Power Pact 1933*. Madison, Wisconsin, 1965.

KERTESZ, STEPHEN, ed., *The Fate of East Central Europe: Hopes and Failures of American Foreign Policy*. Notre Dame, Indiana, 1956.

KOLKO, GABRIEL, The Politics of War. New York, 1968.

LAURENS, FRANKLIN D., *France and the Italo-Ethiopean Crisis 1935-1936*. The Hague, 1967.

LEE, ARTHUR GOULD, *Crown Against Sickle*.London, n.d.

_____, Helen, *Queen Mother of Rumania*. London, 1956.

_____, *Special Duties*. London, 1946.

LENDVAI, PAUL, *Eagles in Cobwebs*. Garden City, New York, 1 969.

LUKACS, JOHN A., *The Great Powers and Eastern Europe*. New York, 1953.

MACARTNEY, C. A., *A History of Hungary 1929-1945*. 2 V., New York, 1956, I.

MACHRAY, ROBERT, *The Struggle for the Danube and the Little Entente 1929-1938*. London, 1938.

MALIŢA, MIRCEA, *Romanian Diplomacy: A Historical Survey*. Bucharest, 1970.

MAMATEY, VICTOR S., *The United States and East Central Europe 1914- 1918*. Princeton, New Jersey, 1957.

MATEI, GHEORGHE, *La Roumanie et les problemes du desarmement* (1 919-1934). Bucarest, 1970.

MCNEILL, WILLIAM H., *America, Britain, and Russia, 1941-1946*. London, 1953.

MEDLICOTT, W. N., *The Economic Blockade*. 2 V., London, 1972.

MICAUD, CHARLES A., *The French Right and Nazi German 1933-1939*. New York, 1964.

MOATS, ALICE-LEONE, *Lupescu*. New York, 1955.

MOISUC, VIORICA, *Diplomaţia României şi problema apărării suveranităţii şi independenţei naţionale in perioada martie 1938-mai 1940*. Bucuresti, 1967.

MONTIAS, JOHN MICHAEL, *Economic Development in Communist Rumania*. Cambridge, Massachusetts, 1967.

MOULTON, HAROLD; PASVOLSKI, LEO, *War Debts and World Prosperity*. New York, 1932.

NAGY-TALAVERA, NICHOLAS M., *The Green Shirts and the Others*. Stanford, California, 1970.

NEDELCU, FLOREA, "Cu privire la politica extern4 a Romaniei in perioada guvernării Goga-Cuza", *Studii privind politica externă a României 1919-1939*. Bucureşti, 1969.

NORTHEDGE, F. S., *The Troubled Giant: Britain Among the Great Powers 1916-1939*. New York, 1966.

OPREA,I.M., *Nicolae Titulescu's Diplomatic Activity*.Bucharest,1 968.

PAVEL, PAVEL, *Why Rumania Failed*. London, 1944.

PEARTON, MAURICE, *Oil and the Romanian State*. London, 1971.

PETRIC, A; TUTUI, GH., *L'instauration et la consolidation du regime democratique populaire en Roumanie*. *Bucarest*, 1964.

_____, *L'unification du mouvement ouvrier de Roumanie*. Bucarest, 1 967.

PHILLIPS, CABELL, *The Truman Presidency*. Baltimore, Maryland, 1966.

POPESCU-PUTURI, ION, ed., *La contribution de la Rournanie a la victoire sur le fascisme*. Bucharest, 1965.

POPESCU-PUTURI, ION, and others, eds., *La Roumanie pendant la deuxieme guerre mondiale*, Bucarest, 1964.

POPESCU-PUTURI, ION, "L'importance historique de l'insurrection armee d'aout 1944," *Nouvelles etudes d'histoire*. Bucharest, 1965.

POPISTEANU, CRISTIAN, *Romania si Antanta Balcanica*. Bucu resti, 1968.

PRATT, JULIUS W., "Cordell Hull," *The American Secretaries of State and their Diplomacy*. Ed. Robert H. Ferrell, New York, 1964, XII, XIII.

PROST, HENRI, *Destin de la Roumanie*. Paris, 1954.

ROBERTS, HENRY L., *Rumania: Problems of an Agrarian State*. New Haven, Connecticut, 1951.

ROCK, WILLIAM, Appeasement on Trial. New York, 1966.

_____, *Neville Chamberlain*. New York, 1969.

ROUCEK, JOSEPH S., Contemporary Roumania and Her Problems. Stanford, California, 1932.

SCOTT, WILLIAM EVANS, *Alliance Against Hitler*. Durham, North Carolina, 1962.

SCURTU, IOAN, *"La contribution de la Roumanie a la guerre antihitlerienne," Nouvelles Etudes d'histoire.* Bucarest, 1970.

SERBANESCO, D. G. R., *Ciel rouge sur la Roumanie.* Paris, 1952.

SETON-WATSON, HUGH, *The East European Revolution.* New York, 1951.

SETON-WATSON, R. W., *Treaty Revision and the Hungarian Frontiers.* London, 1934.

SHERWOOD, ROBERT E., *Roosevelt and Hopkins. An Intimate History.* New York, 1948.

SMITH, GADDIS, *American Diplomacy During the Second World War, 1941-1945.* New York, 1965.

SPECTOR, SHERMAN DAVIS, *Rumania at the Paris Peace Conference.* New York, 1962.

STEINBERG, ALFRED, *The Man from Missouri.* New York, 1962.

TOYNBEE, ARNOLD J., *Survey of International Affairs 1926.* London, 1928.

_____, *Survey of International Affairs 1927.* London, 1929.

ULAM, ADAM B., *Expansion and Coexistence.* New York, 1968.

WALKER, RICHARD L; CURREY, GEORGE, "James F. Byrnes," *The American Secretaries of State and their Diplomacy.* Ed. Robert H. Ferrell, New York, 1965, XIV.

WEINBERG, GERHARD L., *The Foreign Policy of Hitler's Germany.* Chicago, 1970.

WERTH, ALEXANDER, *Russia at War 1941- 945.* New York, 1964.

WHALEY, BARTON, *Codeword Barbarossa.* Cambridge, Massachusetts, 1973.

WOLF, ROBERT LEE, *The Balkans in Our Time.* Cambridge, Massachusetts, 1965.

WOODWARD, SIR LLEWELLYN, *British Foreigh Policy in the Second World War.* 3 V., London, 1970-1 971.

_____,ZIVKOVA, L., "British Economic Policy in the Balkans on the Eve of World War 11," *Studia Balcanica.* 4, Sofia, 1971.

Periodicals and Unpublished Monographs

BABICI, ION, "Actions de solidarite du peuple roumain avec la lutte heroique du peuple d'Ethiopie contre l'agression fasciste (1935-1936)," *Revue Roumaine d'Histoire.* 6 (1967), II,257-273.

BĂLTEANU, BORIS, "Relaţiile guvernului S. U. A. cu regimul fascist din România (septembrie 1940 iunie 1942)," *Studii, Revista de istorie,* 11 (1958), Vl, 77-99.

———, "Situaţtia politica a României in preajma instaurării regimului democrat-popular," *Studii, Revista de istorie.* 10 (1957), II, 69-94.

BARBU, C; IONESCU, V. GH., "Contibuţia comitetelor de Front unic muncitoresc in anii 1944-1 947 la realizarea unităţii clasei muncitoare din România,"*Studii, Revista de istorie.* 20(1967),123-144.

BRADDICK, HENDERSON B., "*The Hoare-Laval Plan: A Study in International Politics,*" Review of Politics. 24 (1962), 342-364.

BRENNAN, BARRY, "The Soviet Conquest of Rumania," *Foreign Affairs.* 30 (April 1952), 466-487.

BR'CGEL, J. W., "Das Soviet Ultimatum an Rumanien im Juni 1940," *Vierteljahrshefte fur Zeitgeschichte.* 4 963), 404-417.

CAMPUS, ELIZA, "Le caractere europeen des traites bilateraux conclus par la Roumanie dans la decade 1920-1930,"*Revue Roumaine d'Histoire.* 12 (1973), VI, 1067-1093.

———, "Pozitia internaţională a României in anii 1938-1940," *Studii, Revista de istorie.* 26 (1973), VI, 1139-1159.

CHIPER, IOAN, "lstoriografia străină despre insurecţia armată din august 1944 din România," *Studii, Revista de istorie.* 22 (1 969), IV, 733-759.

CIMPONERIU, ECATERINA, "Criza guvernării antonesciene in lunile care au precedat istoricul act de la 23 august 1944," *Studii, Revista de istorie.* 22 (1969), IV, 633-653.

CONSTANTINESCU-IAŞI, P., "L'insurrection d'aout 1944," *Revue d'Histoire de la Deuxieme Guerre Mondiale.* 18 (1 968), 70, 39-55.

CRETZIANU, ALEXANDER, "The Rumanian Armistice Negotiations: Cairo 1944," *Journal of Central European Affairs.* 11 (1951), 235-265.

_____, "The Soviet Ultimatum to Roumania (26 June, 1940)," *Journal of Central European Affairs.* 9 (1 951), 396-402.

DEUTSCH, R., "The Foreign Policy of Romania and the Dynamics of Peace (1932-1936)," *Revue Roumaine d'Histoire.* 5(1966), I,121 -132.

DEVASIA, THOMAS A., "The United States and the Formation of Greater Romania 1914-1918: A Study in Diplomacy and Propaganda," Unpublished Doctoral Thesis, Department of History, Boston College, 1970.

Diplomaticus, "The New Regime in Roumania," *Fortnightly.* 143 (January- June, 1938), 580-587.

GIURESCU, DINU C., "La diplomatie roumaine et le Pacte des Quatre (1933)," *Revue Roumaine d'Histoire.* 8 (1 969), I, 77-102.

"Inside Roumania," *New Statesman and Nation.* 17 (January-June, 1939), 450-451.

MELBOURNE, ROY M., "Rumania: Nazi Satellite," Unpublished Doctoral Thesis, University of Pennsylvania, 1951.

MERGEL, GEORG, "Rumanien: Von der Kapitulation zur Volksrepublik," *Ost-Europea.* 3 (Juni, 1 953), 213-219.

MOISUC, VIORICA, "Orientations dans la politique exterieure de la Roumanie apres le Pacte de Munich," *Revue Roumaine d'Histoire.* 5 (1 966), II, 327-340.

NANO, FREDERICK, "The First Soviet Double Cross," *Journal of Central European Affairs.* 12 (1 952), 236-258.

NEDELCU, FLOREA, "Carol al Il-lea şi garda de fier - de la relaţii amicale la criză - (1930-1937)," *Studii, Revista de istorie.* 24 (1971), V, 1009-1 028.

PENDLE, GEORGE, "Rumania 1939," *Fortnightly.* 145 (January-June, 1939), 315-31 9.

PETRIC, ARON, "Proclamarea republicii populare române şi semnificaţia sa istorică," *Studii, Revista de istorie.* 25 (1972), VI, 1143-1157.

RUSENESCU, MIHAI, "Istoriografia Românească privind insurecţia antifascistă din august 1944 şi urmările sale," *Studii, Revista de istorie.* 22 (1969),1V, 717-732.

SCURTU, IOAN Pozitia P. C. R. fata de partidele 'istorice' in timpul guvernului Rădescu," *Seria Stiinţe sociale Istorie,* "Lupta partidelor politice in alegerile parlamentare din decembrie 1937," Studii, Revista de istorie. 20 (1967), I,145-162.

_____, ". 15 (166), 169-195.

SIMION, A,, "Les conditions politiques du diktat de Vienne (30 aout 1940), *Revue Roumaine d'Historie.* 11 (1 972), III,447-472.

TECLU, IACOB, "La participation de L'armee Roumanie a la guerre antihitlerienne," *Revue Roumaine d'Histoire.* 1 (1962), I, 163-198.

TEODORESCU, V., "Aspecte ale folosirii parlamentului de către forţele democratice conduse de Partidul Comunist Român (decembrie 1946-decembrie 1947)," *Studii şi materiale de istorie contemporană.* Bucuresti, 1962, 395-436.

The American Journal of International Law, Supplement V. 16 (1 922), 148-153.

TURCUS, D., "Din lupta condusă de P.C.R. pentru demascarea şi scoaterea elementelor fasciste din aparatul de stat, instituţii şi intreprinderi (23 august 1944-6 martie 1945)," *Studii şi materiale de istorie contemporana.* Bucuresti, 1962, 299-331.

ŢUŢUI GHEORGHE, "Dezvoltarea Partidului Comunist Român in anii 1944-1948," *Anale de istorie.* 16 (1970), 3-15.

_____, "Infringerea de către forţele revoluţionare a acţiunilor antidemocratice şi antiguvernamentale intreprinse de partidele politice reacţionare şi de monarhie (august 1945 - ianuarie 1946)," *Studii, Revista de istorie.* 20 (1967), VI, 1093-1114.

_____, "La position de la monarchie dans la vie politique de la Roumanie (aout 1944 - novembre 1946)," *Revue Roumaine d'Histoire.* 11 (1972), VI, 953-963.

_____, "Partidul Social-Democrat din Romania In perioada luptei pentru instaurarea puterii democrat populare (august 1944 - martie 1945)," *Studii, Revista de istorie.* 27 (1974), III, 343-362.

UDREA, TRAIAN, "Condițiile istorice ale formării frontului național democratic," *Studii, Revista de istorie.* 17 (1964), IV, 835-858.

_____, "La politique exterieure de la dictature legionnaire Antonescienne (septembre 1940 - janvier 1941)," *Revue Roumaine d'Histoire.* 10 (1971), VI, 971-990.

_____, "L'attitude des principaux partis et organisations politiques a l'egard du developpement democratique de la Roumanie apres le 23 aout 1944," Revue Roumaine d'Histoire. 11 (1972), V, 813-832.

UDREA, TRAIAN; CHIPER, IOAN, "La seconde guerre mondiale dans l'historiographie Roumaine," *Revue Roumaine d'Histoire.* 13 (1974), IV, 647-664.

VARGA, V. A., "Atitudinea guvernului român burghezo-moșieresc față de tratativele anglo-franco-sovietice din anul 1939," *Studii, Revista de istorie.* 13 (1960), IV, 51-72.

_____, "Din lupta maselor conduse de P. C. R. pentru instaurarea regimului democrat-popular (ianuarie - 6 martie 1945)," *Studii si materiale de istorie contemporana.* Bucuresti, 1962, 335-372.

ZAHARIA, GHEORGHE, "La Roumanie et la resistance antifasciste du centre et du sud-est europeen en 1935-1941," *Revue Roumaine d'Histoire.* 12 (1973), II, 279-298.

_____, "L'insurrection nationale antifasciste d'aout 1944 et son importance," Revue Roumaine d'Histoire. 13 (1974), IV, 589-606.

Newspapers and Magazines

Curentul, 1942-1944.
Newsweek, 1938-1941.
New York Times, 1938-1947.
Porunca Vremii, 1942-1944.
The Manchester Guardian, 1938-1947.
The Times (London), 1938-1947.
Time, 1938-1941.

American Romanian Academy of Arts and Sciences,
ARA Publisher www.AmericanRomanianAcademy.org
Contact us: info@AmericanRomanianAcademy.org

www.ingramcontent.com/pod-product-compliance
Lightning Source LLC
Chambersburg PA
CBHW060250100426
42742CB00011B/1696